Keys to Music Bibliography, No. 2

KEYS TO MUSIC BIBLIOGRAPHY

Prepared under the auspices of the
School of Library Science, Kent State University

Edited by Guy A. Marco

International Bibliography of Discographies

Classical Music and Jazz & Blues, 1962–1972

A Reference Book

for Record Collectors, Dealers, and Libraries

by

David Edwin Cooper

WITH A PREFACE BY GUY A. MARCO

1975

LIBRARIES UNLIMITED, INC., Littleton, Colo.

LIBRARIES UNLIMITED, INC.
P.O. Box 263
Littleton, Colorado 80120

Library of Congress Cataloging in Publication Data

Cooper, David E   1944–
    International bibliography of discographies.

    (Keys to music bibliography ; no. 2)
    Includes index.
    1. Music—Discography—Bibliography. 2. Jazz music—
Discography—Bibliography. 3. Blues (Songs, etc.)—
Discography—Bibliography. I. Title. II. Series.
ML113.C655I6   016.78   75-4516
ISBN 0-87287-108-8

To *MARY*,

my best friend and wife,

who saw me through it all

PREFACE

Parallels between discography and bibliography on historical-technical-purposeful grounds, have been drawn recently (notably by Gordon Stevenson) and with much persuasiveness. To elaborate one element of the analogy, we might describe the stages in recording of sound through the historical terminology of the book. There was a Manuscript Period, in which the recording of sound was literally and simply by hand: the transcriber listened, and wrote down what he heard as best he could, in musical notation. (Early research in primitive and folk music depended entirely on this demanding technique.) There was an Incunabula Period, in which mechanical means of capturing sound were issuing their first productions—rather less successfully, to be sure, than the work of fifteenth-century printers. As spiritual equivalents to the printed works of the sixteenth-nineteenth centuries we have the 78-rpm discs: efficient and often beautiful in their achievements, but lacking the dimensions which only a later technology could offer. The Contemporary Period of book publishing is characterized by its vast output, variety of formats, and—at its best—high artistry of color and design. Analogies to the new worlds of multi-channel, multi-format recordings are self evident.

But the history of sound recording is very short, compared with the 5,000 years in which humans have written down words: it begins only in the nineteenth century. So it is not surprising that bibliography in all its forms is far advanced over its parallel discipline, discography. Indeed, discographical scholarship is a creature of our own time, and many readers of these paragraphs were born before the term "discography" had even been coined. Enumerative discographical research is not yet complete for the early phases of sound recording, and the discal flood which began in 1949 is only vaguely under control. Names like Hain, Copinger, Stillwell, Proctor, Panzer, Pollard, Wing: these remain without counterparts in the slightly ordered chaos of the disc and tape. But there is a young Besterman, although David Cooper would modestly disclaim the honor of such an association. For Cooper has begun a serious and vital endeavor, comparable in scope if not in actual dimension, as significant to discographical history as Besterman's work has been for the universe of print. Cooper's 1,908 entries are a slight total when set against the 40,000+ of Besterman's first edition, but they appear to cover their field about as well—within the limitations imposed. Every user of this invaluable

7

compendium will hope that Cooper, like Besterman and other patient masters of the bibliographic art, will persist in his work through many revisions, editions, and expansions.

Hopefully too, "Keys to Music Bibliography" will now (after this long delay between numbers one and two) persist as well, and bring forth a series to live up to Walter Gerboth's prefatory expectation in the first issue: "invaluable to the student, the scholar, and the librarian."

Guy A. Marco
Kent State University

TABLE OF CONTENTS

INTRODUCTION

The *International bibliography of discographies* represents an extensively revised and expanded version of an opus prepared and submitted a year ago as a master's research paper for the Kent State University School of Library Science under the more modest title *Bibliography of discographies*. The instigation for preparing this work was the need for a comprehensive and systematic reference source that would organize and provide access to the abundance of discographical materials throughout the world—an undertaking, unfortunately, long overdue.

Discographies, which have for some time constituted an important element of the reference literature in music, are generally taken to be selective or complete listings of musical recordings typical of one composer, performer, or group of performers; but a discography may also be a classified list of the recordings of a particular company or of a particular subject or musical style. The broader interpretation of the word has been applied in the preparation of this bibliography.

A discography is a performing arts tool that is analogous to a bibliography in the literary arts. The importance of discographies lies not only in their providing access to the recorded sound "literature" but also in their often providing much supplementary information about the music, the performers, and the recordings.

The word "international" has been added to the title of the present work because of the international character of music and recordings; recognizing the achievements of discographers and encouraging cooperation among discographers in all parts of the world will serve the interests of all. Part III of this work is devoted to a summary of basic current national discographical resources; though it is hardly as complete as could be desired, this checklist attempts to facilitate access to and dissemination of discographical information across national boundaries. Another aspect of the national character of the present work is its indication of the language of materials when it is other than English and its indication of the country of origin for composers and performers of classical music. Altogether, 21 languages and 37 countries are represented. The range extends from the discographies of Rumanian pianist Dinu Lipatti (in Rumanian—see C766, C771, C772) to Masaaki Awamura's Japanese *Jazz record book* (see J121).

The subject range of this work is restricted to Western classical music and jazz and blues. Thus, not many discographies that include spoken-word recordings and Eastern classical, folk, ethnic, tribal, and pop music will be found here. However, a few essentially folk and popular music discographies were included on the grounds that they touch upon areas of jazz or blues or musical comedy.

The range of quantity and quality in the discographical materials compiled is quite broad, extending from "recommended recordings" lists of only a few items to massive record encyclopedias such as *WERM* (see C350), and from record lists that omit even company issue numbers to marvels of discographical thoroughness and precision like Rust's *Jazz records 1897-1942* (see J204). Furthermore, the discographical materials included are not restricted simply to lists of recordings. A few discographical essays appear (for example, Dixon and Godrich's *Recording the blues*—see J3) and also some record reviews in a few subjects that might otherwise be difficult to approach (like, for instance, Weinstock's "The world of the zarzuela"—C343). For reasons of space, manufacturers' catalogs have been excluded from this work. However, retrospective label discographies have been included.

No criteria regarding length, detail, and thoroughness were used in compiling this bibliography. To the contrary, the interests of musical enthusiasts, students, and amateur collectors were kept much in mind. The numerously cited historical survey texts and composer-and-his-works studies with listening lists will enable the layman to pursue an integrated reading-listening program of self-education to whatever extent he may desire. The "general guides and historical surveys" and "buyers' guides" sections of this bibliography were particularly designed to serve these people as well as others who wish to keep up with the current record market. General review items do not appear in the "buyers' guides" sections unless they cover releases of at least a full year at once. Prominent periodical review sources are listed in the summary of national discographical activities (Part III).

Publications of the years 1962 through 1972 are most fully covered in this bibliography, but materials included are not strictly limited to those years. Discographies of the past eighteen months have been included, insofar as they came to the attention of the author, as well as a few projected publications known to him. Pre-1962 publications have been added so far as could be justified by: 1) their not appearing in previous bibliographies of discographies; 2) their serving as the basis for the later discographical works; or 3) their continuing importance and general merit. Certainly the sections on historical recordings and labels would be much diminished in value had the meritorious publications of earlier decades been omitted.

The ideal bibliography of discographies would be comprehensive for all publications in all languages in all subjects for all time—an undertaking scarcely within the range of a single individual, even a most diligent researcher. Consequently, the author has sought to provide a compilation of recent discographical materials which functionally supplements and extends a few other readily available bibliographies. Those works which may be most effectively used in tandem with this publication are:

Bruun, Carl L., and John Gray. A bibliography of discographies. *Recorded Sound, I (#7, July 1962), 206-13. [Covers classical music only. Most useful for its compilation of performer discographies prior to 1962.]

Carl Gregor, Duke of Mecklenburg. International jazz bibliography: jazz books from 1919 to 1968. Strasbourg, Éditions P. H. Heitz; Baden-Baden, Verlag Heitz GmbH, 1969. 198 p. [Author listing of monographs in jazz and blues up to 1968 with an indication (by the abbreviation "disc.") for works which include a discography. Well indexed.]

Carl Gregor, Duke of Mecklenburg. 1970 supplement to international jazz bibliography & international drum & percussion bibliography. Graz, Universal Edition, 1971. 59, 43 p. [Contains additions and corrections as well as updating of the above work. Not indexed, but has separate section of monographic discographies.]

Index to [the British Institute of Recorded Sound] Bulletin 1-18 and Recorded Sound 1-44. *Recorded Sound,* #44 (Oct. 1971), 805-27. [Classical and jazz discographies indexed here also appear in Bruun and Gray or in this author's work, but the index also includes discographies in other fields such as ethnic and folk musics, Eastern classical music, spoken-word recordings, wildlife sounds recordings, etc. Also indexes BIRS reviews of major discographical publications.]

Merriam, Alan P. A bibliography of jazz. Philadelphia, The American Folklore Society, 1954. 145 p. [Author listing of writings on jazz, with predominance of periodical articles. Covers roughly 1890 through 1950. Citations containing a discography include the indication "Disc." Well indexed.]

Reisner, Robert George. The literature of jazz; a selective bibliography. New York, New York Public Library, 1959. 63 p. [Author listing of writings on jazz, with predominance of periodical articles. Covers roughly 1920 through 1958. Citations containing a discography include the indication "discography."]

Selective bibliographies of the most essential discographical literature appear notably in these books:

Duckles, Vincent Harris. Music reference and research materials; an annotated bibliography. 3d ed. New York, The Free Press; London, Collier-Macmillan, 1974. 526 p. "Discographies": pp. 407-426.

Kennington, Donald. The literature of jazz; a critical guide. London, Library Association, 1970; Chicago, American Library Association, 1971. 142 p. "Reference sources": pp. 65-90.

The author has been advised that a listing of discographies published during the 1973 calendar year will appear in the Association of Recorded Sound Collections [ARSC] Journal later this year (Vol. VI, #2). It is hoped that such a listing will become a regular (and indeed *invaluable*) feature of the journal.

Two recent English publications unfortunately cover much the same ground as this author's work, but in a much narrower sense. They are:

Foreman, Lewis. Discographies: a bibliography of catalogues of recordings, mainly relating to specific musical subjects, composers and performers. London, Triad Press, 1973. 65 p.

Moon, Pete. Bibliography of jazz discographies [1960-1969]. London, British Institute of Jazz Studies, 1970. 24 p.

These bibliographies were compiled contemporaneously with this author's work, and they are evidently more selective and parochial in intent. Since these publications seem little known and available outside the British Isles except to the hardiest of record enthusiasts, the author decided against trying to coordinate his work with theirs.

Some final remarks may be helpful for the reader in utilizing this bibliography to fullest advantage. The arrangement is hierarchical by subject, by author, and then by title—an arrangement that should facilitate the rapid location of discographies dealing with a particular subject or person. However, the index provides a much fuller subject analysis than could be attained through arrangement alone. Hence, the index should be consulted before the user may safely conclude that he has located all possible sources relevant to a particular subject.

The index is also inclusive of authors, distinctive monographic titles, and series as well as subjects—all within a single alphabetical sequence. The title indexing is mainly exclusive of biographies, which may best be approached by subject or author.

Secondary sources were used to a great extent in locating materials, but the author sought to examine and verify each item insofar as could possibly be done. Inevitably, some obscure items could not be verified at all; neither could all the variations of editions and imprints of more common works be fully researched and verified at all points without creating unreasonable delays for the publisher. Where the pagination of a discography within a monograph could not be found, the phrase "includes discography" was used to indicate that the discography was a secondary, probably appended feature of the work cited.

Generally, the details that are lacking are of such minor value that they could hardly justify omitting the difficult-to-locate items or further delaying preparations for publication. Any remaining questionable points will, it is hoped, be resolved in the second edition; to this end, the author would welcome comments, additions, and corrections to his work.

David Edwin Cooper
Buffalo, New York

ACKNOWLEDGMENTS

I would like to acknowledge the roles of several individuals during the conception, construction, and realization of the work at hand. I am deeply indebted to Guy A. Marco, Dean of the School of Library Science at Kent State University, who was instrumental in directing my awareness to this lacuna in music bibliography and who advised the preparation of the initial version of this work as a research paper for the K.S.U. School of Library Science. I am indeed honored that Dean Marco has selected this work to appear as the second issue of the "Keys to music bibliography" series.

James B. Coover, Curator of the Music Library of the State University of New York at Buffalo, Paul T. Jackson of Recorded Sound Research, Peoria, Illinois, and Edward E. Colby, Music Librarian of Stanford University, contributed in no small measure toward improving the revised version of the bibliography by reading the research paper and generously offering the benefit of their experience and additional resources.

The *International bibliography of discographies* was compiled primarily through research in several of the more distinguished music collections of the Eastern United States. My indebtedness extends to so many people at these institutions that I must acknowledge them in the corporate sense rather than individually. The following libraries granted me access to their catalogs and collections and deftly fielded my inquiries, whether in person or by mail:

Library of Congress, Washington, D.C. (Edward Waters, Head of the Music Division)

Library & Museum of the Performing Arts, New York Public Library, New York, N.Y. (Frank C. Campbell, Chief of the Music Division)

Boston Public Library, Boston, Mass. (Ruth M. Bleecker, Head of the Music Research Division)

Cleveland Public Library, Cleveland, Ohio (Stephen Matyi, Head of the Fine Arts Department)

Buffalo and Erie County Public Library, Buffalo, N.Y. (Norma Jean Lamb, Head of the Music Department)

Sibley Music Library, Eastman School of Music, Rochester, N.Y. (Ruth Watanabe, Head Librarian)

State University of New York at Buffalo Libraries, Buffalo, N.Y. (James B. Coover, Curator of the Music Library)

Kent State University Libraries, Kent, Ohio (Desirée De Charms, Music Librarian)

A final note of gratitude is due to my wife, Mary Margetta Lonas Cooper, who constructed the author and title portions of the index and who persevered with me through many ups and downs while this work was in preparation.

D. E. C.

PART I

CLASSICAL MUSIC

SECTION A

CLASSICAL GENERAL GUIDES, BUYERS' GUIDES, AND SUBJECTS

GENERAL GUIDES AND HISTORICAL SURVEYS

C1 Alexander, William P. Music heard today. Dubuque, Ia., W. C. Brown, 1966. 170 p. Includes discographies.

C2 Alexander, William P., and Leroy Williams. Music heard today. Rev. ed. Dubuque, Ia., W. C. Brown, 1969. 178 p. Includes discography.

C3 Angoff, Charles. Fathers of classical music. [Reprint of the New York, 1947 edition.] Freeport, N.Y., Books for Libraries Press, 1969. 164 p. Discography: pp. 153-161.

C4 Bookspan, Martin. 101 masterpieces of music and their composers. Garden City, N.Y., Doubleday, 1968. 511 p. "Checklist of recommended recordings": pp. 467-487.

Bookspan, Martin. 101 masterpieces of music and their composers. Rev. and updated ed. Garden City, N.Y., Doubleday, 1973. 465 p. Includes discographical commentary.

C5 Candé, Roland de. La musique: histoire, dictionnaire, discographie. Paris, Éditions du Seuil, 1971. 687 p. In French. Discography: pp. 623-661.

C6 Cross, Milton. The Milton Cross new encyclopedia of the great composers and their music. Revised and expanded. Garden City, N.Y., Doubleday, 1969. 2v. (1284 p.) "Basic works for the record library": pp. 1185-1192.

C7 Dufourcq, Norbert. Petite histoire de la musique européenne. Nouvelle édition revue et mise à jour. Paris, Larousse, 1969. 136 p. In French. Discography: pp. 121-126.

C8   Fiske, Roger. Listening to music; a guide to enjoyment. New ed. rev. London, G. G. Harrap, 1962. 64 p. Discography: p. 64.

C9   Graziosi, Giorgio. Introduzione all'ascolto. Milano, Ricordi, 1965. 148 p. In Italian. "Indicazioni discografiche": pp. 137-145.

C10   Harman, Richard Alec, Anthony Milner, and Wilfrid Howard Mellers. Man and his music; the story of musical experience in the West. London, Barrie and Rockliff, 1962. 1204 p. New York, Oxford University Press, 1962. 1172 p. Includes discographies.

C11   Hemel, Victor van. Kort overzicht van de muziekgeschiedenis ten dienste van muziekbeoefenaars en -liefhebbers. 9. bijgewerkte druk. Antwerpen, Cupido-Uitgaven, 1965. 120 p. In Flemish. Discography: pp. 116-118.

C12   Hughes, Donald. Let's have some music! A guide for young music-lovers. 2d ed. London, Museum Press, 1965. 140 p. Includes discographies.

C13   Hurd, Michael. An outline history of European music. London, Novello, 1968. 132 p. Discography: pp. 119-123.

C14   Knaurs Weltgeschichte der Musik. Von Kurt Honolka und andere. München, D. Knaur, 1968. 640 p. In German. Bibliography and discography: pp. 609-625.

C15   Londoño Alvarez, Alberto. De la música, la enfermedad y los perfumes. Manizales, Impr. Departamental de Caldas, 1966. 140p. In Spanish. Discography: p. 101.

C16   McGehee, Thomasine (Cobb). People and music. Revised by Alice D. Nelson. Boston, Allyn and Bacon, 1968. 452 p. Includes discographies.

C17   Machlis, Joseph. The enjoyment of music; an introduction to perceptive listening. Rev. ed. New York, W. W. Norton, 1963. 701 p. Includes discographies.

      Machlis, Joseph. The enjoyment of music; an introduction to perceptive listening. Shorter ed. rev. New York, W. W. Norton, 1963. 498 p. Includes discographies.

C18   McKinney, Howard Decker, and William Robert Anderson. Music in history; the evolution of an art. 3d ed. New York, American Book Co., 1966. 820 p. Discography: pp. 819-820.

C19   Miller, William Hugh. Introduction to music appreciation; an objective approach to listening. Rev. ed. Philadelphia, Chilton Book Co., 1970. 345 p. Discography: pp. 277-330.

C20   Montigny, René. Histoire de la musique. Paris, Éditions Payot, 1964. 374 p. In French. Discography: pp. 345-359.

C21   Müller-Marein, Josef, and Hannes Reinhardt. Das musikalische Selbstportrait von Komponisten, Dirigenten, Instrumentalisten, Sängern unserer Zeit. Hamburg, Nannen-Verlag, 1963. 508 p. In German. Discography: pp. 461-497.

C22   Musik for enhver. V: Musikkens historie 1-2. [n.p.,] Arbejdernes oplysningsforbund i Danmark, 1959-60. 2v. In Danish. Includes discographies.

C23   Oxtoby, Charles. Wat is musiek. Kaapstad, Tafelberg-Uitgewers, 1964. 133p. In Dutch. Includes discography.

C24   Praeger history of Western music. Ed. by Frederick William Sternfeld. Discographies by Philip L. Miller. New York, Praeger, 1973– . 5v. [In preparation; for volumes already issued, see index.]

C25   Robertson, Alec, and Denis William Stevens, eds. A history of music. New York, Barnes & Noble, 1963, 1965, 1968. 3v. Includes discographies.
C26   Smoldon, William Lawrence. A history of music. London, H. Jenkins, 1965. 472 p. Includes discographies.

C27   Walter, Don C. Men and music in Western culture. New York, Appleton-Century-Crofts, 1969. 244 p. Includes discographies.

C28   Witold, Jean. Découverte de la musique. Paris, B. Grasset, 1962. 254 p. In French. Includes discography.

C29   Young, Percy Marshall. The enjoyment of music. London, E.M.I. Records, 1968. 192 p. Includes discography.

C30   Young, Percy Marshall. Great ideas in music. New York, D. White Co., 1968. 211 p. Discography: pp. 203-205.

Ancient and Medieval Music

C31   Barker, John W. Spanish medieval music. *American Record Guide*, XXIX (June 1963), 776-77.

C32   Barker, John W. Treasury of early music. *American Record Guide*, XXX (Oct. 1963), 96-100.

C33   Burkhalter, A. Louis. Ancient and oriental music, by Romain Goldron [pseud.]. H. S. Stuttman; distributed by Doubleday, 1968. 127 p. Discography: pp. 121-125.

C34   Burkhalter, A. Louis. Byzantine and medieval music, by Romain Goldron [pseud.]. H. S. Stuttman; distributed by Doubleday, 1968. 127 p. Discography: pp. 121-125.

C35   Burkhalter, A. Louis. Minstrels and masters, by Romain Goldron [pseud.]. H. S. Stuttman; distributed by Doubleday, 1968. 125 p. Discography: pp. 121-125.

C36   Burkhalter, A. Louis. Triomphe de la polyphonie, par Romain Goldron [pseud.]. Lausanne, Éd. Rencontre, 1966. 127 p. In French. Discography: pp. 122-125.

C37   Coover, James B., and Richard Colvig. Medieval and Renaissance music on long-playing records. (Detroit studies in music bibliography, 6) Detroit, Information Services, 1964. 122 p.

C38   Coover, James B., and Richard Colvig. Medieval and Renaissance music on long-playing records: supplement, 1962-1971. (Detroit studies in music bibliography, 26) Detroit, Information Coordinators, 1973. 258 p.

C39   Link, Helmut, and Helmut Uhlig. Meisterwerke der Musik auf Schallplatten von den Anfängen bis Bach und Händel; ein kritischer Kommentar. Berlin, C. Heymann, 1963. 91 p. In German.

C40   Sternfeld, ed. Music from the Middle Ages to the Renaissance. (Praeger history of Western music, 1) London, Weidenfeld & Nicolson, 1973. 524 p. Discography by Philip L. Miller: pp. 431-437.

C41   Thomson, James C. Music through the Renaissance. Dubuque, Ia., W. C. Brown, 1968. 165 p. Discography: pp. 145-151.

Renaissance and Baroque Music

C42   Barker, John W. From Capital—the notable EMI series: Music in alten Städten und Residenzen—with discography. *American Record Guide*, XXX (Nov. 1963), 202-06.

C43   Blaukopf, K. Sehnsucht nach dem Barock? *Phono*, VIII (#4, 1962), 69-70. In German.

C44   Burkhalter, A. Louis. Music of the Renaissance, by Romain Goldron
       [pseud.]. H. S. Stuttman; distributed by Doubleday, 1968. 127 p.
       Discography: pp. 122-125.

C45   Burkhalter, A. Louis. La musique et l'humanisme, par Romain
       Goldron [pseud.]. Lausanne, Éd. Rencontre, 1966. 127 p. In
       French. Discography: pp. 122-125.

C46   Burkhalter, A. Louis. Naissance de l' opéra et du style concertant,
       par Romain Goldron [pseud.]. Lausanne, Éd. Rencontre, 1966. 127 p.
       In French. Discography: pp. 122-125.

C47   Splendeur de la musique baroque, par Romain Goldron [pseud.].
       Lausanne, Éd. Rencontre, 1966. 128 p. In French. Discography:
       pp. 122-125.

C48   Guiomar, M. Chansons et polyphonies de la Renaissance en France et
       en Italie. *Disques*, #127 (Feb. 1962), 106-07. In French.

C49   Noble, A. Music of courts and kings; a survey of recent recordings.
       Recorded Sound, #21 (Jan. 1966), 19-25.

C50   Records in review. *The Consort.* v. 1 - . 1945- . [An occasional
       feature in this annual publication.]

C51   Wangermée, Robert. Flemish music and society in the fifteenth and
       sixteenth centuries. English version by Robert Erich Wolf.
       Brussels, Éditions Arcade; New York, Praeger, 1968. 349 p. Discog-
       raphy: pp. 329-341.

Classical and Romantic Music

C52   Burkhalter, A. Louis. Les débuts du romantisme, par Romain Goldron
       [pseud.]. Lausanne, Éd. Rencontre, 1966. 127 p. In French. Discog-
       raphy: pp. 122-125.

C53   Burkhalter, A. Louis. Du romantisme à l'expressionnisme, par Romain
       Goldron [pseud.]. Lausanne, Éd. Rencontre, 1967. 127 p. In French.
       Discography: pp. 122-125.

C54   Burkhalter, A. Louis. L'éveil des écoles nationales, par Romain
       Goldron [pseud.]. Lausanne, Éd. Rencontre, 1966. 127 p. In French.
       Discography: pp. 122-125.

C55   Burkhalter, A. Louis. Naissance et apogée du classicisme, par Romain
       Goldron [pseud.]. Lausanne, Éd. Rencontre, 1966. 127 p. In
       French. Discography: pp. 122-125.

C56   Landon, H. C. Robbins. Tagebuch einer sentimentalen Reise ins
      Land hinter der Klassik auf alten Poststationen: Plattenstatt
      Pferdewechsel. *Phono*, VIII (#4, 1962), 75-77. In German.

C57   Morse, Peter. Grieg, Sibelius and Kilpinen vocal music. Utica, N.Y.,
      Jerome F. Weber, 1974. [Scheduled for publication.]

C58   Morse, Peter. Schubert/Schumann/Brahms choral music. (Weber dis-
      cography series, 5) Utica, N.Y., Jerome F. Weber, 1970. 8, 6, 12 p.

      Morse, Peter. Schubert/Schumann/Brahms choral music. (Weber dis-
      cography series, 5) Rev. ed. Utica, N.Y., Jerome F. Weber, 1974.
      [Scheduled for publication.]

C59   Naur, Robert. Veje til den klassiske musik. København, Nordisk
      polyphon akts., 1964. 133 p. In Danish. Includes discographies.

C60   Schonberg, Harold C. The collector's Chopin and Schumann.
      (Keystone books in music) Philadelphia, Lippincott, 1959. 256 p.

C61   Weber, Jerome F. Loewe and Franz [Lieder] . (Weber discography
      series, 8) Utica, N.Y., Jerome F. Weber, 1971. 20 p.

Contemporary Music

C62   Barraud, Henry. Pour comprendre les musiques d'aujourd'hui. Paris,
      Éditions du Seuil, 1968. 222 p. In French. Discography: pp. 217-220.

C63   Boretz, Benjamin, and Edward T. Cone, eds. Perspectives on
      Schoenberg and Stravinsky. Princeton, N.J., Princeton University
      Press, 1968. 284 p. Discographies: pp. 251-284.

C64   Cohn, Arthur. The collector's twentieth-century music in the Western
      Hemisphere. (Keystone books in music) Philadelphia, Lippincott,
      1961. 256 p.

C65   Cohn, Arthur. Twentieth-century music in Western Europe; the com-
      positions and the recordings. Philadelphia, Lippincott, 1965; New
      York, Da Capo, 1972. 510 p. Includes discographies.

C66   Curjel, Hans. Synthesen. Vermischte Schriften zum Verstandnis der
      neuen Musik. Hamburg, Claasen, 1966. 207 p. In German. Discog-
      raphy: pp. 187-205.

C67   Degens, R. N. Contemporary music on gramophone records. *Sonorum
      Speculum*, #15 (June 1963), 33-38. In English and German.

C68   Dibelius, Ulrich. Moderne Musik 1945-1965. München, Deutscher Bücherbund, 1968. 392 p. In German. Discography: pp. 359-368.

C69   Fierz-Bantli, G. Auf der Suche nach den Klassikern der Moderne. *Phono*, VIII (#5, 1962), 98-99. In German.

C70   Goléa, Antoine. Vingt ans de musique contemporaine. Paris, Éditions Seghers, 1962. 2v. in 1. In French. Includes discographies.

C71   Harder, Paul O. Bridge to 20th century music; a programed course. Boston, Allyn and Bacon, 1973. 287 p. "Discography and films": pp. 271-277.

C72   Hemel, Victor van. Over moderne muziek en komponisten. 3. bijgewerkte druk. Antwerpen, Cupido-Uitgaven, 196? 182 p. In Flemish. Discography: pp. 176-178.

C73   Hodeir, André. La musique depuis Debussy. Paris, Presses universitaires de France, 1961. 222 p. In French. Includes discography.

C74   Hodeir, André. Since Debussy; a view of contemporary music. Translated by Noel Burch. London, Secker & Warburg; New York, Grove Press, 1961. 256p. Discography: pp. 243-250.

C75   Howard, John Tasker. This modern music; a guide for the bewildered listener. [Reprint of the New York, 1957 edition.] Freeport, N.Y., Books for Libraries Press, 1969. 234 p. Discography: pp. 217-224.

C76   Meyer-Denkmann, Gertrud. Struktur und Praxis neuer Musik im Unterricht; Experiment und Methode. Wien, Universal Edition, 1972. 288 p. In German. Discography: pp. 273-282.

C77   Morse, Peter. Debussy and Ravel vocal music. (Weber discography series, 11) Utica, N.Y., Jerome F. Weber, 1973. 38 p.

C78   Pfluger, Rolf. Diskographie der Wiener Schule. *Österreichische Musikzeitschrift*, XXIV (May-June 1969), 353-58+ In German.

C79   Radiodiffusion-Télévision française. Répertoire international des musiques expérimentales: studios, oeuvres, équipements, bibliographie. Paris, Radiodiffusion-Télévision française, 196? 56 p. In French. Includes discography.

C80   Rauchhaupt, Ursula von, comp. Die Streichquartette der Wiener Schule; Schoenberg, Berg, Webern. Eine Dokumentation. München, H. Ellermann, 1971? 185 p. In German. Discography: pp. 183-185.

C81   Roy, Jean. Journées de musique contemporaine de Paris, 1968. Varèse, Xénakis, Bério, Pierre Henry, oeuvres, études, perspectives. Paris, la "Revue Musicale," 1968. 2v. In French. Discography: v. 2, pp. 29-31.

C82   Samuel, Claude. Panorama de l'art musical contemporain, avec des textes inédits. Paris, Éditions Gallimard, 1962. 838 p. In French. Discography: pp. 783-813.

C83   Schaeffer, Pierre. La Musique concrète. Paris, Presses Universitaires de France, 1967. 128 p. In French. Discography: pp. 126-127.

C84   Sternfeld, Frederick William. Music in the modern age. (Praeger history of Western music, 5) New York, Praeger, 1973. 515 p. Discography by Philip L. Miller: pp. 443-461.

BUYERS' GUIDES

C85   Arntsen, Ella. Musikkbiblioteket; hjelpebok for bibliotekarer, Oslo, Statens bibliotektilsyn, I kommisjon: A/L Biblioteksentralen, 1963. 205 p. In Norwegian. Discography: pp. 179-200.

C86   The art of record buying. London, E.M.G. Handmade Gramophones. v. 1– . 1938– . [An occasional publication; frequency varies.]

C87   Basis-catalogus van klassieke musiekwerken voor openbare bibliotheken. Ed. by the Vlaamse Vereniging voor Bibliotheek- en Archiefpersoneel. Bruxelles, Ministerie van Nederlandse Cultuur Dienst der Openbare Bibliotheken, 1972. 65 p. In Flemish.

C88   Benjamin, Edward. The restful in music. New Orleans, Restful Music, 1970. 131 p.

C89   Capel, Vivian. The music lover's all-in-one gramophone book. London, Focal Press, 1970?

C90   Catalog of open reel tapes. New York, Barclay-Crocker, 1973. 96 p. [Periodically supplemented through *Reel news*.]

C91   Commission for the White House Record Library. The White House record library. Washington, White House Historical Association, 1973. 105 p.

C92   Consumers Union reviews classical recordings, by CU's music consultant and the editors of *Consumer Reports*. Indianapolis, Bobbs-Merrill Co., 1972. 376 p.

C93   The critics' choice. *The Gramophone*. [Appears in the December issue every year.]

C94   La Discothèque idéale. Paris, Éditions universitaires, 1970. 455 p. In French.

       La Discothèque idéale. Rev. ed. Paris, Éditions universitaires, 1973. 443 p. In French.

C95   Døssing, Bo, and Søren Winther. Mønsterkatalog over grammofon-plader. Slagelse, Slagelse Centralbibliothek, 1971. 80 p. In Danish.

C96   Ecke, Christoph. Ewiger Vorrat klassischer Musik auf Langspielplat-ten; ein Wegweiser. Hamburg, Rowohlt. v. 1– . 1959– . In German.

C97   Eidleman, Mary Landry, and others. "Now" recordings for teen-agers. *Top of the News*, XXVIII (#2, Jan. 1972), 145-51.

C98   Freed, Roger. The year's best recordings. *The Saturday Review*. [Appears in the last November issue every year.]

C99   Great recordings of the decade: the classics. *High Fidelity/Musical America*, XXI (Apr. 29, 1971), 62-69.

C100   Greenfield, Edward, Ivan March, and Denis Stevens. A guide to the bargain classics. Blackpool, Long Playing Record Library, 1962-64. 2v.

C101   Greenfield, Edward, Ivan March, and Denis Stevens. The Penguin guide to bargain records. Blackpool, Long Playing Record Library, 1966. 499 p.

C102   Greenfield, Edward, Ivan March, and Denis Stevens. The second Penguin guide to bargain records. Blackpool, Long Playing Record Library, 1970. 584 p.

C103   Greenfield, Edward, Ivan March, and Denis Stevens. The third Pen-guin guide to bargain records. Blackpool, Long Playing Record Library, 1972. 328 p.

C104   Greenfield, Edward, Ivan March, and others. The great records. Blackpool, Long Playing Record Library, 1967. 201 p.

C105   Greenfield, Edward, Ivan March, Denis Stevens, and Robert Layton. Stereo record guide. Blackpool, Long Playing Record Library. v. 1– . 1960– . [Eight volumes to date, periodically updating for new releases.]

C106 Gronow, Pekka, and Ilpo Saunio. Äänilevytieto. Levyhyllyn käsikirja. Porvoo, W. Söderström; Helsinki, WSOY, 1970. 361 p. In Finnish.

C107 Hemming, Roy. Discovering music; a guide to stereo records, cassettes and cartridges. New York, Four Winds, 1974.

C108 High Fidelity annual records in review. Great Barrington, Mass., Wyeth. v. 1– . 1955– . [Title varies.]

C109 Koehler & Volckmar, Musik-Schallplatten; klassische und moderne Musik in hervorragenden Interpretationen auf Langspielplatten der führenden Markenfirmen. Koehler & Volckmar, 196? 112 p. In German.

C110 Layton, Robert. Recommended recordings; a basic library. London, The Gramophone, 1966. 40 p.

C111 Libraphone, inc. Listening library of LP recordings. Long Branch, N.J., Libraphone. v. 1– . 1961– .

C112 Lory, Jacques. Guide des disques. Paris, Buchet-Chastel, 1967. 434 p. In French.

Lory, Jacques. Guide des disques. 2d ed. Paris, Buchet-Chastel, 1968. 459 p. In French.

Lory, Jacques. Guide des disques. 3d ed. Paris, Buchet-Chastel, 1971. 416 p. In French.

C113 Lundblad, Bengt. De bästa grammofonskivorna. Lund, Bibliotekstjänst, 1964. 134 p. In Swedish.

Lundblad, Bengt. De bästa grammofonskivorna. 2d ed. Lund, Bibliotekstjänst, 1966. 181 p. In Swedish.

C114 McArthur, Edwin, and William E. Stolze. Guide to good listening; the new handbook for building your record library. St. Louis, Aeolian Company of Missouri, 1964. 28 p.

C115 Maleady, Antoinette O. Record and tape reviews index. Metuchen, N.J., Scarecrow Press. v. 1– . 1972– .

C116 Maselli, Gianfranco. Il cercadischi. Guida alla formazione di una discoteca dal Medioevo ai nostri giorni. Milano, A. Mondadori, 1972. 304 p. In Italian.

C117 Pinchard, Max. Ma discothèque classique; un choix des meilleurs enregistrements. Verviers, Gérard, 1963. 158 p. In French.

C118   Polart index of record reviews. Detroit, Polart. v. 1-9. 1960-68.

C119   Preview of the coming season's records. *High Fidelity/Musical America.* [Appears in September issues.]

C120   Russcol, Herbert. Guide to low-priced classical records. New York, Hart, 1969. 831 p.

C121   Stevenson, Gordon. The practical selector. *Library Journal*, LXXXVII (May 1, 1963), 1819-22.

C122   Taubman, Hyman Howard. How to build a record library. [Reprint of the Garden City, 1953 edition.] Westport, Conn., Greenwood, 1970. 94 p.

C123   Taubman, Hyman Howard. The New York Times guide to listening pleasure. New York, Macmillan, 1968. 328 p. Discography: pp. 255-319.

C124   White, Ralph D. Collector's reference catalogue of private recordings on LP. McKinney, Texas, Ralph D. White [P.O. Box 658]. 3v. [In preparation.]

C125   Wilson, William John, ed. The stereo index: a complete catalogue of every recommended stereo disc. 3d ed. London, Wilson Stereo Library, 1967. 174 p.

Wilson, William John, ed. The stereo index: a complete catalogue of every recommended stereo disc. 4th ed. London, Wilson Stereo Library, 1969. 262 p.

SUBJECTS AND GENRES

American Music

C126   Edwards, Arthur C., and William Thomas Marrocco. Music in the United States. Dubuque, Ia., W. C. Brown, 1968. 179 p. Discography: pp. 143-158.

C127   Ellsworth, R. Americans on microgroove—a discography. *High Fidelity*, VI (July 1956), 63-69; (Aug. 1956), 60-66.

C128   Hall, David. CRI: a sonic showcase for the American composer. *Library Journal*, LXXXVII (May 1, 1963), 1826-29.

Hall, David. CRI: a sonic showcase for the American composer. [Reprint with revisions.] *American Composers' Alliance Bulletin,* XI (#2-4, 1963), 21-29.

C129   Howard, John Tasker, and George Kent Bellows. A short history of music in America. New York, Thomas Y. Crowell Co., 1967. 496 p. "Recordings of American music": pp. 429-456.

C130   Keats, S. American music on LP records—an index. *Juilliard Review*, Spring 1955, 31-43; Fall 1955, 48-51; Winter 1955/56, 24-33; Fall 1956, 17-20; Winter 1956/57, 33-39; Fall 1957, 36-40.

C131   McClellan, W. Recordings and new American music [selected 20th-century composers]. *Music Journal*, XXIII (Dec. 1965), 40-46.

C132   Mellers, Wilfrid Howard. Music in a new found land. New York, A. A. Knopf; London, Barrie and Rockliff, 1964. 543 p. Discography by Kenneth W. Dommett [excluding jazz and blues portion]: pp. 452-478, 511-519.

C133   Sablosky, Irving L. American music. Chicago, University of Chicago Press, 1969. 228 p. Discography: pp. 206-213.

Australian Music

C134   Brumby, Colin. Discography of Australian music. *Australian Journal of Music Education*, I (Oct. 1967), 51-52.

C135   Covell, Roger. Australia's music; themes for a new society. Melbourne, Sun Books, 1967. 356 p. Discography: pp. 307-313.

C136   McCredie, Andrew D. Musical composition in Australia, including select bibliography and discography. Canberra, Advisory Board, Commonwealth Assistance to Australian Composers, 1969. 34 p. Discography: pp. 29-31.

C137   Plush, Vincent. Discography of music by Australian composers. *Studies in Music*, #6 (1972), 68-85. Contents: Agnew, Ahern, Aked, Antill, Badger, Bainton, Banks, Benjamin, Bonighton, Boyd, Brumby, Burnard, Butterley, Conyngham, Cuckson, Cugley, Dobie, Douglas, Dreyfus, Eagles, Edwards, English, Evans, Exton, Farr, Findlay, Ford, Fowler, Gifford, Glanville-Hicks, Grainger, Gross, Hanson, A. Hill, M. Hill, Holland, Hollier, Hughes, Humble, Hurst, Hutchens, Hyde, James, Jenkins, Jones, Kay, Keats, Le Gallienne, Lovelock, Mather, Meale, Nickson, Overman, Penberthy, Peters, Phillips, Rorke, Sculthorpe, Sitsky, Sutherland, Tahourdin, Tibbits, Tregaskis, Trumble, Tunley, Werder, Wesley-Smith, Williamson.

Austrian Music

C138   Blaukopf, Kurt. Musik aus Österreich. Ein diskographisches Verzeichnis, das einen Überblick über die wichtigsten Werke in möglichst repräsentativen Aufnahmen bietet. Wien, Österreichische Gesellschaft für Musik, 1968. 32 p. In German.

Ballet Music

C139   Rycken, Hendrik. Verhalen gespeeld bij fonoplaten. Lier, J. van In, 1965? 56 p. In Dutch. Includes discography.

Band Music

C140   Band record guide. Evanston, Ill., The Instrumentalist, 1971. 108 p.

C141   Bibliography of band recordings. *The Instrumentalist*, XI (Oct. 1956), 60-70.

C142   Dondeyne, Désiré. Nouveau traité d'orchestration, à l'usage des harmonies, fanfares et musiques militaires. Paris, H. Lemoine, 1969. 368 p. In French. Discography (4 p.) inserted.

Bassoon and Contrabassoon

C143   Langwill, Lyndesay Graham. The bassoon and contrabassoon. London, E. Benn; New York, W. W. Norton, 1965. 269 p. "Discography of bassoon players": pp. 223-258.

Belgian Music

C144   Centre belge de documentation musicale, Brussels. Music in Belgium; contemporary Belgian composers. Brussels, A. Manteau, 1964. 158 p. "A brief list of recordings": pp. 141-158.

C145   Wangermée, Robert. La musique belge contemporaine. Bruxelles, La renaissance du livre, 1959. 151 p. In French. Includes discographies.

Berlin

C146   Reinold, Helmut. Berlin als Musikstadt, die Jahre 1910-1960. Freiburg i. Br., Fono-Verlagsgesellschaft, 1962. 32 p. In German. Discography: pp. 28-32.

Black Music

C147 De Lerma, Dominique René, ed. Black music in our culture. Kent,
      Ohio, Kent State University Press, 1970. 263 p. Discographies:
      pp. 181-199.

C148 De Lerma, Dominique René. A discography of concert music by
      black composers. (Afro-American music opportunities association
      resource papers, 1) Minneapolis, AAMOA Press, 1973. 29 p.

C149 Southern, Eileen. The music of black Americans: a history. New
      York, W. W. Norton, 1971. 552 p. Bibliography and discography:
      pp. 511-532.

Brass Instruments

C150 Bridges, Glenn D. Pioneers in brass. Detroit, Sherwood Publications,
      1965. 113 p. Includes discographies.

      Bridges, Glenn D. Pioneers in brass. Rev. ed. Detroit, Sherwood
      Publications, 1968. 135 p. Includes discographies.

Brazilian Music

C151 Andrade, Mario de. Ensaio sôbre a música brasileira. 3. ed. São Paulo,
      Livraria Martins Editora, 1972. 188 p. In Portuguese. Includes discog-
      raphy.

Canadian Music

C152 Canada on records. *Musicanada,* #26 (Jan.-Feb. 1970), entire issue.

C153 Canadian Music Centre, Toronto. Catalogue of chamber music avail-
      able on loan from the library of the Canadian Music Centre. Toronto,
      Canadian Music Centre, 1967. 288 p. In English and French. Includes
      a discography of Canadian chamber music.

C154 MacMillan, Keith. Canadian notes for Notes [includes a discography
      of new recordings of Canadian music] . *Notes,* XXIV (#2, Dec. 1967),
      245-50.

Catalan Music

C155   Una Década de música catalana. 1960-1970. Barcelona, Exposició muntada per Joventuts Musicals, 1970. 114 p. In Catalan, English, French, German, and Spanish. Includes discographies.

Chamber Music

C156   Gammond, Peter, and Burnett James. Music on record, a critical guide: volume 3, chamber and instrumental music. London, Hutchinson, 1963. 185p.

C157   Materials for miscellaneous instrumental ensembles. Washington, Music Educators National Conference, 1960. 89 p. Includes discography.

Children's Music

C158   Bustarret, Anne. Disques pour nos enfants, avec une discographie commentée. Paris, Gamma, 1970. 91 p. In French.

C159   New York Library Association. Children's and Young Adult Services Section. Recordings for children. 2d ed., rev. New York, New York Library Association, 1964. 43 p.

Choral Music

C160   Jacobs, Arthur, ed. Choral music: a symposium. Baltimore, Penguin Books, 1963. 444 p. "Recommended gramophone records": pp. 427-436.

C161   Johnson, D. The Mass since Bach. *High Fidelity*, VIII (Apr. 1958), 81-82; (May 1958), 85-90.

C162   Kirby, Lewis M. A catalog of sacred music. Alexandria, Va., Seminary Books Service, Record Dept., 196? 79 p.

C163   Kirchberg, K. Der Männerchor—eine Discographie. *Musikhandel*, XIII (#5, 1962), 219; (#6, 1962), 253-54. In German.

C164   Religious Record Index, Dayton, Ohio. Official religious record index. Dayton, Ohio, Religious Record Index, 1961. 132 p. Supplements, 1962– .

C165   Routley, Erik. Twentieth century church music. New York, Oxford University Press, 1964. 244 p. Discography: pp. 235-239.

C166   Royal School of Church Music. A selected list of church music recordings. Croydon, Royal School of Church Music, 1967. 12 p.

Christmas Music

C167   Especially for Christmas. *American Record Guide*, XXX (Dec. 1963), 283-87.

C168   Nettel, Reginald. Carols, 1400-1950; a book of Christmas carols. Bedford, Eng., Gordon Fraser Gallery, 1956. 112 p. Discography: pp. 109-110.

C169   Reinold, Helmut, ed. Mittelalterliche Weihnacht. Freiburg i Br., Fono-Verlagsgesellschaft, 1962. 32 p. In German. Discography: pp. 29-32.

Clarinet

C170   Eberst, Anton. Klarinet i klarinetisti. Novi Sad, Yugoslavia, Forum, 1963. 160 p. In Serbo-Croatian. Discography: pp. 117-150.

C171   Gilbert, Richard. The clarinetists' solo repertoire; a discography. New York, Grenadilla Society, 1972. 100 p.

C172   Walker, Bonnie Hicks. Recordings for the clarinet and the recording artists. Augusta, Ga., Walker, 1969. 63 p.

Clavichord

C173   Cooper, Kenneth. The clavichord in the eighteenth century. Unpublished Ph.D. dissertation, Columbia University, 1971. 289 p. Includes "list of all extant clavichord recordings."

C174   Wagner, Lavern J. The clavichord today, part 2. *Periodical of the Illinois State Music Teachers Association,* VII (#1, Summer 1969), 1-16. Includes discography.

Composer as Performer

C175   Douglas, John R. The composer and his music on record. *Library Journal*, XCII (#6, Mar. 15, 1967), 1117-21.

C176   Mueller von Asow, Erich Hermann. Komponistinnen-Discographie. Berlin, Mueller von Asow, 1962. 153 p. In German.

Concerto

C177   Young, Percy Marshall. Concerto. Boston, Crescendo Publishers, 1968. 168 p. "Index of works and recordings": pp. 155-162.

C178   Wooldridge, David. Conductor's world. London, Barrie & Rockliff, 1970. 379 p. Discography: pp. 349-363. Contents: Wilhelm Furtwängler, Erich Kleiber, Otto Klemperer, Serge Koussevitsky, Clemens Krauss, Willem Mengelberg, Charles Munch, Artur Nikisch, Leopold Stokowski, Richard Strauss, Bruno Walter, and Felix Weingartner.

Czechoslovakian Music

C179   Gardavský, Čeněk. Les Compositeurs tchécoslovaques contemporains. [Translation by Mojimir Vanék.] Prague, Panton, 1966. 562 p. In French; also available in English edition. Discography: pp. 539-562.

Danish Music

C180   Ketting, K. Recorded Danish music. *Dansk Musiktidsskrift,* XLVII (special issue, 1971), 133-36.

C181   Nationaldiskoteket, København. Edition Balzer—a history of music in sound in Denmark. København, Nationaldiskoteket, 1966. 12 p.

Dutch Music

C182   Rayment, M. Donemus recordings. *Musical Opinion,* LXXXVIII (May 1965), 468-69.

Education

C183   Bédard, Yves. Oeuvres commentées à l'usage des professeurs d'education musicale. Montreal, Leméac, 1968. 132 p. In French. Discography: p. 131.

C184   Campanini, Cesare. I racconti delle note; testo di educazione musicale per la Scuola media secondo il nuovo programma ministeriale. Bergamo, Edizioni Carrara, 1964. 176 p. In Italian. Discography: pp. 175-176.

C185   Contemporary Music Project for Creativity in Music Education. Experiments in musical creativity. Washington, Music Educators National Conference, 1966. 86 p. Includes discographies.

C186 Demus, Jörg. Abenteuer der Interpretation. Wiesbaden, F. A. Brockhaus, 1967. 248 p. In German. Discography: pp. 231-244.

C187 Dinkla, H. Muzikale vorming voor leerlingen van het voortgezet onderwijs. 3. druk. Den Haag, G. B. van Goor Zonen, 1966. 200 p. In Dutch. Discography: p. 6.

C188 Ellis, Don. The new rhythm book. North Hollywood, Calif., Ellis Music Enterprises, 1972. 101 p. Discography: pp. 95-101.

C189 Gagnard, Madeleine. L'initiation musicale des jeunes. Tournai, Casterman, 1971. 139 p. In French. Discography: pp. 137-138.

C190 Hügler, Walter. Schallplatten-Verzeichnis für den Musikunterricht. Trossingen, Württemberg, Verlag Der Harmonikalehrer, 1965. 11 p. In German.

C191 Joint Committee of the California Music Educators Association and the Music Committee of the California Association for Supervision and Curriculum Development. Teachers guide to music in the elementary school. Sacramento, Calif., State Dept. of Education, 1963. 149 p. Includes discographies.

C192 Monsour, Sally, and Margaret Perry. A junior high school music handbook. Englewood Cliffs, N.J., Prentice-Hall, 1963. 135 p. Includes discography.

Monsour, Sally, and Margaret Perry. A junior high school music handbook. 2d ed. Englewood Cliffs, N.J., Prentice-Hall, 1970. 147 p. "Recordings of contemporary music for classroom use": pp. 127-129.

C193 New York State Bureau of Secondary Curriculum Development. Teaching general music; a resource handbook for grades 7 and 8. Albany, SUNY State Education Dept., 1966. 180 p. Includes discographies.

C194 RCA Victor educational and library catalog. New York, RCA Victor Educational Sales. [An annual publication.]

C195 Raebeck, Lois, and Lawrence Wheeler. New approaches to music in the elementary school. Dubuque, Ia., W. C. Brown, 1964. 310 p. Includes discographies.

Raebeck, Lois, and Lawrence Wheeler. New approaches to music in the elementary school. 2d ed. Dubuque, Ia., W. C. Brown, 1969. 389 p. Includes discographies.

C196   Righi, Franceline. L'Éducation musicale à l'école primaire. Lyon,
        C. R. D. P., 1968? 195 p. In French. Discography: pp. 179-188.

C197   Runkle, Aleta, and Mary LeBow Eriksen. Music for today's boys and
        girls; sequential learning through the grades. Boston, Allyn and Bacon,
        1966. 280 p. Includes discographies.

        Runkle, Aleta, and Mary LeBow Eriksen. Music for today's boys and
        girls; sequential learning through the grades. 2d ed. Boston, Allyn and
        Bacon, 1970. 410 p. Includes discographies.

C198   Sasso, Silvestro. Dal ritmo all'espressione. Corso di educazione
        musicale ad uso degli istituti magistrali, delle scuole magistrali e delle
        scuole corali. Milano, Principato. v. 1– . 1970– . In Italian. Discog-
        raphy: v. 1, pp. 274-276.

C199   Thiel, Jörn. International anthology of recorded music. Wien,
        München, Jugend und Volk, 1971. 208 p.

C200   Weerts, Richard. How to develop and maintain a successful wood-
        wind section. West Nyack, N.Y., Parker, 1972. 204 p. Includes
        discography.

C201   Westphal, Frederick W. Guide to teaching woodwinds. Dubuque, Ia.,
        W. C. Brown, 1962. 315 p. Discography: pp. 281-285.

C202   Wills, Vera G., and Ande Manners. A parent's guide to music lessons.
        New York, Harper & Row, 1967. 274 p. Discography: pp. 75-83.

C203   Winters, Geoffrey. An introduction to group music making; a
        practical guide for the non-specialist. London, New York, Chappell,
        1967. 59 p. Discography: p. 59.

Electronic Music

C204   Davies, Hugh. A discography of electronic music and musique
        concrète. *Recorded Sound,* #14 (Apr. 1964), 205-24.

C205   Frank, P. A discography of electronic music on recordings. *BMI, The
        Many Worlds of Music,* Summer 1970, 14-22.

C206   Oram, Daphne. An individual note: of music, sound and electronics.
        London, Galliard; New York, Galaxy Music, 1972. 145 p. "List of
        records": pp. 129-136.

C207 Preiberg, Fred K. Musica ex machina: über das Verhältnis von Musik und Technik. Berlin, Ullstein, 1960. 299 p. In German. Discography: pp. 263-281.

C208 Russcol, Herbert. The liberation of sound: an introduction to electronic music. Englewood Cliffs, N.J., Prentice-Hall, 1972. 315 p. Discography: pp. 243-264.

C209 Schwartz, Elliott. Electronic music; a listener's guide. New York, Praeger, 1973. 306 p. Discography: pp. 293-298.

English Music

C210 Mason, Colin. Music in Britain, 1951-1962. London, Longmans, Green, 1963. 56 p. Discography: pp. 51-56.

C211 Mellers, Wilfrid Howard. Harmonious meeting; a study of the relationship between English music, poetry and theatre, ca. 1600-1900. London, D. Dobson, 1965. 317 p. Discography: pp. 309-311.

Experimental Music

C212 An incomplete discography of experimental music. *Inter-American Music Bulletin*, #14 (Nov. 1959), 3.

Film, Radio, and Television music

C213 Limbacher, James L. A selected list of recorded musical scores from radio, television, and motion pictures. Dearborn, Mich., Dearborn Public Library, 1960. 21 p.

Limbacher, James L. A selected list of recorded musical scores from radio, television, and motion pictures. 4th ed. Dearborn, Mich., Dearborn Public Library, 1967. 48 p.

C214 Smolian, Steven. A handbook of film, theater, and television music on record, 1948-1969. New York, Record Undertaker, 1970. 2v. in 1 (64 p., 64 p.)

Flute

C215 Ballantine, Bill. The flute; an introduction to the instrument. New York, F. Watts, 1971. 127 p. Discography: pp. 115-122.

C216 Burks, Aldine K. Follow the pipers; a guide to contemporary flute artists and teachers. Westfield, N.Y., Burks, 1969. 181 p. Includes discographies.

C217 Girard, Adrien. Histoire et richesses de la flûte. Paris, Librarie Gründ, 1953; New York, McGinnis and Marx, 1956. 143 p. In French. Discography: pp. 129-134.

C218 Lasocki, D. R. G. The Baroque flute and its role today. *Recorder and Music Magazine*, II (#4, Feb. 1967), 96+

C219 Reinold, Helmut, ed. Die Flöte. Freiburg i Br., Fono-Verlagsgesellschaft, 1963. 32 p. In German. Discography: pp. 22-32.

C220 Roberts, Alice. Discography of the flute. Master's research paper, Kent State University School of Library Science, 1972. 72 p.

French Horn

C221 Uggen, S. A French horn discography. *The Instrumentalist*, XXIV (Mar. 1970), 59-61.

French Music

C222 Bloch, Francine. La disque en France. Paris, La documentation française, 1967. In French.

C223 Davies, Laurence. The gallic muse. South Brunswick, N.J., A. S. Barnes, 1969. 230 p. Discography: pp. 207-218.

C224 Demuth, Norman. French opera; its development to the Revolution. Sussex, Artemis Press, 1963; Chester Springs, Pa., Dufour Editions, 1964. 337 p. Discography: pp. 323-329.

C225 Moortgat, Gabriël. Xvie [i.e., Zestiende], xviie & xviiie eeuwse Franse orgelmeesters. Brugge, Verbeke-Loys, 1963. 107 p. In Flemish. Discography: pp. 103-107.

C226 Roy, Jean. Présences contemporaines; musique française: Satie, Koechlin, Roussel, Schmitt, Varèse, Migot, Honegger, Milhaud, Poulenc, Jaubert, Sauguet, Jolivet, Lesur, Messiaen, Ohana, Dutilleux, Nigg, Jarré, Boulez, Bondon, avec un index des oeuvres et des disques. Paris, Nouvelles Éditions Debresse, 1962. 488 p. In French. Includes discographies.

C227 Stricker, Rémy. La musique française du romantisme à nos jours. Paris, La documentation française, 1966. 96 p. In French. Discography: pp. 94-95.

C228 Vendée, G. Disques de musique française—1968-1969. *Le Courrier Musical de France*, #25 (1969), 32-43; #26 (1969), 111-15; #27 (1969), 191-99. In French.

German Music (East)

C229 Berlin. Stadtbibliothek. Abteilung Musikbibliothek und Phonothek. Musik und Literatur der DDR auf Schallplatten. Eine Diskographie zum 20. Jahrestag d. DDR. Zusammengestellt von Achim Rohde. Berlin, Berliner Stadtbibliothek, 1969. 38 p. In German.

Guitar and Lute

C230 Frank, M. H. Lute and guitar. *Listen*, I (Feb. 1964), 21.

C231 Miller, C. The lute on discs. *The Guitar Review*, #27 (Oct. 1963), 22-26.

Harp

C232 Harp News reference record list: 1950-1960. *Harp News*, III (#2, 1960), 11-16.

Hungarian Music

C233 Contemporary Hungarian composers. Gyula Czigány, responsible editor. Budapest, Editio Musica, 1970. 156 p. Discography: pp. 144-156.

Instrumental Music

C234 Discothèque de France. Répertoire des interprètes; musique classique, instruments. Rédigé par Bernard Marrey. Paris, Discothèque de France, 1972. 43 p. In French.

Instruments

C235 Corneloup, Marcel. L'Orchestre et ses instruments, initiation musicale à travers les grandes oeuvres. Paris, les Presses d'Ile-de-France, 1965? 239 p. In French. Discography: pp. 231-233.

C236   Rattalino, Piero. Gli strumenti musicali. Milano, Ricordi, 1968. 166 p.
        In Italian. "Nota discografica": pp. 159-161.

Latin American Music

C237   New recordings of music of the Americas. *Inter-American Music
        Bulletin*, #77 (May 1970), 16-17.

C238   Trigo de Sousa, A. Discografía seleccionada de compositores ameri-
        canos. *Arte Musical*, XXXIII (#25-26, 1967), 83-88. In Portuguese.

Library Catalogs

C239   Aarhus, Denmark. Statsbibliotek. Fortegnelse over musikplader.
        Klassisk musik og folkemusik. Aarhus, Carstens, 1968. 127 p. In
        Danish.

C240   Bibliotekscentralen, København. Grammofonplaader i undervisningen.
        København, Bibliotekscentralen, 1971. 30 p. In Danish.

C241   British Broadcasting Corporation. Gramophone Record Library. BBC
        Gramophone Record Library; archive commercial gramophone
        records. London, BBC, 1963. 2v.

C242   British Broadcasting Corporation. Transcription Service. Index of
        all current BBC transcription recordings. London, BBC, 197?

C243   British Institute of Recorded Sound, London. Central gramophone
        library catalogue. London, BIRS, 1965. 235 p.

C244   British Institute of Recorded Sound, London. Music by British com-
        posers of the twentieth century—handlist of tape recordings in the
        Institute's collection. London, BIRS, 1967.

C245   Canadian Music Centre, Toronto. Recordings of works by Canadian
        composers included in the library of the Canadian Music Centre.
        Toronto, Canadian Music Centre, 1967? 11 p.

C246   Dartmouth Electronic Music Studio. Catalog of tape holdings. 2d ed.
        Hanover, N.H., Dartmouth College, 1970. 44 p.

C247   Discothèque de Paris. Catalogue de la discothèque centrale. Paris,
        Discothèque de Paris, 1970? 960 p. In French.

C248   Indiana. University. School of Music. Latin American Music Center.
        Music from Latin America available at Indiana University: scores,

tapes and records. Ed by Juan A. Orrego-Salas. Bloomington, Ind., Latin American Music Center, Indiana University, 1971. 412 p. Catalog of tape recordings: pp. 191-380.

C249   Louisiana. State Library, Baton Rouge. Dimensions in listening; recordings, spoken and musical. Baton Rouge, Louisiana State Library, 1970. 99 p.

C250   Louisiana. State Library, Baton Rouge. Recordings collection. Baton Rouge, Louisiana State Library, 1963. 43 p.

C251   New Mexico. University. Fine Arts Library. A discography of Hispanic music in the Fine Arts Library of the University of New Mexico. Ed. by Ned Sublette. Albuquerque, Fine Arts Library, University of New Mexico, 1973. 110 p.

C252   RAI-Radiotelevisione italiana. Direzione programmi radio. Discoteca centrale. Catalogo della discoteca storica. 1ª serie. Roma, RAI—Radiotelevisione italiana, Servizio archivi, 1969. 3v. In Italian.

C253   Radiodiffusion Outre-Mer. Phonothèque centrale de la *SCRAFOM;* enregistrements musicaux. Paris, Radiodiffusion Outre-Mer, 1961-62. 2v. In French.

C254   Radiodiffusion-Télévision française. Archives sonores service phono-graphique. Catalogue des disques microsillons. Paris, Radiodiffusion-Télévision française, 196? In French.

C255   Rome. Centro Nazionale Studi di Musica Popolare. Catalogo sommario delle registrazioni, 1948-1962. Roma, Centro Nazionale Studi di Musica Popolare, 1963. 279 p. In Italian.

C256   Stanford University Libraries. Audio catalog of the undergraduate library. 4th ed. Stanford, Calif., J. H. Meyer Memorial Library, 1971?

C257   Suffolk, East, England. County Library. Gramophone record catalogue. Ipswich, Suffolk, East Suffolk County Library, 1969. 225 p.

C258   Washington (State) University. Phonoarchive. History in sound; a descriptive listing of the KIRO-CBS collection of broadcasts of the World War II years and after, in the Phonoarchive of the University of Washington. Ed. by Milo Ryan. Seattle, University of Washington Press, 1963. 617 p.

Lithuanian Music

C259   Tauragis, Adeodatas. Lithuanian music; past and present. Translated
        by M. Ginsburgas and N. Kameneckaite. Gintaras, Vilnius, 1971.
        223 p. Discography: pp. 215-224.

Lüdenscheid

C260   Pahl, Helmut. Diskographie von Stadt und Kreis Lüdenscheid. 2. erw.
        Aufl. [Previously published under the title Lüdenscheider Interpreten
        auf Schallplatten.] Lüdenscheid, Stadtverwaltung, Hauptamt,
        Stadtarchiv, 1970. 129 p. In German.

Mechanical Musical Instruments

C261   Waard, R. de. From music boxes to street organs. Translated by
        Wade Jenkins. New York, Vestal Press, 1967. 263 p. Discography:
        pp. 258-259.

Musical Comedy

C262   Alphabetical directory to original cast & soundtrack albums. *Cash
        Box*, XXV (Apr. 11, 1964, supplement), 4.

C263   Bosch, Jack. Prisma operettegids, door G. di Foresta. Utrecht, Het
        Spektrum, 1962. 198 p. In Dutch. Includes discographies.

C264   Burton, Jack. The blue book of Broadway musicals. [Reprint of the
        1952 edition with additional material by Larry Freeman.] Watkins
        Glen, N.Y., Century House, 1969. 327 p. Includes discography.

C265   Engel, Lehman. The American musical theater; a consideration. New
        York, CBS Records; distributed by Macmillan, 1967. 236 p. Discog-
        raphy: pp. 208-214.

C266   Kreuger, M. A discography of original-cast Capitol albums. *The
        American Record Guide*, XXXII (Oct. 1965), 181.

C267   Kreuger, M. A discography of original-cast Columbia albums. *The
        American Record Guide*, XXXII (Dec. 1965), 329-37.

C268   Kreuger, M. A discography of original-cast Decca LP albums. *The
        American Record Guide*, XXXII (Sep. 1965), 76-77.

C269 Kreuger, M. For the collector of Broadway musicals—a discography of RCA Victor LP original-cast albums. *The American Record Guide*, XXXI (July 1965), 1044-46.

C270 Limbacher, James L. Theatrical events; a selected list of musical and dramatic performances on long-playing records. 5th ed. Dearborn, Mich., Dearborn Public Library, 1968. 95 p.

C271 Stambler, Irwin, Vern Bushway, and others. Encyclopedia of popular music. New York, St. Martin's Press, 1965. 353 p. Discography: pp. 341-353.

Norwegian Music

C272 Kortsen, Bjarne. Contemporary Norwegian orchestral music. Bergen, Forfatteren, Solbakken 17, 1969. 458 p. Includes discography.

C273 Kortsen, Bjarne. Modern Norwegian chamber music. 2d ed. Haugesund, Kortsen, 1969. 174 p. "Norwegian works available on records": p. 174.

Opera

C274 Berlin. Deutsche Musik-Phonothek. Die Oper im xx. Jahrhundert; Diskographie. Teilkatalog hrsg. anlässlich des Kongresses "Zeitgenössisches Musiktheater" in Hamburg, Juni 1964. Berlin, Deutsche Musik-Phonothek, 1964. 123 p. In German.

C275 Bibliographie und Diskographie: Zeitgenoessisches Musiktheater. *Musik und Bildung*, III (Nov. 1971), 556-63. In German.

C276 Ewen, David. The book of European light opera. New York, Holt, Rinehart and Winston, 1962. 297 p. Discography: pp. 274-277.

C277 Galatopoulos, Stelios. Italian opera. London, Dent, 1971. 179 p. "List of records": pp. 165-166.

C278 Gammond, Peter, and Burnett James. Music on record, a critical guide: opera and vocal music. London, Hutchinson, 1963. 452 p.

C279 Guerre, Gisèle. Opéra-comique in the nineteenth century. [n.p.,] Guerre, 1966. 76 p. Discography: p. 75.

C280 Harris, Kenn. Opera recordings; a critical guide. New York, Drake, 1963. 328 p.

C281   Herzfeld, Friedrich. Schallplattenführer für Opernfreunde. Frankfurt am Main, Verlag Ullstein, 1962. 296 p. In German.

C282   Hughes, Patrick Cairns. Glyndebourne; a history of the festival opera. London, Methuen, 1965. 307 p. "The Glyndebourne recordings": pp. 298-300.

C283   Jacobs, Arthur, and Stanley Sadie. The opera guide. London, H. Hamilton, 1964. 370 p. Discography: pp. 365-370.

C284   Jacobs, Arthur, and Stanley Sadie. The Pan book of opera. London, Pan Books, 1964. 500 p. Discography: pp. 489-495.

C285   Költzsch, Hans. Der neue Opernführer. Stuttgart, Steingrüben, 1968. 558 p. In German. Discography: pp. 524-535.

C286   Lualdi, Adriano. La bilancia di Euripide; dieci libretti d'opera. Milano, dall'Oglio Editore, 1969. 658 p. In Italian. Discography: pp. 647-651.

C287   Natan, Alex. Primo uomo; grosse Sänger der Oper. Basel, Basilius Presse, 1963. 152 p. In German. Discography: pp. 121-147.

C288   Steyn, Louis. Die Afrikaanse operagids. Kaapstad, Human & Rousseau, 1964. 295 p. In Dutch. Discography: pp. 293-294.

C289   The Victor book of the opera. 13th ed., revised by Henry W. Simon. New York, Simon and Schuster, 1968. 475 p. Discography: pp. 459-467.

C290   Vsesoiuznaia studiia gramzapisi. Opernaia i kamerno-vokal' naia muzyka. Moskva, 1961. 68 p. [Citation transliterated from the Russian.] In Russian.

C291   Worbs, Hans Christoph. Welterfolge der modernen Oper. Berlin, Rembrandt Verlag, 1967. 190 p. In German. Discography: pp. 181-182.

Orchestral Music

C292   Gammond, Peter, and Burnett James. Music on record, a critical guide: orchestral music. London, Hutchinson, 1962. 2v. (191 p., 199 p.)

Organs

C293   Armstrong, William Howard. Organs of America; the life and work of David Tannenburg. Philadelphia, University of Pennsylvania Press, 1967. 154 p. Discography: p. 145.

C294   Hoverland, John Allyn. Organs on record: an annotated discography of performances in selected European countries (Austria, Denmark, Germany, The Netherlands, Norway, Sweden and Switzerland). Master's research paper, Kent State University School of Library Science, 1973. 54 p.

C295   Laade, Wolfgang. Klangdokumente historischer Tasteninstrumente: Orgeln, Kiel- und Hammerklaviere. Diskographie. Zürich, Musikverlag zum Pelikan, 1972. 133 p. In German.

C296   Prick van Wely, Max Arthur. Het orgel en zijn meesters. 2. geheel herziene druk. Den Haag, Kruseman, 1965. 374 p. In Dutch. Discography: pp. 354-359.

C297   Schäfer, Ernst. Laudatio organi; eine Orgelfahrt. Leipzig, Deutscher Verlag für Musik, 1972. 21 p. [of text; plates, discographies and index also included.] In German.

Percussion Instruments

C298   Bartlett, Harry R. Guide to teaching percussion. Dubuque, Ia., W. C. Brown, 1964. 168 p. Discography: pp. 162-163.

C299   Houston, R. Percussion ensemble and solo recordings. Miami, University of Miami Music Library, 1971?

Piano

C300   Ballantine, Bill. The piano; an introduction to the instrument. New York, F. Watts, 1971. 128 p. Discography: pp. 110-123.

C301   Chapin, Victor. Giants of the keyboard. Philadelphia, Lippincott, 1967. 189 p. Discography: pp. 181-182.

C302   Goldsmith, H. The romantic piano concerto—a discography. *High Fidelity*, XI (May 1961), 64-69; (June 1961), 65-68.

C303   Kaiser, Joachim. Great pianists of our time. Translated by David Wooldridge and George Unwin. London, Allen and Unwin, 1971. 230 p. Discography by F. F. Clough: pp. 219-226.

C304 Kaiser, Joachim. Grosse Pianisten in unserer Zeit. München, Rütten u. Loening, 1965; Gütersloh, Bertelsmann-Lesering; Gütersloh, Kelen; Wien, Buchgemeinschaft, 1967. 230 p. In German "Schallplattenverzeichnis": pp. 219-226.

C305 Range, Hans Peter. Von Beethoven bis Brahms. Einführung in die konzertanten Klavierwerke der Romantik. Lahr/Schwarzw., Schauenburg, 1967. 233 p. In German. Includes discographies.

Plainchant

C306 Bescond, Albert Jacques. Le chant grégorien. Paris, Buchet-Chastel, 1972. 319 p. In French. Discography: pp. 312-313.

C307 De Sutter, Ignace. De Schoonheid van het Gregoriaans. Bruxelles, Belgische Radio en Televisie, 1969. 56 p. In Flemish. Includes discography.

C308 Laade, Wolfgang. Die Geschichte der liturgischen Musik der Östkirchen auf Schallplatten. *Schallplatte und Kirche*, XXXIX (#5, Sep.-Oct. 1969), 109-14; XL (#3, May-June 1970), 225-33. In German.

C309 Nicholson, David. Singing in God's ear. New York, Desclee Co., 1959. 123 p. Discography: pp. 119-123.

C310 Passalacqua, Cosma. Biografia del gregoriano. Milano, Nuova accademia editrice, 1963. 378 p. In Italian. Discography: pp. 361-363.

C311 Semaine d'études internationales, Fribourg, 1965. Le chant liturgique après Vatican II. Paris, Éditions Fleurus, 1966. 248 p. In French. Discography: p. 203.

Polish Music

C312 Dziębowska, Elźbieta. Polska współczesna kultura muzyczna, 1944-1966. Kraków, Polskie Wydawn. Muzyczne, 1968. 457 p. In Polish. Discography: pp. 422-426.

C313 Panek, Waclaw. Dyskografia i piśmiennictwo muzyczne na Łuzycach po 1945 roku. *Muzyka*, XV (#2, 1970), 117-22. In Polish.

Russian Music

C314 Cecil, Winifred. Russian songs and singers. *The Saturday Review*, XLVI (Dec. 28, 1963), 48-49.

C315   Four Continents Book Corporation, New York. Russian music on records. New York, Four Continents Book Corporation, 1967.

C316   Gardner, Johann von. Diskographie des russischen Kirchengesangs. 7. Folge. Östkirchliche Studien, XIX (#1, 1969), 23-42. In German.

C317   Weinstock, H. Russian opera on microgroove. High Fidelity, V (Nov. 1955), 105-18.

St. Cecilia

C318   Landon, H. C. Robbins. Music's St. Cecilia [i.e., music written for or about music's patron saint]. Hifi/Stereo Review, XVII (#4 Apr. 1967), 59-63.

Scandinavian Music

C319   Wallner, Bo. Vår tids musik i Norden. Från 20-tal till 60-tal. Stockholm, Nordiska musikförlaget; København, Wilhelm Hansen Musikforlag; Oslo, Norsk musikforlag, 1968. 435 p. In Swedish. Discography: pp. 383-402.

Solo Song

C320   Clark, R. S. A basic library of German Lieder. Stereo Review, XXII (June 1969), 67-72.

C321   Neef, Wilhelm. Das Chanson; eine Monographie. Leipzig, Koehler & Amelang, 1972. 270 p. In German. Discography: pp. 255-270.

C322   Prawer, Siegbert Salomon, ed. The Penguin book of Lieder. Baltimore, Penguin Books, 1964. 208 p. Discography: pp. 194-200.

C323   Stahl, Dorothy. A selected discography of solo song. (Detroit studies in music bibliography, 13) Detroit, Information Coordinators, 1968. 90 p.

C324   Stahl, Dorothy. A selected discography of solo song: supplement, 1968-1969. (Detroit studies in music bibliography, 13) Detroit, Information Coordinators, 1970. 95 p.

C325   Stahl, Dorothy. A selected discography of solo song: a cumulation through 1971. (Detroit studies in music bibliography, 24) Detroit, Information Coordinators, 1972. 137 p.

C326   Tschulik, Norbert. Lieder aus Österreich; eine kleine Geschichte des Kunstliedes von Walther von der Vogelweide bis heute. Wien, Bergland Verlag, 1964. 119 p. In German. Discography: pp. 111-115.

Swedish Music

C327   Aahlén, Carl-Gunnar. Svensk skivförteckning 1964-66. *Svensk Tidskrift för Musikforskning*, L (1968), 199-232. In Swedish.

C328   Aahlén, Carl-Gunnar. Svensk skivförteckning 1967-68. *Svensk Tidskrift för Musikforskning*, LI (1969), 225-50. In Swedish.

C329   A basic library of Swedish music on record. Swedish music—past and present, a special edition of *Musikrevy*, 1967, 101-05.

C330   Connor, Herbert. Samtal med tonsättare. Stockholm, Natur och kultur, 1971. 223 p. In Swedish. Biographies, lists of works, bibliographies and discographies: pp. 193-218.

C331   Percy, G. Svensk seriös musik paa skiva. *Musikrevy*, XX (#7, 1965), 289-92+ In Swedish.

C332   Wallner, Bo, comp. 40 [i.e., Fyrtio] -tal. En klippbok om Måndagsgruppen och det svenska musiklivet. Stockholm, Institutet för rikskonserter; Solna, Seelig, 1971. 112 p. In Swedish. Discography: p. 111.

Swiss Music

C333   Fierz, G. Schweizer Musik auf Schallplatten. *Schweizerische Musikzeitung*, C (#2, 1960), 105-06. In German.

C334   Radio [Swiss compositions]. *Schweizerische Musikzeitung,* CX (#1, 1970), 55-56. In German.

C335   Schweizerischer Tonkünstlerverein. 40 [i.e., Vierzig] Schweizer Komponisten der Gegenwart. Amriswil, Bodensee-Verlag, 1956. 236 p. In German, French, or English edition. Includes discographies.

Symphonies

C336   Rauchhaupt, Ursula von, ed. Die Welt der Symphonie. Hamburg, Polydor International GmbH, 1972. 324 p. In German. Discography: pp. 318-320.

Trombone

C337   Mergenthaler, Wilhelm, Paul Beinhauer, and Richard Lörcher.
        Handreichung für Posaunenbläser. Wuppertal, Aussaat Verlag, 1964.
        110 p. In German. Discography: p. 110.

Trumpet

C338   Lowrey, Alvin L. Trumpet discography. Denver, National Trumpet
        Symposium; distributed by Theodore Front [Los Angeles], 1972.
        3v. (109 p. total) Contents.—v. 1: Maurice André.—v. 2: individual
        trumpet performers.—v. 3: brass ensembles.

Viola d'amore

C339   Arazi, Ishaq. D'amore con amore. *American String Teacher*, XIX
        (#4, 1969), 7-10+ In English.

Violin

C340   Ballantine, Bill. The violin; an introduction to the instrument. New
        York, F. Watt, 1971. 127 p. Discography: pp. 116-121.

C341   Creighton, James. Discopaedia of the violin 1889-1971. Toronto,
        University of Toronto Press, 1973. 1004 p.

Women Composers

C342   Mueller von Asow, Erich Hermann. Komponistinnen-Discographie
        [compositions by women]. *Musikerziehung*, XV (#2, 1961), 94-96.
        In German.

Zarzuela

C343   Weinstock, H. The world of the zarzuela. *The Saturday Review*,
        XXXVIII (May 28, 1955), 33.

SECTION B

CLASSICAL HISTORICAL RECORDINGS
AND LABEL DISCOGRAPHY

GENERAL SOURCES

C344 Arnold's Archive. Collector's guide to recorded excerpts: Broadway shows and musical comedy, 1890-1940. Grand Rapids, Mich., Arnold's Archive, 1971?

C345 Bauer, Robert. Addenda to The new catalogue of historical records, 1898-1908/09. *The Record Collector*, II (Nov. 1947); III (June 1948); (July 1948); (Aug. 1948). [See C347 below.]

C346 Bauer, Robert. Historical records. Milan, Martucci, 1937. 294 p.

C347 Bauer, Robert. The new catalogue of historical records, 1898-1908/09. London, Sidgwick & Jackson, 1947. 495 p. [Revision of C346 above; for addenda to this work, see C345 above and C354 below.]

Bauer, Robert. The new catalogue of historical records, 1898-1908/09. Facsimile reprint. London, Sidgwick & Jackson, 1970. 495 p.

C348 Bescoby-Chambers, John. The archives of sound; including a selective catalogue of historical violin, piano, spoken, documentary, orchestral, and composer's own recordings. Longfield, Surrey, Oakwood, 1966. 253 p.

C349 Celletti, Rodolfo, ed. Le grandi voci; dizionario critico-biografico dei cantanti con discografia operistica. Roma, Istituto per la collaborazione culturale, 1964. 1044 cols. In Italian.

C350 Clough, Francis F., and G. J. Cuming. The world's encyclopaedia of recorded music. [Includes first supplement bound with this volume.] London, Sidgwick & Jackson, 1952. 890 p.

Clough, Francis F., and G. J. Cuming. The world's encyclopaedia of recorded music. Supplement II: 1951-1952. London, Sidgwick & Jackson, 1953. 262 p.

Clough, Francis F., and G. J. Cuming. The world's encyclopaedia of recorded music. Supplement III: 1953-1955. London, Sidgwick & Jackson, 1957. 564 p.

Clough, Francis F., and G. J. Cuming. The world's encyclopaedia of recorded music. [Reprint of all the above.] Westport, Conn., Greenwood Press, 1966, 1970. 3v.

C351 Deakins, Duane D., Elizabeth Deakins, and Thomas Grattelo. Comprehensive cylinder record index. Stockton, Calif., Duane Deakins, 1956-1961. 5v. Contents.—v. 1: Edison amberol records.—v. 2: Edison standard records.—v. 3: Edison blue amberol records.—v. 4: Indestructible records.—v. 5: U.S. everlasting non-breakable records.

C352 Douglas, John R. Classic recordings for a song [i.e., budget-label LP reissues]. *Library Journal*, XCVI (#4, Feb. 15, 1971), 597-607. Partial contents: Ansermet, Argenta, Backhaus, Beecham, Boulanger, Cantelli, Cortot, De Sabata, Flagstad, Furtwängler, Gieseking, Haskil, Horowitz, Hotter, A. Kipnis, Landowska, L. Lehmann, Lipatti, Mitropoulos, Monteux, Munch, Poulenc, Ravel, Reiner, Rodzinski, Rosbaud, Scherchen, Schnabel, Solomon, Talich, Toscanini, Walter.

C353 Frankfurt am Main. Deutsches Rundfunkarchiv. Die ersten vier Jahrzehnte unseres Jahrhunderts im Spiegel einer Berliner Schallplattensammlung. Frankfurt am Main, Deutsches Rundfunkarchiv, 1966. 2v. In German.

C354 Freestone, J. Addenda to Bauer's The new catalogue of historical records, 1898-1908/09. *The Gramophone*, XXIX (July 1951), 338; XXX (May 1953), 360. [See C347 above.]

C355 Freestone, J. Unpublished records. *Record News*, I (Mar. 1957), entire issue.

C356 Girard, Victor, and Harold M. Barnes. Vertical-cut cylinders and discs: a catalogue of all "hill-and-dale" recordings of serious worth made and issued between 1897-1932 circa. London, British Institute of Recorded Sound, 1964. 234 p.

Girard, Victor, and Harold M. Barnes. Vertical-cut cylinders and discs: a catalogue of all "hill-and-dale" recordings of serious worth made and issued between 1897-1932 circa. Rev. ed. London, British Institute of Recorded Sound, 1971. 196 p.

C357 Gramophone Shop, inc., New York. The Gramophone Shop encyclopedia of recorded music. Ed. by R. D. Darrell. New York, Gramophone Shop, 1936. 574 p.

Gramophone Shop, inc., New York. The Gramophone Shop encyclopedia of recorded music. 2d ed., ed. by George Leslie. New York, Simon and Schuster, 1942. 558 p.

Gramophone Shop, inc., New York. The Gramophone Shop encyclopedia of recorded music. 3d ed., ed. by Robert H. Reid. New York, Gramophone Shop, 1948. 639 p.

Gramophone Shop, inc., New York. The Gramophone Shop encyclopedia of recorded music. [Reprint of the 3d ed., ed. by Robert H. Reid.] Westport, Conn., Greenwood Press, 1970. 639 p.

C358 Hurst, P. G. The golden age recorded. London, Sidgwick & Jackson, 1947.

Hurst, P. G. The golden age recorded. New and rev. ed. Lingfield, Surrey, Oakwood Press, 1963. 187 p. Discography: pp. 149-187.

C359 Limbacher, James L. Broadway on records, 1900-1960, a selected list of musical and dramatic performances on long-playing records. Dearborn, Mich., Dearborn Public Libraries, 1961. 8 p.

C360 Moses, Julian Morton. Collectors' guide to American recordings 1898-1925. New York, American Record Collectors' Exchange, 1949. 200 p. [See companion volume, C361 below.]

C361 Moses, Julian Morton. Price guide to collectors' records. New York, American Record Collectors' Exchange, 1952. 28 p.

Moses, Julian Morton. Price guide to collectors' records. Rev. ed. including revised value chart. New York, American Record Collectors' Exchange, 1967. 28 p.

C362 Rust, Brian A. L. London musical shows on records 1894-1954. London, British Institute of Recorded Sound, 1958. 207 p. [Includes supplement: chronological list of musical productions 1894-1954. 13 p.]

C363 Thorens, S. C. Catalogue sheets, 1907-1914. London, London Phonograph and Gramophone Society, 1967. 40 p.

C364 Voices of the past. Lingfield, Surrey, Oakwood Press. v. 1– . 1956– . [Nine volumes issued to date; contents analyzed in C365-C373 below.]

C365 Voices of the past, v. 1. Bennett, John R. A catalogue of vocal recordings from the English catalogues of The Gramophone Company (1898-1899), The Gramophone Company Limited (1899-1900), The Gramophone & Typewriter Company Limited (1901-1907), and The Gramophone Company Limited (1907-1925). Lingfield, Surrey, Oakwood Press, 1956. 238, xlvii p.

C366 Voices of the past, v. 2. Bennett, John R. A catalogue of vocal recordings from the Italian catalogues of The Gramophone Company Limited (1899-1900), The Gramophone Company (Italy) Limited (1899-1909), The Gramophone Company Limited (1909), Compagnia Italiana del Grammofono (1909-1912), and Società Nazionale de Grammofono (1912-1925). Lingfield, Surrey, Oakwood Press, 1957. 178 p.

C367 Voices of the past, v. 3. Bennett, John R. Dischi Fonotipia, including supplement (1958) and addenda (1964). Lingfield, Surrey, Oakwood Press, 1958, 1964. 88, 77 p.

C368 Voices of the past, v. 4. Bennett, John R., and Eric Hughes. The International Red Label catalogue of 'DB' & 'DA' His Master's Voice recordings, 1924-1956. Book I: 'DB' (12 inch). Lingfield, Surrey, Oakwood Press, 1961. 400 p.

C369 Voices of the past, v. 5. Smith, Michael. The catalogue of 'D' & 'E' His Master's Voice recordings. Lingfield, Surrey, Oakwood Press, 1961? 131, xviii p.

C370 Voices of the past, v. 6. Bennett, John R., and Eric Hughes. The International Red Label catalogue of 'DB' & 'DA' His Master's Voice recordings, 1924-1956. Book 2: 'DA.' Lingfield, Surrey, Oakwood Press, 1964. 233 p.

C371 Voices of the past, v. 7. Bennett, John R., and Wilhelm Wimmer. A catalogue of vocal recordings from the 1898-1925 German catalogues of The Gramophone Company Limited, Deutsche Grammophon A.-G. Lingfield, Surrey, Oakwood Press, 1967. 404 p.

C372   Voices of the past, v. 8. Smith, Michael, and Ian Cosens. Smith Graphophone Company, ltd.; English celebrity issues: D and LB series, L and LX series, X and PB series, 7000 and PX series, ROX and SDX series, YB series. Lingfield, Surrey, Oakwood Press, 1970? 240 p.

C373   Voices of the past, v. 9. Bennett, John R. A catalogue of vocal recordings from the 1898-1925 French catalogues of The Gramophone Company Limited, Compagnie française du gramophone. Lingfield, Surrey, Oakwood Press, 1971? 304 p.

LABEL DISCOGRAPHY

American Gramophone Society Records

C374   Mecinski, H. R. American Gramophone Society (Addison Foster) record numbers (mauve and gold series). *The Record Collector*, VIII (June 1953), entire issue.

Association Phonique des Grands Artistes Records

C375   Girard, Victor. Association Phonique des Grands Artistes (APGA). *The Record Collector*, IX (March 1954), entire issue.

Bettini Records

C376   Bettini catalogs for June 1898, April 1900, June 1901. Stanford, Calif., Stanford University, 1965. 3v.

C377   Catalogue général des disques Bettini, année 1904. *The Record Collector*, XVII (#1-2, 1967), whole issue. In French.

Canadian Victor Records

C378   Manning, E. Canadian Victor numbers. *Record News*, V (Nov. 1960), entire issue.

Columbia Records

C379   Favia-Artsay, Aida. Columbia's 1903 grand opera series. *Hobbies*, LXVIII (Oct. 1963), 30-31.

C380 Kleeburg, Fred M. Columbia's 1903 grand opera series: first recordings of opera in America. *American Record Guide*, XXIX (June 1963), 772-75.

Dacapo Records

C381 Liliedahl, Karleric. Dacapo. (Nationalfonotekets diskografier 10) Stockholm, Kungliga biblioteket, 1969. 23 p. In Swedish.

Danish His Master's Voice Records

C382 Rosenberg, Herbert. The Danish His Master's Voice "DA" and "DB" series 1936-1952. København, Nationaldiskoteket, 1965. 35 p.

Edison Records

C383 Adrian, Karlo. Numerical list of Edison Bell: Winner, parts 1-3. Bournemouth, Talking Machine Review, 1970.

C384 Annand, H. H. The complete catalogue of the United States Everlasting Indestructible cylinders, 1905-1913. Bournemouth, City of London Phonograph & Gramophone Society, 1966. 38 p.

C385 Annand, H. H. Numerical catalogue of all British blue amberol Edison cylinder records, 1912-1915. Hillingdon, Middlesex, Annand, 1960. 1v. (unpaged)

C386 Betz, Peter C. Edison concert cylinder records: a catalogue of the series issued 1899-1901. Bournemouth, City of London Phonograph & Gramophone Society, 1968. 20 p.

C387 Carter, Sydney H. The complete catalogue of Edison gold moulded two-minute cylinder records, 1901-12. [Foreign series.] Worthing, Carter, 1965. 3v.

C388 Carter, Sydney H. The complete catalogue of the Edison amberol cylinder records. Worthing, Carter, 1963. 1v. (unpaged)

C389 Carter, Sydney H. The complete catalogue of the Edison blue amberol cylinder records. Worthing, Carter, 1963-64. 3v.

C390 Freestone, J. Edison cylinders. *The Gramophone*, XXXI (Apr. 1954), 371.

C391   Koenigsberg, Allen. Edison cylinder records, 1889-1912, with an illustrated history of the phonograph. New York, Stellar Productions, 1969, lxii, 159 p.

C392   Walsh, J. A. March, 1901, catalog of Edison 'concert' cylinders. *Hobbies*, LXXI (Nov. 1966), 37-38+; (Dec. 1966), 37-38; (Jan. 1967), 37.

C393   Wile, Raymond R. Edison disc sales figures (82,000-84,000 series), 1919/20. *Association of Recorded Sound Collections Journal*, III (#2-3, Fall 1971), 60-78.

English Brunswick Records

C394   Riemens, L. Brunswick Hall of Fame. *The Record Collector*, V (Apr. 1950), entire issue.

English Columbia Records

C395   Gray, John. Columbia [English] LX series. *Bulletin of the British Institute of Recorded Sound*, #15-16 (Spring 1960), 14.

C396   Hughes, Eric. Columbia [English] LB series. *Bulletin of the British Institute of Recorded Sound*, #15-16 (Spring 1960), 8-14.

Eterna Records

C397   Markowski, L., and H. P. Mueller. Schallplatten-Übersicht [Eterna label]. *Musik und Gesellschaft*, XIX (Feb. 1969), 126-31. In German.

Fonotipia Records

C398   Bennett, John R. Dischi Fonotipia: a golden treasury. Ipswich, Record Collector Shop, 1953. 88 p. [For a republication of this work with supplement and addenda, see C367 above.]

C399   Witten L. The Paris Fonotipias; a tragedy. *The Record Collector*, XII (#1-2, Jan.-Feb. 1958), 38-43.

G & T Records

C400 Hevingham-Root, L., and P. G. Hurst. The London Red G & T's of 1902. *The Record Collector*, XIII (Mar.-Apr. 1960), 2-47; (May 1960), 67-68.

Gramophone Company Records

C401 Gramophone Company, ltd. Catalogue of "Red label" Gramophone records 1904. 1st ed., reprinted with September to November supplements. Bournemouth, E. Bayly, 1972. 20 p.

Monarch Records

C402 Gramophone Company, ltd. Catalogue of twelve-inch Monarch records . . . March 1904. 1st ed., reprinted with supplements. Bournemouth, E. Bayly, 1972. 35 p.

National Gramophone Records

C403 Excerpts from the record catalog, National Gram-o-phone Company, April, 1899. *Record Research*, #83 (Apr. 1967), 8-9.

Phonotype Records

C404 Dennis, James F. E. Phonotype records. *The Record Collector*, VIII (Sep. 1953), entire issue.

RCA Victor Records

C405 Smolian, Steven. Da capo [complete numerical listing of RCA Victor "Red Seal" albums collated from many sources]. Covers LM 1-LM 1967. *American Record Guide*, XXX-XXXI (May 1964-Apr. 1965), [several pages each in most of those monthly issues].

Resia Records

C406 Liliedahl, Karleric. Resia inkl. 4-melodi och 4-schlager. (National-fonotekets diskografier 9) Stockholm, Kungliga biblioteket, 1969. 48 p. In Swedish.

Scandinavian His Master's Voice Records

C407   Nationaldiskoteket, København. The Scandinavian His Master's Voice M-series, 1920-1933. København, Nationaldiskoteket, 1966. 47 p.

Sonora Records

C408   Englund, Björn. Sonora IV. E 5000-serien, 6000-serien, 9000-serien, K 9500-serien. (Nationaldiskotekets diskografier 8) Stockholm, Kungliga biblioteket, 1968. 35 p. In Swedish.

C409   Englund, Björn. Sonora V, VI. 2000/3000-serien. (Nationalfonotekets diskografier 11,12) Stockholm, Kungliga biblioteket, 1969. 2v. (74 p., 73 p.) In Swedish.

C410   Englund, Björn. Sonora VII. 7000-serien del 1. (Nationalfonotekets diskografier 13) Stockholm, Kungliga biblioteket, 1972. 70 p. In Swedish.

Victor Records

C411   Léon, Jacques Alain. Catálogo numérico dos discos vocais Victor Sêlo Vermêlho [Numerical catalogue of Red-Seal Victor vocal records] . Part I (500-9999). Part II (10,000-18,546). Niteroi, Brazil, Batista, 1964, 1968. 2v. In Portuguese.

C412   Walsh, J. Early Victor phonographs and catalogs. *Hobbies*, LXXII (Jan. 1968), 36+; (Feb. 1968), 36+; (Mar. 1968), 37-38+; (Apr. 1968), 36+; (May 1968), 37.

C413   Walsh, J. Victor double-faced records that were remade. *Hobbies*, LXX (Nov. 1965), 35-36; (Dec. 1965), 36-37+.

C414   Williams, Frederick P. The times as reflected in the Victor Black Label military band recordings from 1900 to 1927. *Association of Recorded Sound Collections Journal*, IV (#1-2-3, 1972), 33-46.

Zonophone Records

C415   Walsh, J. Early Zon-o-phone record catalogs. *Hobbies*, LXX (Jan. 1966), 37.

C416   Wolf, A. Zonofono celebrity records. *The Record Collector*, II (Oct. 1947), entire issue.

SECTION C

CLASSICAL COMPOSER
AND PERFORMER DISCOGRAPHY

ABSIL, JEAN (Belgian composer)

C417   Guide, Richard de. Jean Absil; vie et oeuvre. Tournai, Casterman, 1965. 228 p. In French. Discography: pp. 213-214.

ALBERT, EUGEN D' (German pianist and composer)

C418   Eugene d'Albert [discography]. *Antique Records*, #1 (Nov. 1972), 11-12.

ALSEN, ELSA (Norwegian soprano)

C419   Vesper, E. Elsa Alsen. *The Record Collector*, XV (#1, Jan. 1963), 5-12.

ANCONA, MARIO (Italian baritone)

C420   Moran, W. R. Mario Ancona (1860-1931). *The Record Collector*, XVI (#5-6, 1965), 131-39.

ANSERMET, ERNEST (Swiss conductor and composer)

C421   Gavoty, Bernard. Ernest Ansermet. Aufnahmen von Jean Mohr. Deutsch von A. H. Eichmann. Genf, R. Kister, 1961. 34 p. In German. Discography: pp. 32-34.

ANSORGE, CONRAD (German pianist)

C422   Conrad Ansorge's Polyphon recordings. 78 RPM, #2 (1968), 6.

ARLEN, HAROLD (real name, HYMAN ARLUCK; American composer, songwriter, singer)

C423   Jablonski, Edward. Harold Arlen: happy with the blues. Garden City, N.Y., Doubleday, 1961. 286 p. "Selected discography": pp. 262-273.

ARNOLDSON, SIGRID (Swedish soprano)

C424   Sigrid Arnoldson—diskografi. *Musikrevy*, XXVII (#1, 1972), 39.

ARRAU, CLAUDIO (Chilean pianist)

C425   Gavoty, Bernard. Claudio Arrau. Geneva, R. Kister, 1962. 34 p. In French; English and German editions were also simultaneously published. Discography: pp. 30-32.

AUSTRAL, FLORENCE (Australian soprano)

C426   White, D., and W. Hogarth. Florence Austral. *The Record Collector*, XIV (#1-2, 1961), 22-29; (#7-8, 1961), 168-69.

BACH, CARL PHILIPP EMANUEL (German composer)

C427   Barford, Philip. The keyboard music of C. P. E. Bach, considered in relation to his musical aesthetic and the rise of the sonata principle. London, Barrie and Rockliff, 1965; New York, October House, 1966. 186 p. Discography: pp. 179-180.

BACH, JOHANN CHRISTIAN (German composer)

C428   J. C. Bach on records. *High Fidelity*, XII (June 1961), 36-37+

BACH, JOHANN SEBASTIAN (German composer)

C429   Broder, Nathan. The collector's Bach. (Keystone books in music) Philadelphia, Lippincott, 1958. 192 p.

C430 Buchet, Edmond Édouard. Jean-Sébastien Bach après deux siècles d'études et de témoignages. Paris, Buchet-Chastel, 1968. 313 p. In French. Discography: pp. 263-302.

C431 Buchet, Edmond Édouard. Jean-Sébastien Bach, l'oeuvre et la vie. Paris, Les Libraires associés, 1963. 268 p. In French. "Discographie critique et comparée": pp. 246-267.

Brandenburg Concerti

C432 Higbee, Dale. J. S. Bach's music for recorder on records. Part I: the Brandenburg concerti, BMV 1046-1051. *American Recorder*, IX (#4, Fall 1968), 116-23.

Cantatas

C433 Broder, Nathan. The Bach cantatas; a discography. *High Fidelity*, XII (Aug. 1962), 44-47+

Chamber and Orchestral Works

C434 Broder, Nathan. Bach—the chamber and orchestral music. *High Fidelity*, VI (May 1956), 86-99.

Choral Works

C435 Broder, Nathan. Bach—the choral works. *High Fidelity*, V (Sep. 1955), 79.

C436 Broder, Nathan. The Bach Passions and oratorios—a discography. *High Fidelity/Musical America*, XVI (July 1966), 46-47+.

C437 Miller, Philip L. For the first time, Bach's St. Luke's Passion. *American Record Guide*, XXIX (Feb. 1963), 438.

C438 Wienke, G. Bach: Hohe Messe in H-moll; eine vergleichende Discographie. *Phono*, VIII (#4, 1962), 79+ In German.

Concerti, Keyboard

C439 Finally, all twelve of Bach's keyboard concerti. *American Record Guide*, XXX (Nov. 1963), 534.

Die Kunst der Fuge

C440   Chailley, Jacques. L'art de la fugue de J.-S. Bach; étude critique des sources, remise en ordre du plan, analyse de l'oeuvre. Paris, A. Leduc, 1971. 89 p. In French. Discography: pp. 81-85.

BÄCK, SVEN-ERIK (Swedish composer)

C441   Bäck, Sven-Erik. Verkförteckning 1945-1966. *Nutida Musik*, X (#3-4, 1966-67), 20+ In Swedish.

BAKER, JANET (English soprano)

C442   Blyth, Alan. Janet Baker. London, Ian Allen, 1973. 64 p. Discography: pp. 61-64.

BANTOCK, GRANVILLE (English composer)

C443   Foreman, R. L. Sir Granville Bantock: a discography. *Recorded Sound*, #32 (Oct. 1968), 338-42.

BARBER, SAMUEL (American composer)

C444   Broder, Nathan. Samuel Barber. New York, G. Schirmer, 1954. 111 p. Discography: pp. 104-107.

BARBIROLLI, JOHN (English conductor)

C445   Kennedy, Michael. Barbirolli, conductor laureate. London, MacGibbon and Kee, 1971. 416 p. Discography: pp. 341-402.

C446   Reid, Charles. John Barbirolli: a biography. London, Hamilton; New York, Taplinger, 1971. 446 p. Discography: pp. 432-436.

C447   Stone, Ralph. The Barbirolli recordings. *Le Grand Baton*, Nov. 1970, 31-59; May 1971, 33.

C448   Walker, Malcolm. Barbirolli on disc. *Opera* (England), XXI (Mar. 1970), 198-205.

C449   Walker, Malcolm. Barbirolli's early recordings. *Antique Records*, #2 (May 1973), 28-30.

BARENBOIM, DANIEL (Israeli pianist and conductor)

C450   Pleijel, B. Daniel Barenboim. *Musikrevy*, XXIV (#2, 1969), 59-60+
In Swedish.

BARTÓK, BÉLA (Hungarian composer and pianist)

C451   Citron, Pierre. Bartók. Paris, Éditions du Seuil, 1963. 187 p. In
French. Discography: pp. 182-185.

C452   Clough, Francis F., and G. J. Cuming. The works of Béla Bartók on
records. *Tempo*, #13 (Autumn 1949), 39-41.

C453   Frankenstein, A. Bartók on microgroove. *High Fidelity*, VI (Oct.
1956), 121-30.

C454   Geraedts, Henri, and Jaap Geraedts. Béla Bartók. 2., geheel
bijgewerkte druk. Haarlem, H. J. Gottmer, 1961. 191 p. In Dutch.
Includes discography.

C455   Kraus, Egon. Bibliographie und Diskographie: Béla Bartók. *Musik und
Bildung*, III (#10, Oct. 1971), 494-96. In German.

C456   Mari, Pierrette. Bartók. Paris, Hachette, 1970. 96 p. In French. Discography: p. 94.

C457   Nordwall, Ove. Béla Bartók. Traditionalist—modernist. Stockholm,
Nordiska musikförlaget, 1972. 127 p. In Swedish and English. Discography: pp. 119-125.

C458   Nordwall, Ove. Förteckning over av Bartók inspelade grammo-
fonskivor. *Musik-Kultur*, XXXII (#7, 1968), 6-7. In Swedish.

C459   Szabolcsi, Bence, ed. Béla Bartók; Weg und Werk. Schriften und
Briefe. Leipzig, Philipp Reclam, 1968. 205 p. In German. Includes
discography.

       Szabolcsi, Bence, ed. Béla Bartók; Weg und Werk. 2d ed. München,
Deutscher Taschenbuch Verlag, 1972. 381 p. In German. Discography:
pp. 311-323.

C460   Ujfalussy, Jósef. Béla Bartók. Translated by Ruth Pataki. Budapest,
Corvina Press, 1971. 459 p. Discography by Laszlo Somfai:
pp. 443-452.

BATHORI, JANE (French mezzo)

C461   Barnes, Harold M. Jane Bathori discography. *Recorded Sound*, #4 (Oct. 1961), 109-10.

BAX, ARNOLD (English composer)

C462   Foreman, R. L. Arnold Bax: a discography. *Recorded Sound*, #29-30 (Jan.-Apr. 1968), 277-83.

BEECHAM, THOMAS (English conductor)

C463   The Beecham discography. *Le Grand Baton*, Aug.-Nov. 1969, whole double issue.

C464   Botsford, W. The Beecham discography. *American Record Guide*, XXXIII (May 1967), 742-47; (June 1967), 930-32; (July 1967), 1009-12; (Aug. 1967), 1078-81; XXXIV (Oct. 1967), 150-51; (Nov. 1967), 244-45; (Feb. 1968), 506-10; (Apr. 1968), 686-89.

C465   Botsford, W. Sir Thomas and the gramophone, 1910-1960. *High Fidelity/Musical America*, XV (June 1965), 45-48+

C466   Stone, Ralph. The Beecham recordings up to 1932. *Le Grand Baton*, Feb. 1967, 21-29.

C467   Stone, Ralph. A discography of the recordings made with the London Philharmonic Orchestra by Sir Thomas Beecham during the "golden era" (1932-1939). *Le Grand Baton*, I (1964), 24-31.

BEETHOVEN, LUDWIG VAN (German composer)

C468   The Beethoven cycle. *Philips*, Autumn 1969, 14-21.

C469   Boucourechliev, André. Beethoven. Paris, Éditions du Seuil, 1963. 191 p. In French. Discography: pp. 180-183.

C470   Briggs, John. The collector's Beethoven. (Keystone books in music) Philadelphia, Lippincott, 1962. 152 p.

C471   Freed, Roger. Beethoven by the numbers [all Beethoven recordings currently available in the United States]. *The Saturday Review*, LIII (Nov. 28, 1970), 67.

C472   Gyimes, Ferenc, and Veronika Vavrinecz. Beethoven müvei hangle-
        mezen. Diszkográfia. Budapest, Allami Gorkij Könyvtár, 1971. 186 p.
        In Hungarian; summaries in German and Russian. Includes discography.

C473   Hoke, Hans Gunter, ed. Ludwig van Beethoven. Gesamtausgabe
        anlässlich der Beethoven-Ehrung der Deutschen Demokratischen
        Republik 1970. Verzeichnis der Veröffentlichungen bis 1970
        [Schallplattenkatalog]. Berlin, VEB Deutsche Schallplatten, 1970.
        56 p. In German.

C474   Hughes, Rosemary. Beethoven: a biography with a survey of books,
        editions and recordings. (The concertgoers companions) London,
        Bingley, 1970. 114 p. Discography by Brian Redfern: pp. 91-105.

C475   Ley, Stephan. Beethoven. Sein Leben in Selbstzeugnissen, Briefen und
        Berichten. Wien, Berlin, Neff, 1971. 432 p. In German. Discography:
        pp. 421-432.

C476   The recordings of Beethoven as viewed by the critics of High Fidelity.
        Great Barrington, Mass., Wyeth Press, 1971. 173 p.

C477   Stuttgart. Stadtbücherei. Ludwig van Beethoven zum 200. Geburtstag.
        Noten, Schallplatten, Bücher aus d. Beständen d. Musik-abt.
        Zusammengestellt von Brigitte Willberg. Stuttgart, Stadtbücherei,
        1970. 106 p. In German. Includes discography.

C478   Witold, Jean. Ludwig van Beethoven; l'homme et son oeuvre. Paris,
        Seghers, 1964. 190 p. In French. Includes discography.

Chamber Music

C479   Marsh, R. C. Beethoven on records: the chamber music. *High Fidelity/
        Musical America*, XX (May 1970, sec. 1), 60-68+

Choral Works

C480   Landon, H. C. Robbins. Beethoven on records: the choral music.
        High Fidelity/Musical America, XX (Feb. 1970, sec. 1), 70-72+

Concerti

C481   Goldsmith, H. Beethoven on records: the concertos. *High Fidelity/
        Musical America*, XX (Aug. 1970), 51-56+; (Sep. 1970, sec. 1), 66-68.

Fidelio and Lieder

C482   Harewood, Earl of. Opera on the gramophone: "Fidelio." *Opera* (England), XX (Mar. 1969), 199-208.

C483   Movshon, G. Beethoven on records: "Fidelio" and the songs. *High Fidelity/Musical America*, XX (Jan. 1970, sec. 1), 81-85+

Orchestral Works

C484   Hamilton, D. Beethoven on records: the orchestral music. *High Fidelity/Musical America*, XX (July 1970, sec. 1), 62-65+

Piano Music

C485   Anson, G. Beethoven: the piano music in 1970 [with discography]. *American Music Teacher*, XX (#1, 1970), 30-35; (#2, 1970), 30-33+

C486   Goldsmith, H. Beethoven on records: the piano music. *High Fidelity/ Musical America*, XXI (Jan. 1971), 61-64+

Piano Sonatas

C487   Goldsmith, H. Beethoven on records: the piano sonatas. *High Fidelity/ Musical America*, XX (Oct. 1970), 63-66+

Quartets, Strings

C488   Morgan, R. P. Beethoven on records: the string quartets. *High Fidelity/Musical America*, XX (Apr. 1970, sec. 1), 73-76+

C489   Schuhmacher, G. Beethovens Streichquartette—eine Diskographie. *Musica*, XXII (#4, 1968), 309-11. In German.

Quartets, Strings, Op. 18

C490   Finscher, L. Was fordert die ideale Interpretation von Beethovens op. 18? Versuch einer kritischen Diskographie der Streichquartette. *Phono*, XI (#2, 1964), 43-46. In German.

Symphonies

C491 Burke, C. G. The Beethoven symphonies reconsidered. *High Fidelity*, VII (Jan. 1957), 95-105.

C492 Chantavoine, Jean. Les symphonies de Beethoven. Paris, Belfond, 1970. 232 p. In French. Discography: pp. 223-231.

C493 Lang, Paul Henry. Beethoven on records: the symphonies. *High Fidelity/Musical America*, XX (Dec. 1970), 49-50+

C494 Luten, C. J. Ludwig van Beethoven's nine symphonies. *American Record Guide*, XXX (Sep. 1963), 10-12.

BELLINI, VINCENZO (Italian composer)

C495 Shawe-Taylor, Desmond. A "Puritani" discography. *Opera* (England), XI (June 1960), 387-395.

BENDER, PAUL (German basso)

C496 Dennis, James. Paul Bender. *The Record Collector*, XVII (#11, 1968), 255-56.

BERG, ALBAN (Austrian composer)

C497 Forneberg, Erich. Wozzeck von Alban Berg. Berlin, R. Lienau, 1963. 87 p. In German. Includes discography.

BERLIN, IRVING (American composer)

C498 Jay, Dave. The Irving Berlin songography; 1907-1966. New Rochelle, N.Y., Arlington House, 1969. 172 p. Includes discography.

BERLIOZ, HECTOR (French composer)

C499 Ballif, Claude. Berlioz. Paris, Éditions du Seuil, 1968. 192 p. In French. Discography: pp. 184-187.

C500 Berlioz . . . célébration de son centenaire. La Tronche-Montfleury, "Cahiers de l'Alpe," 1969. 140 p. In French. Discography: pp. 137-140.

C501   Delaye-Didier-Delorme, Henriette. Hector Berlioz; ou, Le chant désespéré. Lyon, *EISE*, 1964. 121 p. In French. Discography: pp. 119-121.

C502   Demarquez, Suzanne. Hector Berlioz. Lausanne, La Guilde du livre; Paris, Seghers, 1969. 192 p. In French. Discography: pp. 183-186.

C503   From the discography of Hector Berlioz (1803-1869). *Philips*, Winter 1969, 23.

C504   Hofmann, M. R. Discographie d'Hector Berlioz. *Journal Musical Francais*, #179 (Apr. 1969), 34. In French.

C505   Jacobson B. Berlioz on records—an appraisal. *High Fidelity/Musical America*, XIX (Mar. 1969), 56-60+

C506   Schreiber, U. Berlioz und die Schallplatte—eine diskografische Skizze. *Hifi-Stereophonie,* IX (Feb. 1970), 127-32. In German.

C507   Seroff, Victor Ilyitch. Hector Berlioz. New York, Macmillan, 1967. 168 p. Discography: pp. 162-163.

BERNAC, PIERRE (French baritone)

C508   Hughes, E., and P. Saul. Pierre Bernac discography. *Recorded Sound*, #18 (Apr. 1965), 322-27.

BERNSTEIN, LEONARD (American conductor)

C509   Ewen, David. Leonard Bernstein; a biography. London, W. H. Allen, 1967. 175 p. Discography: pp. 166-167.

C510   Ewen, David. Leonard Bernstein; a biography for young people. Philadelphia, Chilton Book Co., 1967. 180 p. Includes discography.

C511   Weber, Jerome F. Leonard Bernstein, a composer discography. *Association of Recorded Sound Collections Journal*, VI (#1, 1974), 30-39.

BERWALD, FRANZ (Swedish composer)

C512   Andersson, Ingvar. Franz Berwald. II: Källhänvisningar och person-register. Diskografi. Stockholm, Norstedt, 1971. 87 p. In Swedish. Includes discography by Carl-Gabriel Stellan Mörner.

C513   Mörner, Carl-Gabriel Stellan. Franz Berwald (1796-1868). En diskografi med anledning av jubileumsåret 1968. *Bibliotedsbladet*, LIII (#8, 1968), 964-67. In Swedish.

BILLQUIST, ULLA (Swedish singer)

C514   Bredevik, Gunnar. Ulla Billquist. (Nationalfonotekets diskografier 502) Stockholm, Kungliga biblioteket, 1970. 56 p. In Swedish.

BIZET, GEORGES (French composer)

C515   Robert, Frédéric. Georges Bizet; l'homme et son oeuvre. Paris, Seghers, 1965. 191 p. In French. Includes discography.

BJÖRLING, JUSSI (Swedish tenor)

C516   F. T. H. The Björling recordings—a select discography. *Le Grand Baton*, Feb. 1967, 13-18.

C517   Nationaldiskoteket, København. Jussi Björling: a record list. København, Nationaldiskoteket, 1969. 84 p.

C518   Seemungal, Rupert P. A complete discography of Jussi Björling. 3d ed. Port of Spain, Trinidad, Seemungal, 1964. 45 p.

BLACK, ANDREW (Scottish baritone)

C519   Greaves, S. C. Andrew Black; an appreciation by a fellow Glaswegian [includes discography]. *The Record Collector*, XIV (#9-10, 1962), 197-200.

BLISS, ARTHUR (English composer)

C520   Thompson, Kenneth L. The works of Sir Arthur Bliss. *Musical Times*, CVII (Aug. 1966), 666-673.

Thompson, Kenneth L. The works of Sir Arthur Bliss. [Published as monograph.] London, Novello, 1966.

Thompson, Kenneth L. The works of Sir Arthur Bliss. Rev. ed. London, Novello, 1971.

BOCCHERINI, LUIGI (Italian composer)

C521   Gérard, Yves. A thematic, bibliographical and critical catalogue of the works of Luigi Boccherini. London, New York, Oxford University Press, 1969. 716 p. Discography: pp. 687-694.

BOECK, AUGUST DE (Belgian composer)

C522   Pols, André M. Het leven van A. de Boeck. Brussel, D. A. P. Reinaert Uitg., 1966. 43 p. In Flemish. Discography: p. 43.

BÖHM, KARL (German conductor)

C523   Roemer, Margaret. Karl Böhm. Berlin, Rembrandt Verlag, 1966. 64 p. In German. Discography: pp. 27-31.

C524   Werba, R. Karl Böhm Diskographie. *Österreichische Musikzeitschrift*, XXIV (Aug. 1969), 489-93. In German.

BORI, LUCREZIA (Spanish soprano)

C525   Lucrezia Bori: the discography. *Record Advertiser*, Jan.-Feb. 1971, 8-15.

BORONAT, OLIMPIA (Polish soprano)

C526   Witten, L. C. A discography of Olimpia Boronat, Countess Rzewuska, 1867?-1934, soprano. *The Record Collector*, XX (#6-7, 1972), 160-63.

BOSTON SYMPHONY ORCHESTRA

C527   Helm, E. New man in Boston [includes Boston Symphony recordings]. *Musical America*, LXXXII (Dec. 1962), 6-7+

BOULEZ, PIERRE (French composer and conductor)

C528   Derrien, Jean-Pierre. Pierre Boulez. *Musique en Jeu*, I (1970), 103-32. In French.

BOULT, ADRIAN CEDRIC (English conductor)

C529   Clough, Francis F., and G. J. Cuming. Discography [of Sir Adrian Boult]. *The Music Yearbook*, II (1973-74), 170-86.

BRAGA, FRANCISCO (Brazilian composer)

C530   Rio de Janeiro. Biblioteca Nacional. Exposiçao comemorativa do centenário do nascimento de Francisco Braga (1868-1945). Rio de Janeiro, Biblioteca Nacional, 1968. 84 p. In Portuguese. Discography: pp. 54-56.

BRAHMS, JOHANNES (German composer)

C531   Bruyr, José. Brahms. Paris, Éditions du Seuil, 1965. 188 p. In French. Discography: pp. 184-188.

C532   Dale, Kathleen. Brahms: a biography with a survey of books, editions & recordings. (The concertgoers companions) London, Bingley; Hamden, Conn., Archon Books, 1970. 118 p. Discography by Brian Redfern: pp. 96-110.

C533   Laufer, J. Brahms. Paris, Éditions du Scorpion, 1963. 188 p. In French. Discography: pp. 165-175.

Chamber and Keyboard Music

C534   Affelder, P. The chamber music of Brahms on records—sonatas, keyboard music, instrumental miscellany. *High Fidelity*, V (Mar. 1955), 72-82.

Lieder

C535   Weber, Jerome F. Brahms Lieder. (Weber discography series, 4) Utica, N.Y., Jerome F. Weber, 1970. 20 p.

   Weber, Jerome F. Brahms Lieder. 2d ed. [Scheduled for publication in 1976.]

Orchestral Music

C536   Burke, C. G. Brahms—the orchestral music on microgroove. *High Fidelity*, VI (April 1956), 97-98; (Sep. 1956), 77-84.

BRITTEN, BENJAMIN (English composer)

C537 Barker, F. G. Britten on record. *Music & Musicians*, XII (Nov. 1963), 41.

C538 Mitchell, Donald. Britten on records. *Disc*, Autumn 1951, 54-55.

C539 Mitchell, Donald, and Hans Keller, eds. Benjamin Britten; a commentary on his works from a group of specialists. London, Rockliff, 1952. 410 p. Discography: pp. 352-360.

    Mitchell, Donald, and Hans Keller, eds. Benjamin Britten; a commentary on his works from a group of specialists. [Reprint ed.] Westport, Conn., Greenwood Press, 1972. 410 p. Discography: pp. 352-360.

BROUWENSTIJN, GRÉ (Dutch soprano)

C540 Igesz, B. Portrait of an artist: Brouwenstijn on records. *American Record Guide*, XXVI (#6, Feb. 1960), 410-13.

BRUCKNER, ANTON (Austrian composer)

C541 Diether, Jack. Bruckner and Mahler in the first decade of LP. *Chord and Discord*, II (#8, 1958), 91-111.

C542 Gallois, Jean. Bruckner. Paris, Éditions du Seuil, 1971. 189 p. In French. Discography: pp. 187-189.

C543 Lancelot, Michel. Anton Bruckner, l'homme et son oeuvre. Paris, Seghers, 1964. 191 p. In French. Includes discography.

C544 Nowak, Leopold. Anton Bruckner, Musik und Leben. Wien, Österreichischer Bundesverlag, 1964. 110 p. In German. Discography: pp. 97-100.

C545 Taishoff, S. Bruckner on microgroove. *High Fidelity*, VIII (Mar. 1958), 89-97.

Sacred Music

C546 Diether, Jack. From Angel, DGG and Amadeo, a feast of Bruckner's church music. *American Record Guide*, XXIX (July 1963), 850-52.

Vocal Music

C547   Weber, Jerome F. Bruckner [vocal music other than lieder]. (Weber discography series, 10) Utica, N.Y., Jerome F. Weber, 1971. 34 p.

Weber, Jerome F. Bruckner [vocal music other than lieder]. 2d ed. Utica, N.Y., Jerome F. Weber, 1973.

BUDAPEST QUARTET

C548   Smolian, Steven. Four decades of the Budapest Quartet—a discography, 1926-1966 [includes personnel history]. *American Record Guide*, XXXVII (Dec. 1970), 220-24+

BURIAN, KARL (Czech tenor)

C549   Brew, D., and G. Sova. Karel Burian. *The Record Collector*, XVIII (#7, 1969), 156-64.

BURKE, THOMAS

C550   Winstanley, S. Thomas Burke: a discography. 78 RPM, Nov. 1969, 33-34.

BURKHARD, WILLY (Swiss composer)

C551   Willy-Burkhard-Gesellschaft. Willy Burkhard, 17. April 1900-18. Juni 1955. Werkverzeichnis. Liebefeld, Willy-Burkhard-Gesellschaft, 1968. 32 p. In German. Discography: p. 32.

BUSCH, FRITZ (German conductor)

C552   Busch, Grete. Fritz Busch; Dirigent. Frankfurt am Main, S. Fischer, 1970. 366 p. In German. Discography: pp. 334-354.

BUSH, GEOFFREY (English composer)

C553   Tape recordings of music by Geoffrey Bush in the collection of the British Institute of Recorded Sound. *Recorded Sound*, #40 (Oct. 1970), 694-95.

BUSONI, FERRUCCIO BENVENUTO (Italian composer and pianist)

C554   Aahlén, Carl Gunnar. Grammofonens veteraner: Ferruccio Busoni (1866-1924). *Musikrevy*, XXVI (#5, 1971), 299-301. In Swedish.

C555   Saul, P., comp. Busoniana [works recorded by Busoni and works by Busoni recorded by others] . *Recorded Sound*, I (#8, 1962), 256-61.

BUTT, CLARA (English alto)

C556   Clara Butt: the records. *Record Advertiser*, Nov.-Dec. 1971, 4-8; Jan.-Feb. 1972, 2-9.

BUTTERWORTH, GEORGE SAINTON KAYE (English composer)

C557   Thompson, Kenneth L. A Butterworth catalogue. *Musical Times,* CVII (Sep. 1966), 771-72.

CABANILLES, JUAN BAUTISTA JOSÉ (Spanish composer)

C558   Garcia Ferreras, Arsenio. Juan Bautista Cabanilles; sein Leben und sein Werk. (Die Tientos für Orgel) Regensburg, G. Bosse, 1973. 184 p. In German. Discography: p. 179.

CAGE, JOHN (American composer)

C559   Kostelanetz, Richard, comp. John Cage. New York, Praeger, 1970. 237 p. Discography: pp. 211-230.

CALLAS, MARIA (real name, MARIA CALOGEROPOULOS; American soprano)

C560   Hamilton, David. The recordings of Maria Callas. *High Fidelity*, XXIV (Mar. 1974), 40-48.

CANTELLI, GUIDO (Italian conductor)

C561   Goldsmith, Harris. Guido Cantelli: his legacy on records. *Le Grand Baton*, Feb. 1966, 3-14.

CARUSO, ENRICO (Italian tenor)

C562 Favia-Artsay, Aida. Caruso on records: pitch, speed and comments for all the published records of Enrico Caruso, complete with two special Caruso stroboscopes. Valhalla, N.Y., Historic Records, 1965. 218 p.

C563 Freestone, John, and Harold John Drummond. Enrico Caruso; his recorded legacy. London, Sidgwick and Jackson, 1960; Minneapolis, T. S. Denison, 1961. 130 p.

C564 Mouchon, Jean Pierre. Enrico Caruso, 1873-1921, sa vie et sa voix, étude psychophysiologique, physique, phonétique et esthétique. Langres, Impr. du Petit-Cloître, 1966. 108 p. In French. Discography: pp. 95-102.

CASALS, PABLO (Spanish cellist, conductor and composer)

C565 Ginzburg, Lev Solomonovich. Pablo Kazal's. Moskva, Muzyka, 1966. [Citation transliterated from the Russian.] 244 p. In Russian. Discography: pp. 213-219.

C566 Kirk, H. L. Pablo Casals; a biography. New York, Holt, Rinehart and Winston, 1974. 692 p. Discography, compiled by Teri Noel Towe: pp. 568-625.

C567 Müller-Blattau, Joseph Maria. Casals. Berlin, Rembrandt Verlag, 1964. 64 p. In German. Discography: pp. 28-31.

C568 Pablo Casals. Columbia M5 30069, 1970. 5 records with notes. Casals discography (6 p.) laid in.

CASELLA, ALFREDO (Italian composer)

C569 Hughes, E., and G. C. Stonehill. Alfredo Casella: a discography. *Recorded Sound*, #28 (Oct. 1967), 237-40.

CHABRIER, EMMANUEL (French composer)

C570 Robert, Frédéric. Emmanuel Chabrier; l'homme et son oeuvre. Catalogue des oeuvres. Discographie. Paris, Seghers, 1970. 190 p. In French. Discography: pp. 183-186.

CHAUSSON, ERNEST (French composer)

C571   Gallois, Jean. Ernest Chausson; l'homme et son oeuvre. Paris,
        Seghers, 1967. 193 p. In French. Discography: pp. 190-191.

CHOPIN, FRÉDÉRIC (Polish composer)

C572   Beaufils, Marcel, and others. Chopin. Paris, Hachette, 1965. 281 p.
        In French. "Catalogue commentée & discographie critique":
        pp. 257-281.

C573   Grenier, Jean. Frédéric Chopin; l'homme et son oeuvre. Paris,
        Seghers, 1964. 181 p. In French. Discography: pp. 173-179.

C574   Holcman, J. The honor roll of recorded Chopin, 1906-1960. *The
        Saturday Review*, XLIII (Feb. 27, 1960), 44-45+

C575   Schonberg, H. Frédéric Chopin. *High Fidelity*, V (June 1955),
        78-89.

C576   Seroff, Victor Ilyitch. Frédéric Chopin. New York, Macmillan,
        1964. 118 p. "Selected discography": pp. 113-115.

C577   Walker, Alan, ed. Frédéric Chopin; profiles of the man and the musi-
        cian. London, Barrie & Rockliff, 1966; New York, Taplinger, 1967.
        334 p. Discography: pp. 301-32.

CLEVELAND ORCHESTRA

C578   Marsh, Robert Charles. The Cleveland Orchestra. Cleveland, World
        Pub. Co., 1967. 205 p. Discography: pp. 189-200.

C579   Meyers, Betty. Discography of the Cleveland Orchestra and Cleveland
        Pops Orchestra, 1924-1970. Master's research paper, Kent State
        University School of Library Science, 1972. 185 p.

COATES, ERIC (English composer and violist)

C580   Brown, Nathan. A[n Eric] Coates discography. *Le Grand Baton*,
        Feb. 1969, 4-14.

COATES, JOHN (English tenor)

C581   John Coates: the recordings. *Record Advertiser*, Mar.-Apr. 1972, 4-6.

COLE, MAURICE

C582 Mitchell, John. Maurice Cole: a discography. *Recorded Sound*, #29-30 (Jan.-Apr. 1968), 291-92.

COPELAND, GEORGE (American pianist)

C583 Moore, J. George Copeland Discography. *Recorded Sound*, #25 (Jan. 1967), 142-47.

COPLAND, AARON (American composer, conductor and pianist)

C584 Berger, Arthur. Aaron Copland. New York, Oxford University Press, 1953. 120 p. Discography: pp. 107-112.

C585 Berger, Arthur. An Aaron Copland discography. *High Fidelity*, V (July 1955), 64-69.

C586 Hamilton, David. Aaron Copland: a discography of the composer's performances. *Perspectives of New Music*, IX (#1, 1970), 149-54.

C587 Hamilton, David. The recordings of Copland's music. *High Fidelity/ Musical America*, XX (Nov. 1970), 64-66+

CORTOT, ALFRED (French pianist)

C588 Alfred Cortot e i suoi dischi. *Musica e Dischi*, XVIII (July 1962), 45. In Italian.

COUPERIN, FRANÇOIS, LE GRAND (French composer)

C589 Charlier, Henri. François Couperin. Lyon, Éditions et Impr. du Sud-Est, 1965. 124 p. In French. Discography: p. 121.

CROOKS, RICHARD (American tenor)

C590 Mackiggan, K. S. Richard Crooks [includes discography by C. I. Morgan]. *The Record Collector*, XII (May 1959), 125-34; Oct. 1959), 147-55.

C591 Moran, W. R. Correspondence [corrections to Crooks discography]. *The Record Collector*, XII (Dec.-Jan. 1959/60), 258-61.

C592   Morgan, C. I. Addenda to the Richard Crooks discography. *The Record Collector*, XX (#11-12, 1972), 266-70.

C593   Morgan, C. I. Richard Crooks' discography. *Record Advertiser,* Sep.-Oct. 1972, 8-12; Nov.-Dec. 1972, 2-16; Jan.-Feb. 1973. 17.

DAVIES, BENJAMIN GREY (Welsh tenor)

C594   Ben Davies: the records. *Record Advertiser*, July-Aug. 1971, 4-9.

DAVIES, TUDOR (Welsh tenor)

C595   The Tudor Davies discography. *Record Advertiser*, May-June 1972, 19-21; July-Aug. 1972, 1-9.

DAVIS, COLIN (English conductor)

C596   Blyth, Alan. Recordmasters: Colin Davis. Shepperton, Middlesex, Allan, 1972. 64 p. Discography: pp. 60-64.

DEBUSSY, CLAUDE (French composer)

C597   Barraque, Jean. Debussy. Paris, Éditions du Seuil, 1962. 189 p. In French. Discography: pp. 183-189.

C598   Discographie selective de Claude Debussy. *Le Courrier Musical de France*, #24 (1968), 235. In French.

C599   Goldsmith, H. Debussy on microgroove. *High Fidelity*, XII (Sep. 1962), 66-69+; (Oct. 1962), 98-99.

C600   Goléa, Antoine. Claude Debussy; l'homme et son oeuvre. Paris, Seghers, 1965. 191 p. In French. Discography: pp. 173-184.

C601   Hart, P. Debussy on records. *Music Magazine*, CLXIV (Aug. 1962), 37.

C602   Holcman, J. Debussy on disc; 1912-1962. *The Saturday Review*, XLV (Aug. 25, 1962), 34-35.

C603   Osborne, C. L. Debussy on microgroove. *High Fidelity*, XII (Nov. 1962), 84+

Le Martyre de Saint Sébastien

C604   Discographie [of Le martyre de Saint Sébastien] . *Revue Musicale*, #234 (1957), 81. In French.

Orchestral and Vocal Music

C605   Frankenstein, A. Debussy—orchestral and vocal music. *High Fidelity*, VIII (Jan. 1958), 79-86.

DE LARA, ADELINA (real name, ADELINA TILBURY; English pianist and composer)

C606   De Lara, Adelina, and Clare Abrahall. Finale. London, Burke, 1955. 222 p. Discography: pp. 219-222.

De Lara, Adelina, and Clare Abrahall. Finale. [Reprint edition.] St. Clair Shores, Mich., Scholarly Press, 1972. 222 p. Discography: pp. 219-222.

DELIUS, FREDERICK (English composer)

C607   Glass, Hubert. Reissues for the Delius centenary. *American Record Guide*, XXX (Dec. 1963), 40.

C608   Mayes, Stanley H. Frederick Delius—a man of genius. A discography. *Le Grand Baton*, Jan.-Mar. 1965, 3-16.

C609   Upton, Stuart, and Malcolm Walker. Frederick Delius; a discography. Edgware, Middlesex, Delius Society, 1969. 42 p. [New edition is in preparation.]

DELLER, ALFRED (English countertenor)

C610   Hardwick, John Michael Drinkrow, and Mollie Hardwick. Alfred Deller; a singularity of voice. London, Cassell; New York, F. A. Praeger, 1968. 204 p. Discography: pp. 181-190.

DE MURO, BERNARDO (Italian tenor)

C611   Léon, J. A. Bernardo de Muro—discography. *The Record Collector*, XVIII (#3, 1968), 62-65.

DE RESZKE, JEAN (Polish tenor)

C612   Stratton, John. The recordings of Jean de Reszke. *Recorded Sound*, #27 (July 1967), 209-13.

DÉSORMIÈRE, ROGER (French conductor)

C613   Mayer, Denise, and Pierre Souvtchinsky. Roger Désormière et son temps. Monaco, Éditions du Rocher, 1966. 189 p. In French. Includes discographies.

DESSAU, PAUL (German composer)

C614   Hennenberg, Fritz. Paul Dessau. Leipzig, VEB Deutscher Verlag für Musik, 1965. ?p. In German. Discography: pp. 153-155.

DESTINN, EMMY (Czech soprano)

C615   Dennis, J. Emmy Destinn; discography. *The Record Collector*, XX (#1-2, 1971), 29-47.

C616   Emmy Destinn—Addenda. *The Record Collector*, XX (#4, 1971), 93-94.

DIDUR, ADAMO (Polish basso)

C617   Dennis, J. Didur discography. *The Record Collector*, XVI (#1, 1964), 21-23.

DOHNÁNYI, ERNST VON (Hungarian pianist and composer)

C618   Rueth, Marion Ursula. The Tallahassee years of Ernst von Dohnányi. Master's thesis, Florida State University, 1962. 257 p. Discography: pp. 239-245.

DUNAYEVSKY, ISAAK (Russian composer)

C619   Person, David, comp. I. O. Dunajevskij. A musical-bibliographical reference book. Moskva, Sovetskij Kompositor, 1971. [Citation transliterated from the Russian.] 346 p. In Russian. Includes discography.

DVOŘÁK, ANTONÍN (Czech composer)

C620 Schonberg, Harold C. A Dvořák discography. *High Fidelity*, V (Dec. 1955), 101-110.

EAMES, EMMA (American soprano)

C621 Smolian, Steven. Emma Eames—a discography. *American Record Guide, XXIX (Nov. 1962), 215-17.*

EGK, WERNER (German composer)

C622 Krause, Ernst. Werner Egk; Oper und Ballett. Wilhelmshaven, Heinrichshofens Verlag, 1971. 232 p. In German. Discography: p. 222.

EISLER, HANNS (German composer)

C623 Brockhaus, Heinz Alfred. Hanns Eisler. Leipzig, Breitkopf & Härtel, 1961. 209 p. In German. Includes discography.

ELGAR, EDWARD (English composer)

C624 Kennedy, Michael. Portrait of Elgar. London, New York, Oxford University Press, 1968. 324 p. "Recordings conducted by Elgar": pp. 302-350.

C625 Moore, Jerrold Northrop. An Elgar discography. *Recorded Sound*, II (#9, Jan. 1963), whole issue (48 p.)

Moore, Jerrold Northrop. An Elgar discography. Rev. ed. with errata list. London, BIRS, 1963.

ENDREZE, ARTHUR (English baritone)

C626 Barnes, H. M., and V. Girard. Arthur Endreze (barytone): a discography. *Recorded Sound*, #27 (July 1967), 207-08.

ENGLISH SINGERS

C627 The English Singers: discography. *Recorded Sound*, #20 (Oct. 1965), 380-81.

ERDMANN, EDUARD (Latvian pianist and composer)

C628 Bitter, Christof, and Manfred Schlösser. Begegnungen mit Eduard Erdmann. Darmstadt, Erato-Presse, 1968. ? p. In German. Includes discography.

FALKNER, DONALD KEITH (English basso)

C629 Turner, W. Sir Keith Falkner. *The Record Collector*, XIX (1970), 149-71.

FALLA, MANUEL DE (Spanish composer)

C630 Gauthier, André. Manuel de Falla, l'homme et son oeuvre; catalogue des oeuvres, discographie. Paris, Seghers, 1966. 191 p. In French. Discography: pp. 185-188.

C631 Marsh, R. C. A selective discography of Manuel de Falla. *High Fidelity*, VII (July 1957), 63-66.

FARRAR, GERALDINE (American soprano)

C632 Geraldine Farrar discography; corrections and addenda. *The Record Collector*, XIV (#7-8, 1961), 172-74.

C633 Moran, W. R. Geraldine Farrar. *The Record Collector*, XIII (#9-10, 1960), 196-240.

FAURÉ, GABRIEL-URBAIN (French composer)

C634 Vuillermoz, Émile. Gabriel Fauré. Translated by Kenneth Schapin. Philadelphia, Chilton Book Co., 1969. 265 p. Discography by Steven Smolian: pp. 173-259.

FERRANI, CESIRA (Italian soprano)

C635   Witten, L. C. A discography of Cesira Ferrani, soprano, 1863-1943. *The Record Collector*, XX (#6-7, 1972), 157-59.

FERRIER, KATHLEEN (English alto)

C636   Porter, A. Kathleen Ferrier discography. *The Gramophone*, XXXII (Jan. 1955), 372.

FIEDLER, ARTHUR (American conductor)

C637   Moore, Robert Lowell. Fiedler, the colorful Mr. Pops; the man and his music. Boston, Little, Brown, 1968. 372 p. Discography: pp. 293-364.

FIELD, JOHN (Irish composer)

C638   Doscher, David. A John Field discography. *International Piano Library Bulletin*, Sep. 1968, 34-36.

FISCHER, EDWIN (English pianist and conductor)

C639   Dank an Edwin Fischer. Wiesbaden, Brockhaus, 1962. ? p. In German. Includes discography.

C640   Hughes, E. Edwin Fischer discography. *Recorded Sound*, I (#5, 1961-1962), 158-63.

FISCHER-DIESKAU, DIETRICH (German baritone)

C641   Demus, Jörg, and others. Dietrich Fischer-Dieskau. Berlin, Rembrandt Verlag, 1966. 88 p. In German. Discography: pp. 83-88.

C642   Wolfe, L. A Fischer-Dieskau discography. *The Saturday Review*, XLV (June 30, 1962), 35.

FLAGSTAD, KIRSTEN (Norwegian soprano)

C643   Kirsten Flagstad—Discographie. *Musikhandel*, XIV (Jan. 1963), 12. In German.

C644   Zakariasen, W. The duet of the century: Flagstad and Melchior. *High Fidelity/Musical America*, XX (July 1970, sec. 1), 52-56.

FORSELL, JOHN (Swedish singer)

C645   Liliedahl, Karleric. John Forsell. A discography. Trelleborg, Liliedahl, 1972. 23 p.

FRANCK, CÉSAR (French composer)

C646   Affelder, P. César Franck on microgroove. *High Fidelity*, VII (Mar. 1957), 93-101.

C647   Gallois, Jean. Franck. Paris, Éditions du Seuil, 1966. 192 p. In French. Discography: pp. 187-189.

C648   Mohr, Wilhelm. Caesar Franck. 2., erg. Aufl. Tutzing, H. Schneider, 1969. 345 p. In German. Discography: pp. 197-201.

FREITAS BRANCO, PEDRO DE (Portuguese conductor and composer)

C649   Cassuto, A. Discografía de Pedro de Freitas Branco. *Arte Musical*, XXIX (#20-22, 1963-1964), 379-87. In Portuguese.

FRICSAY, FERENC (Hungarian conductor)

C650   Herzfeld, Friedrich. Ferenc Fricsay; ein Gedenkbuch. Berlin, Rembrandt Verlag, 1964. 116 p. In German. Discography: pp. 110-114.

FRIEDMAN, IGNAZ (Polish pianist)

C651   Ignaz Friedman; a discography. 78 RPM, #3 (1968), 9-12; #4 (1969), 11-14; #5 (1969), 6-13.

FURTWÄNGLER, WILHELM (German conductor)

C652   Gillis, Daniel. Furtwängler recalled. Zurich, Atlantic Verlag; New York, Meredith Press, 1965. 224 p. "Furtwängler on record," by Michael Marcus: pp. 185-221.

C653   Höcker, Karla. Wilhelm Furtwängler; Dokumente, Berichte und Bilder, Aufzeichnungen. Berlin, Rembrandt Verlag, 1968. 152 p. In German. Bibliography and discography: pp. 146-151.

C654   Olsen, Henning Smidth. Wilhelm Furtwängler; a discography. København, Nationaldiskoteket, 1970. 95 p.

C655   Sharpe, Geoffrey. Furtwängler [with list of recordings currently available in England]. *Music Review*, XVI (Feb. 1955), 1-4.

C656   Was Furtwängler hinterlassen hat. *Phono*, XI (#2, 1964), 38-39. In German.

C657   Wilhelm Furtwängler. *Disques*, #69 (Jan. 1955), 48-49. In French.

GARDNER, JOHN LINTON (English composer)

C658   Recordings of John Gardner. *Recorded Sound*, #44 (Oct. 1971), 803-04.

GEORGESCU, GEORGES (Rumanian conductor)

C659   Hoffman, A. Interpretationsstile in der Kunst des Dirigierens: George Georgescu. (Bezüglich seiner Letzten internationalen Tournées.) *Revue Roumaine d'Histoire de l'Art*, I (#1, 1964). 139-50. In German.

C660   Hoffman, A. Stiluri dirijorale: George Georgescu. *Istoria Artei*, XII (#1, 1965), 37-38. In Rumanian.

GERSHWIN, GEORGE (American composer and pianist)

C661   Jablonski, Edward. George Gershwin. New York, Putnam, 1962. 190 p. Includes discography.

C662   Jablonski, Edward. Gershwin after twenty years [with a discography]. *Hi-Fi Music at Home*, July-Aug. 1956, 22-23.

C663   Jablonski, Edward. The Gershwin years. 2d ed. Garden City, N.Y., Doubleday, 1973. 416 p. Discography: pp. 359-387.

C664   Payne, Pierre Stephen Robert. Gershwin. New York, Pyramid Books, 1960; London, Robert Hall, 1962. 157 p. Discography: pp. 119-122.

C665   Rushmore, Robert. The life of George Gershwin. New York, Crowell-Collier; London, Collier-Macmillan, 1966. 178 p. Discography: pp. 167-171.

GERSTER, OTTMAR (German violist and composer)

C666   Laux, Karl. Ottmar Gerster; Leben und Werk. Leipzig, P. Reclam Jun., 1961. 116 p. In German. Includes discography.

GHEDINI, GIORGIO FEDERICO (Italian composer)

C667   Salvetti, Guido. Symphonia. Opera postuma di G. F. Ghedini. *Musicalia*, I (#1, Sep. 1970), 13-16. In Italian.

GIESEKING, WALTER (German pianist)

C668   Gieseking, Walter. So wurde ich Pianist. Wiesbaden, F. A. Brockhaus, 1963. 147 p. In German. Includes discography.

C669   Discographie générale de Walter Gieseking. *Disques*, #83-84 (Dec. 1956), 892-93.

GIESEN, HUBERT (German pianist)

C670   Giesen, Hubert. Am Flügel: Hubert Giesen; meine Lebenserinnerungen. Frankfurt am Main, S. Fischer, 1972. 300 p. In German. Discography: pp. 281-288.

GIGLI, BENIAMINO (Italian tenor)

C671   Gigli, Beniamino. The memoirs of Beniamino Gigli, translated by Darina Silare. London, Cassell, 1957. 277 p. Discography by Mark Ricaldone: pp. 233-270.

C672   Hillier, A. D. Beniamino Gigli—a supplementary discography. *Record Advertiser*, Jan.-Feb. 1973, 2-16; Mar.-Apr. 1973, 5-18; May-June 1973, 2-7.

C673   Smith, F. C. Beniamino Gigli [including complete discography]. *American Record Guide*, XXIV (#6, Feb. 1958), 240-42+

GINASTERA, ALBERTO (Argentinian composer)

C674 Suárez Urtubey, Pola. Alberto Ginastera. Buenos Aires, Ediciones Culturales Argentinas, 1967, 162 p. In Spanish. Discography: pp. 160-161.

GINSTER, RIA (German soprano)

C675 Jones, R. Ria Ginster. *Recorded Sound*, #20 (Oct. 1965), 382-88.

GIORDANO, UMBERTO (Italian composer)

C676 Morini, Mario. Umberto Giordano. Milano, Casa musicale Sonzogno, 1968. 434 p. In Italian. "Discografia giordaniana, a cura di Raffaele Végeto": pp. xiv-lxxiii.

GRAINGER, PERCY ALDRIDGE (Australian pianist and composer)

C677 Hughes, E. The recorded works of Percy Grainger. *Recorded Sound*, #45-46 (Jan.-Apr. 1972), 38-43.

C678 Lawrence, A. F. Records of Percy Grainger as an interpreter. *Recorded Sound*, #45-46 (Jan.-Apr. 1972), 43-48.

C679 Slattery, Thomas C. The wind music of Percy Aldridge Grainger. Unpublished Ph.D. dissertation, University of Iowa, 1967. ? p. Discography: pp. 232-239.

C680 Stonehill, Gerald. Piano rolls played by Percy Grainger. *Recorded Sound*, #45-46 (Jan.-Apr. 1972), 49.

GREEF, ARTHUR DE (Belgian pianist and composer)

C681 Anderson, H. L. The recording sessions of Arthur de Greef. *Recorded Sound*, #29-30 (Jan.-Apr. 1968), 285-91.

GREEF-ANDRIESSEN, PELAGIE (Austrian soprano)

C682 Pelagie Greef-Andriessen [discography]. *Antique Records*, May 1973, 24.

GREENE, HARRY PLUNKET (Irish tenor)

C683   Harry Plunket Greene: the records. *Record Advertiser*, Sep.-Oct. 1971, 3.

C684   Plunket Greene discography. *Recorded Sound*, #32 (Oct. 1968), 329-30.

GRIEG, EDVARD HAGERUP (Norwegian composer)

C685   Aahlén, Carl-Gunnar. Grammofonens veteraner: Edvard Grieg (1843-1907). *Musikrevy*, XXVII (#3, 1972), 155-57.

C686   Pols, André M. Het leven van E. Grieg. Brussels, Reinaert Uitgaven, 1971. 47 p. In Flemish. Discography: pp. 44-47.

GRUMIAUX, ARTHUR (Belgian violinist)

C687   Arthur Grumiaux. *Phonoprisma*, VI (#1, 1963), 19-20. In German.

HÄNDEL, GEORG FRIEDRICH (German composer)

C688   Cudworth, Charles. Handel; a biography, with a survey of books, editions, and recordings. (The concertgoer's companions) Hamden, Conn., Linnet Books; London, Bingley, 1972. 112 p. Discography by Brian Redfern: pp. 90-101.

C689   Pols, André M. Het leven van G. F. Haendel. Brussel, Reinaert Uitgaven, 1970. 48 p. In Flemish. Discography: pp. 43-48.

C690   Sadie, Stanley. Handel. London, J. Calder, 1966. 192 p. Discography: pp. 189-192.

C691   Werke von Georg Friedrich Händel auf Langspielplatten. *Musikerziehung*, XII (June 1959), 231-32; XIII (Sep. 1959), 36-37. In German.

HAHN, REYNALDO (Venezuelan composer)

C692   Barnes, H. M., and V. Girard. Reynaldo Hahn discography. *Recorded Sound*, #21 (Jan. 1966), 16-18.

HAITINK, BERNARD (Dutch conductor)

C693   A Haitink discography. *Records and Recordings*, Sep. 1972, 23.

HAMMOND, JOAN (Australian soprano)

C694   Hammond, Joan. A voice, a life; autobiography. London, Gollancz, 1970. 264 p. Discography: pp. 249-256.

HASKIL, CLARA (Rumanian pianist)

C695   Gavoty, Bernard. Clara Haskil. Portraits de Roger Hauert. Genève, Kister, 1962. 32 p. In French. Discography: pp. 30-32.

HAYDN, FRANZ JOSEF (Austrian composer)

C696   Barbaud, Pierre. Haydn. Paris, Éditions du Seuil, 1957. 191 p. In French. Discography: pp. 186-191.

C697   Burke, Cornelius G. The collector's Haydn. (Keystone books in music) Philadelphia, Lippincott, 1959. 316 p.

C698   Discography of discarded Haydn. *The Saturday Review*, XLIV (Feb. 25, 1961), 63-64.

C699   Redfern, Brian L. Haydn: a biography with a survey of books, editions and recordings. London, Bingley; Hamden, Conn., Archon Books, 1970. 111 p. Discography: pp. 85-104.

C700   Vignal, Marc. Franz-Joseph Haydn; l'homme et son oeuvre. Paris, Seghers, 1964. 191 p. In French. Discography: pp. 180-188.

C701   Werke von Joseph Haydn auf Langspielplatten. *Musikerziehung*, XII (Mar. 1959), 159-63. In German.

Symphonies

C702   Dearling, Robert, and Anthony Hodgson. The symphonies of Joseph Haydn [conducted by Maerzendorfer]. *Records and Recordings*, Feb. 1973, 28-33.

C703   Hodgson, Anthony, and others. Joseph Haydn—the pre-London symphonies [a discography]. *The Haydn Yearbook*, VII (1970), 169-253.

C704   Marsh, R. C. The symphonies of Haydn: a discography. *High Fidelity*, XI (Oct. 1961), 54-56.

HEMPEL, FRIEDA (German soprano)

C705   Wile, Raymond R. The Edison discs of Frieda Hempel. *Association of Recorded Sound Collections Journal*, III (#2-3, Fall 1971), 47-52.

HEROLD, VILHELM (Danish tenor)

C706   Nationaldiskoteket, K\u00f8benhavn. Vilhelm Herold. K\u00f8benhavn, Nationaldiskoteket, 1967?

HESELTINE, PHILIP (pen-name, PETER WARLOCK; English composer)

C707   Marvin, Keith, and C. P. Mills. An inventory of Peter Warlock recordings. *The Peter Warlock Society Newsletter*, #1 (1966), 10-11.

HESS, MYRA (English pianist)

C708   Clough, Francis F., and G. J. Cuming. Myra Hess discography. *Recorded Sound*, #24 (Oct. 1966), 104-06.

HEWARD, LESLIE (English conductor and composer)

C709   Blom, Eric. Leslie Heward 1897-1943. 2d ed. Birmingham, Cornish Bros., 1946. 94 p. Discography: pp. 92-94.

HINDEMITH, PAUL (German composer)

C710   Frankfurt am Main. Deutsches Rundfunkarchiv. Paul Hindemith, 16.11.1895-28.12.1963, als Dirigent und Solist im Rundfunk. Frankfurt am Main, Deutsches Rundfunkarchiv, 1965. 85 p. In German.

C711   Paul Hindemith-werkverzeichnis. Mainz, Schott, 1965. ? p. In German. Discography: pp. 55-59.

C712   Rösner, Helmut, ed. Paul Hindemith—Katalog seiner Werke, Diskographie, Bibliographie, Einführung in das Schaffen. Frankfurt am

Main, Städtische Musikbibliothek, 1970. 60 p. In German. Includes discography.

HISLOP, JOSEPH (Scottish tenor)

C713   Joseph Hislop: a discography. 78 RPM, #4 (1969), 4-8.

HOFMANN, JOSEF (Polish pianist)

C714   Kanski, J. Hofmann na plytach gramofonowych (Jozef Hofmann). *Ruch Muzyczny*, VI (#4, 1962), 4-5. In Polish.

C715   Lawrence, A. F. R., and Gregor Benko. Josef Hofmann discography. *International Piano Library Bulletin*, Summer 1967, 9-16; Fall-Winter 1967, 11-18; May 1968, 3-8; Dec. 1968, 3-5.

HOLBROOKE, JOSEF (English composer)

C716   Foreman, Lewis, and Graham Parlett. Holbrooke discography. *Antique Records*, May 1974. [Scheduled for publication.]

HOLST, GUSTAV THEODORE (English composer)

C717   Short, Michael. Gustav Holst (1874-1934)—a centenary documentation. Unpublished FLA thesis, Library Association, London, 1973. Includes discographies.

HONEGGER, ARTHUR (Swiss composer)

C718   Essai de discographie générale de Honegger. *Disques*, #75-76 (Dec. 1955), 898-99. In French.

C719   Feschotte, Jacques. Arthur Honegger. Lausanne, La Guilde du livre, 1970. 191 p. In French. Discography: pp. 173-177.

C720   Feschotte, Jacques. Arthur Honegger; l'homme et son oeuvre. Paris, Seghers, 1966. 189 p. In French. Discography: pp. 171-177.

C721   Landowski, Marcel, and Marie-Françoise Christout. Honegger. Paris, Éditions du Seuil, 1957. 191 p. In French. Discography: pp. 181-191.

HOTTER, HANS (German baritone)

C722 Wessling, Berndt Wilhelm. Hans Hotter. Bremen, Schünemann, 1966. 141 p. In German. Bibliography and discography: pp. 140-141.

HUBERMAN, BRONISLAW (Polish violinist)

C723 Bronislaw Huberman: a discography. *Record Advertiser*, Nov.-Dec. 1970, 5-7.

IBERT, JACQUES (French composer)

C724 Michel, Gérard. Jacques Ibert; l'homme et son oeuvre. Paris, Seghers, 1968. 192 p. In French. Discography: pp. 176-182.

IRELAND, JOHN (English composer)

C725 Chapman, Ernest. John Ireland; a catalogue of published works and recordings. London, Boosey & Hawkes, 1968. 53 p. Discography: pp. 37-42.

IVES, CHARLES EDWARD (American composer)

C726 Cowell, Henry, and Sidney Cowell. Charles Ives and his music. London, New York, Oxford University Press, 1969. [First published in 1955.] 253 p. Discography: pp. 228-243.

C727 De Lerma, Dominique-René. Charles Edward Ives 1874-1954: a bibliography of his music. Kent, Ohio, Kent State University Press, 1970. 212 p. Discography: pp. 189-212.

C728 Hall, David. Charles Ives: a discography. *Hifi/Stereo Review*, XIII (Oct. 1964), 142-46; (Dec. 1964), 92+

C729 Warren, Richard. Charles E. Ives; discography. (The historical sound recordings publication series, 1) New Haven, Conn., Historical Sound Recordings, Yale University Library, 1972. 124 p.

IVOGÜN, MARIA (real name, INGE VON GUNTHER; Hungarian soprano)

C730 Dennis, J. Maria Ivoguen: discography. *The Record Collector*, XX (#5, 1972), 114-19.

C731   Weihermueller, M. Maria Ivoguen, addenda [discography]. *The Record Collector*, XX (#11-12, 1972), 283-84.

JADLOWKER, HERMANN (Russian tenor)

C732   Kaufman, T., and D. Brew. Hermann Jadlowker discography. *The Record Collector*, XIX (#1-2, 1970), 11-32.

JANÁČEK, LEOŠ (Czech composer)

C733   Racek, Jan. Leoš Janáček. Leipzig, Reclam, 1971. 286 p. In German. Discography: pp. 253-265.

C734   Silverberg, R. A whole man from Moravia; for Leoš Janáček life began at seventy [selective Janáček discography]. *High Fidelity*, XIII (Mar. 1963), 55-57+

JANSSEN, HERBERT (German baritone)

C735   Hart, T. Herbert Janssen. *The Record Collector*, XVI (#11-12, 1966), 256-63.

JAUBERT, MAURICE (French composer)

C736   Porcile, François. Maurice Jaubert, musicien populaire ou maudit? Paris, Les Éditeurs français réunis, 1971. 286 p. In French. Discography: pp. 253-256.

JONES, SISSIERETTA (American soprano)

C737   Daughtry, Willia E. Sissieretta Jones: profile of a black artist. *Musical Analysis*, I (#1, Winter 1972), 12-18.

KARAJAN, HERBERT VON (Austrian conductor)

C738   Haeusserman, Ernst. Herbert von Karajan; Biographie. Gütersloh, C. Bertelsmann, 1968. 319 p. In German. Discography: pp. 303-316.

C739   Werba, R. Karajan-Diskographie. *Österreichische Musikzeitschrift*, XXII (Apr. 1967), 233-35+ In German.

KASCHMANN, GIUSEPPE (German baritone)

C740   Wile, Raymond R. Edison disc recordings of Giuseppe Kaschmann. *Association of Recorded Sound Collections Journal*, III (#2-3, Fall 1971), 52-53.

KEILBERTH, JOSEPH (German conductor)

C741   Freyse, R. Joseph Keilberth, ein Schallplatten-Porträt.*Neue Zeitschrift für Musikwissenschaft*, CXXIV (#11, 1963), 435-39. In German.

KEMPFF, WILHELM (German pianist and composer)

C742   Purkyt, R. Wilhelm Kempff auf Schallplatten. *Phono*, XII (#2, 1965), 36-38. In German.

KERNS, GRACE (American soprano)

C743   Walsh, J. Grace Kerns and John Barnes Wells [includes discography]. *Hobbies*, LXIX (Aug. 1964), 34-36.

KIRKBY-LUNN, LOUISE (English alto)

C744   Richards, J. B. The Kirkby Lunn recordings. *The Record Collector*, XIX (#5-6, 1970), 172-88.

KLEMPERER, OTTO (German conductor)

C745   Klemperer, Otto. Minor recollections. Translated from the German by J. Maxwell Brownjohn. London, D. Dobson, 1964. 124 p. Discography by F. F. Clough and G. J. Cuming: pp. 103-117.

C746   A Klemperer discography. *The Saturday Review*, XLVIII (May 29, 1965), 48-49+

C747   Heyworth, Peter, comp. Conversations with Klemperer. London, Gollancz, 1973. ? p. Discography by Malcolm Walker: pp. 105-122.

KODÁLY, ZOLTÁN (Hungarian composer)

C748   Barna, István. Kodály Zoltán müveinek magyar hanglemezei. *Magyar Zene*, VIII (#2, 1967), 183-88. In Hungarian.

C749   Greenfield, E. Kodály on records. *Tempo*, #63 (Winter 1962-1963), 41-43.

C750   Young, Percy Marshall. Zoltán Kodály, a Hungarian musician. London, E. Benn, 1964. 231 p. Discography: pp. 218-220.

KORJUS, MILIZA (Polish soprano)

C751   Pearmain, J. Miliza Korjus discography. *The Record Collector*, XVI (#2, 1964), 39-45.

KOSHETZ, NINA (Russian soprano)

C752   Liff, V. Nina Koshetz, discography. *The Record Collector*, XVII (#3, 1967), 58-61.

KRAUSS, CLEMENS (Austrian conductor)

C753   Performances by Clemens Krauss: non-commercial recordings in the archives of the West German Radio and the Clemens Krauss-Archiv, Vienna. *Recorded Sound*, #42-43 (Apr.-July 1971), 743-46.

KRUSZELNICKA-BICCIONI, SALOMEA (Ukrainian soprano)

C754   Autrey, R. L. Kruszelnicka discography. *The Record Collector*, XVIII (#4, 1969), 83-88.

KULLMAN, CHARLES (American tenor)

C755   Morgan, C. I. Charles Kullman: discography. *The Record Collector*, XX (#11-12, 1972), 250-58.

LAMBERT, CONSTANT (English composer)

C756   Shead, Richard. Constant Lambert. London, Simon Publications, 1973. ? p. Discography: pp. 187-192.

LANDOWSKA, WANDA (Polish harpsichordist)

C757   Kipnis, I. The legacy of Landowska—a discography. *American Record Guide*, XXVI (Dec. 1959), 239.

C758   Landowska, Wanda. Landowska on music. Ed. by Denis Restout. New York, Stein and Day, 1964; London, Secker and Warburg, 1965. 434 p. Discography: pp. 411-424.

LANDOWSKI, MARCEL (French composer)

C759   Goléa, Antoine. Marcel Landowski; l'homme et son oeuvre. Paris, Seghers, 1969. 191 p. In French. Discography: pp. 181-182.

LAURI-VOLPI, GIACOMO (Italian tenor)

C760   Disco Nacional, Argentina. Lauri-Volpi. *The Record Collector*, XX (#8-10, 1972), 239.

LAZARO, HIPOLITO (Spanish tenor)

C761   Richards, J. B. Hipolito Lazaro. *The Record Collector*, XVI (#3-4, 1964), 52-82.

LEIDER, FRIDA (German soprano)

C762   Leider, Frida. Playing my part. Translated by Charles Osborne. New York, Meredith Press, 1966. 217 p. Discography: pp. 211-214.

LEMNITZ, TIANA (German soprano)

C763   Seeliger, R., and B. Park. Tiana Lemnitz discography. *The Record Collector*, XV (#2, 1963?), 37-43.

LHÉVINNE, JOSEF (Russian pianist)

C764   Anderson, H. L. Josef Lhévinne discography. *Recorded Sound*, #44 (Oct. 1971), 791-96.

LHÉVINNE, ROSINA (Russian pianist)

C765   Anderson, H. L. Rosina Lhévinne discography. *Recorded Sound*, #44 (Oct. 1971), 797.

LIPATTI, DINU (Rumanian pianist and composer)

C766   Băragăuanu, G. Dinu Lipatti compozitor. *Muzica*, XIV (May-June 1964), 72-87. In Rumanian.

C767   Băragăuanu, Grigore, and Dragoş Tănăsescu. Aspects inédits de l'activité de Dinu Lipatti. *Muzica*, XX (#1, Jan. 1970), 47. In French.

C768   Băragăuanu, Grigore, and Dragoş Tănăsescu. Dinu Lipatti. *Muzica*, XXI (#1, Jan. 1971), 37-44. In French.

C769   1970 [i.e., Dix-neuf cent soixante-dix], in memoriam Dinu Lipatti, 1917-1950. Genève, Éditions Labor et Fides, 1970. 131 p. In French. Discography: pp. 125-126.

C770   Lipatti, Anna. Dinu Lipatti. La douleur de ma vie. Genève, Perret-Gentil, 1967. 95 p. In French. Discography: pp. 89-90.

C771   Tănăsescu, Dragoş. Dinu Lipatti. Bucuresti, Editura muzicală, 1971. 224 p. In Rumanian. Discography: pp. 195-208.

C772   Tănăsescu, Dragoş. Lipatti. Bucharest, Meridiane Pub. House, 1965. 98 p. In Rumanian. Discography: pp. 95-98.

LISZT, FRANZ (Hungarian composer)

C773   Jacobson, B. Liszt on records. *High Fidelity/Musical America*, XVIII (Apr. 1968), 51-55.

C774   Leroy, Alfred. Franz Liszt; l'homme et son oeuvre. Paris, Seghers, 1964; Lausanne, La Guilde du livre, 1967. 192 p. In French. Discography: pp. 183-187.

C775   Seroff, Victor Ilyitch. Franz Liszt. New York, Macmillan, 1966; Freeport, N.Y., Books for Libraries Press, 1970. 152 p. Discography: pp. 147-149.

C776   Wessling, Berndt Wilhelm. Franz Liszt, ein virtuoses Leben. München, Piper, 1973. 316 p. In German. Includes discography.

LITVINNE, FÉLIA (real name, FRANÇOISE-JEANNE SCHÜTZ; Russian soprano)

C777   Witten, L. C. A discography of Félia Litvinne, soprano. *The Record Collector*, XX (#6-7, 1972), 147-56; (#11-12, 1972), 283.

LOCATELLI, PIETRO ANTONIO (Italian composer)

C778   Calmeyer, John Hendrik. The life, times and works of Pietro Antonio Locatelli. Unpublished Ph.D. dissertation, University of North Carolina, 1969. 465 p. Includes discography.

LOEWE, CARL (German composer)

C779   Elson, J. Carl Loewe and the nineteenth century German ballad [includes discography]. *The Nats Bulletin*, XXVIII (#1, 1971), 16-19.

LUBIN, GERMAINE (French soprano)

C780   Barnes, H. Germaine Lubin discography. *Recorded Sound*, #19 (July 1965), 367.

LUTYENS, ELIZABETH (English composer)

C781   Hughes, E., and S. Junge. Composer's anthology [Elizabeth Lutyens; includes discography]. *Recorded Sound*, #38 (Apr. 1970), 599-600.

MAAZEL, LORIN (American conductor)

C782   Geleng, Ingvelde. Lorin Maazel; Monographie eines Musikers. Berlin, Rembrandt Verlag, 1971. 135 p. In German. Discography: p. 130.

MACCHI, MARIO (Italian conductor)

C783   Celletti, R. Maria de Macchi. *Musica e Dischi*, XVIII (Aug. 1962), 8. In Italian.

McCORMACK, JOHN (Irish tenor)

C784   Morby, P. Brown wax to blue amberol—and the McCormack cylinders. *The Record Collector*, XVIII (#1-2, 1968), 5-42.

C785   Roe, Leonard F. X. McDermott. John McCormack—the complete discography. London, Charles Jackson, 1956. 93 p.

C786   Roe, Leonard F. X. McDermott. The John McCormack discography. Lingfield, Surrey, Oakwood Press, 1972. 93 p.

C787   Strong, Leonard Alfred George. John McCormack. London, Peter
        Nevill, 1949. 309 p. Discography: pp. 281-309. [Discography
        includes brief listings of artists associated with McCormack as well
        as McCormack himself.]

MACHAUT, GUILLAUME DE (French composer)

C788   Levarie, Siegmund. Guillaume de Machaut. Ed. by John J. Becker.
        New York, Sheed and Ward, 1954. 114 p. Discography: p. 114.

        Levarie, Siegmund. Guillaume de Machaut. Ed. by John J. Becker.
        Reprint ed. New York, Da Capo Press, 1969. 114 p. Discography: p. 114.

MAHLER, GUSTAV (Austrian composer)

C789   Bălan, George. Gustav Mahler sau cum exprima muzica idei.
        Bucureşti, Editura Muzicală a Uniunii Compozitorilor din R.P.R.,
        1964. 195 p. In Rumanian. Discography: pp. 193-195.

C790   Duse, Ugo. Gustav Mahler: introduzione allo studio della vita e delle
        opere. Padova, Marsilio, 1962. 270 p. In Italian. Discography:
        pp. 268-270.

C791   Gustav Mahler—Diskographie. *Hifi-Stereophonie,* X (Apr. 1971),
        364+ In German.

C792   Hall, David. Gustav Mahler: the music, the records. *Hifi/Stereo
        Review,* V (Sep. 1960), 42-49.

C793   Marsh, R. C. A Mahler discography on historical principles. *High
        Fidelity,* VII (May 1957), 81-87.

C794   Mitchell, Donald. Mahler on the gramophone. *Music and Letters,*
        XLI (Apr. 1960), 156-63.

C795   Schreiber, Wolfgang. Gustav Mahler in Selbstzeugnissen und
        Bilddokumenten. Reinbek bei Hamburg, Rowohlt, 1971. 187 p.
        In German. Discography: pp. 183-186.

C796   Trigo de Sousa, A. Mahler e Bruckner em discos. *Arte Musical,*
        XXVIII (#9, 1960), 251-52. In Portuguese.

C797   Vignal, Marc. Mahler. Paris, Éditions du Seuil, 1966. 187 p. In French.
        Discography: pp. 185-187.

C798   Weber, Jerome F. Mahler. (Weber discography series, 9) Utica, N.Y., Jerome F. Weber, 1971. 47 p.

Das Lied von der Erde

C799   Restagno, Enzo. Das Lied von der Erde. *Musicalia*, I (#1, Sep. 1970), 55-59. In Italian.

Symphonies

C800   Fierz, G. Gustav Mahler: eine Diskographie seiner Sinfonien. *Schweizerische Musikzeitung*, C (#3, 1960), 185-88. In German.

C801   Jacobson, B. The Mahler symphonies on records; an analysis of sixty-odd recorded versions currently available. *High Fidelity/Musical America*, XVII (Sep. 1967), 55-59.

MANTELLI, EUGENIA (Italian alto)

C802   Ziering, R. M. Eugenia Mantelli; a discography. *The Record Collector*, XIV (#11-12, 1962), 279-84.

MARCOUX, VANNI (French baritone)

C803   Barnes, H. M. Vanni Marcoux: a discography. *Recorded Sound*, #29-30 (Jan.-Apr. 1968), 269-72.

MARESCOTTI, ANDRÉ FRANÇOIS (Swiss composer)

C804   Goléa, Antoine. André-François Marescotti; biographie, études analytiques. Paris, Société des Éditions Jobert, 1963. 18 p. In French. Discography: p. 18.

MARRINER, NEVILLE (English conductor)

C805   MacLachlin, Don. A Marriner discography: works conducted by Neville Marriner. *Records and Recordings*, June 1972, 23.

MARTINELLI, GIOVANNI (Italian tenor)

C806   Aylward, D. Martinelli on LP records. *Recorded Sound*, I (#8, 1962), 239-41.

C807   Wile, Raymond R. The first Martinelli recordings. *Association of Recorded Sound Collections Journal*, III (#2-3, Fall 1971), 25-46.

MARTINU, BOHUSLAV (Czech composer)

C808   Halbreich, Harry. Bohuslav Martinu. Zurich, Atlantis-Verlag, 1968. 384 p. In German. Discography: pp. 345-348.

MASCAGNI, PIETRO (Italian composer)

C809   Morini, Mario, ed. Pietro Mascagni. Milano, Casa Musicale Sonzogno di Piero Ostali, 1964. 2v. In Italian. Discography: v. 2, pp. 235-280.

MASSENET, JULES (French composer)

C810   Coquis, André. Jules Massenet; l'homme et son oeuvre. Paris, Éditions Seghers, 1965. 190 p. In French. Discography: pp. 181-182.

MATTHAY, TOBIAS (English pianist)

C811   Tobias Matthay. *Recorded Sound*, I (#5, Jan. 1962), 143.

MELCHIOR, LAURITZ (Danish tenor)

C812   Hansen, Hans. Lauritz Melchior; a discography. København, Nationaldiskoteket, 1965. 44 p.

       Hansen, Hans. Lauritz Melchior; a discography. Rev. ed. København, Nationaldiskoteket, 1972. 40 p.

MELCHISSÈDEC, LÉON (French baritone)

C813   Witten, L. C. Léon Melchissèdec. *Antique Records*, #2 (May 1973), 31-33.

MENDELSSOHN, FELIX (German composer)

C814   Köhler, Karl-Heinz. Felix Mendelssohn-Bartholdy. Leipzig, Reclam, 1966. 285 p. In German. "Schallplattenverzeichnis": pp. 253-258.

Elijah

C815   Werner, Jack. Mendelssohn's "Elijah"; a historical and analytical guide to the oratorio. London, Chappell, 1965. 109 p. Discography: pp. 95-105.

Lieder

C816   Stoner, Thomas. Mendelssohn's published songs. Unpublished Ph.D. dissertation, University of Maryland, 1972. 428 p. Includes discography.

Vocal Music

C817   Morse, Peter. Mendelssohn vocal music. (Weber discography series, 6) Utica, N.Y., Jerome F. Weber, 1970. 11 p.

   Morse, Peter. Mendelssohn vocal music. Rev. ed. Utica, N.Y., Jerome F. Weber, 1973. 30 p.

MENGELBERG, WILLEM (Dutch conductor)

C818   Hardie, Robert H. The recordings of Willem Mengelberg—a discography. Nashville, Tenn., Hardie [Dyer Observatory, Vanderbilt University], 1972.

C819   Wolf, Robert. Mengelberg recordings: a discography. *Le Grand Baton,* Aug.-Nov. 1971, 40-54.

MENUHIN, YEHUDI (American violinist)

C820   Magidoff, Robert, and Henry Raynor. Yehudi Menuhin; the story of the man and the musician. 2d ed. London, Hale, 1973. ? p. Discography: pp. 324-340.

C821   Spingel, Hans Otto. Yehudi Menuhin. Berlin, Rembrandt Verlag, 1964. 61 p. In German. Discography: pp. 28-31.

MESSIAEN, OLIVIER (French composer)

C822   Mari, Pierrette. Olivier Messiaen; l'homme et son oeuvre. Paris, Éditions Seghers, 1965. 191 p. In French. Discography: pp. 186-188.

C823   Samuel, Claude. Entretiens avec Olivier Messiaen. Paris, P. Belfond, 1967. 239 p. In French. Discography: pp. 227-231.

MEYERBEER, GIACOMO (real name, JAKOB LIEBMANN BEER; German composer)

C824   Bebb, R., and V. Liff. Opera on the gramophone: "Les Huguenots." *Opera* (England), XX (Aug. 1969), 678-84.

MICHAILOVA, MARIA (Russian soprano)

C825   Barnes, H. M. A discography of Maria Michailova. *Recorded Sound*, #33 (Jan. 1969), 366-80.

MILANOV, ZINKA (Yugoslavian soprano)

C826   Einstein, Edwin K., Jr. Zinka Milanov: a complete discography. *Le Grand Baton*, May 1968, 7-16.

MILHAUD, DARIUS (French composer)

C827   Roy, Jean. Darius Milhaud, l'homme et son oeuvre. Paris, Seghers, 1968. 192 p. In French. Discography: pp. 183-185.

MITROPOULOS, DIMITRI (Greek conductor)

C828   Christopoulou, Maria. Dēmētrēs Mētropoulos: zoē kai ergo. Athens, Yannoukakis, 1971. [Citation transliterated from the Greek.] 248 p. In Greek. Includes discography.

MOERAN, ERNEST JOHN (English composer)

C829   Wild, Stephen. E. J. Moeran. London, Triad Press, 1973. ? p. Discography by Lewis Foreman: pp. 23-31.

MONIUSZKO, STANISLAW (Polish composer)

C830   Prosnak, Jan. Stanislaw Moniuszko. Wyd. 2. Kraków, Polskie Wydawn. Muzyczne, 1968. 204 p. In Polish. Discography: pp. 185-199.

C831   Rudziński, Witold. Moniuszko. Kraków, Polskie Wydawn. Muzyczne, 1969. 283 p. In Polish. Discography: pp. 245-273.

MONTEUX, PIERRE (French conductor)

C832   Monteux, Doris Gerald (Hodgkins). It's all in the music. New York, Farrar, Straus and Giroux, 1965. 272 p. Discography: pp. 233-261.

Monteux, Doris Gerald (Hodgkins). It's all in the music. London, Kimber, 1966. 255 p. Discography: pp. 225-249.

MONTEVERDI, CLAUDIO (Italian composer)

C833   Hagg, W. Monteverdi-Diskographie. *Österreichische Musikzeitschrift,* XXVI (Aug. 1971), 468-71. In German.

C834   Sommerfield, David. A Monteverdi discography. *Current Musicology,* IX (1969), 215-32.

C835   Tellart, Roger. Claudio Monteverdi. Lausanne, La Guilde du livre, 1970. 191 p. In French. Discography: pp. 181-184.

C836   Tellart, Roger. Claudio Monteverdi; l'homme et son oeuvre. Paris, Seghers, 1964. 190 p. In French. Discography: pp. 181-184.

C837   Westerlund, Gunnar, and Eric Hughes. Music of Claudio Monteverdi: a discography. London, British Institute of Recorded Sound, 1972. 72 p.

MOORE, GRACE (American soprano)

C838   Favia-Artsay, A. Grace Moore. *Hobbies,* LXVII (Jan. 1963), 30-31.

MOZART, WOLFGANG AMADEUS (Austrian composer)

C839   Burke, C. G. Mozart on records: a selective discography. *High Fidelity,* VI (Jan. 1956), 71-86.

C840   Hocquard, Jean Victor. Mozart. Nouv. ed. Paris, Éditions du Seuil, 1970. 185 p. In French. Discography: pp. 180-186.

C841   King, Alexander Hyatt. Mozart: a biography with a survey of books, editions and recordings. (The concertgoer's companions) London, Bingley; Hamden, Conn., Archon Books, 1970. 114 p. Discography by Brian Redfern: pp. 88-105.

C842   Lindlar, H. Kleine Mozart-Diskographie. *Phonoprisma*, V (#2, 1962), 33-34. In German.

C843   Mozart by a mile [compositions on LP records]. *Audio*, LIII (Apr. 1969), 18.

C844   Pirie, Peter J. A bibliography of Mozart records [available in England]. *Music Review*, XVII (Feb. 1956), 71-86.

C845   Reinold, Helmut, ed. Der italienische Mozart. Freiburg i Br., Fono-Verlagsgesellschaft, 1962. 31 p. In German. Discography: pp. 26-31.

C846   Seroff, Victor Ilyitch. Wolfgang Amadeus Mozart. New York, Macmillan, 1965. 124 p. Discography: pp. 115-121.

C847   Stearns, Monroe. Wolfgang Amadeus Mozart, master of pure music. New York, F. Watts, 1968. 249 p. Discography: pp. 240-243.

C848   Wolfgang Amadeus Mozart. Zum 175. Todestag am 5. Dezember. Zusammengestellt von Hans-Joachim Kögel und Achim Rohde. Berlin, Berliner Stadtbibliothek, 1966. 41 p. In German. Includes discography.

Così Fan Tutte

C849   Jefferson, A. More letters: "Così" and "Rosenkavalier" discographies. *Opera* (England), XIX (Sep. 1968), 772-73.

Le Nozze di Figaro

C850   Mozart: "Le Nozze di Figaro"; eine Discographie. *Phono*, X (#1, 1963), 18-19. In German.

Operas

C851   Broder, Nathan. The Mozart operas on record. *High Fidelity*, X (Nov. 1960), 56-57.

C852   Klein, H. The supremacy of Mozart [discussion of recorded operatic excerpts. Reprinted from The Gramophone (Dec. 1925 and Feb. 1926).] *Recorded Sound*, #40 (Oct. 1970), 678-88.

C853   Osborne, D. L. The operas of Mozart on microgroove; a discography-in-depth. *High Fidelity/Musical America*, XV (Nov. 1965), 65-72+

Piano Concerti

C854   Broder, Nathan. Mozart: the piano concertos. *High Fidelity*, VIII (Oct. 1958), 111.

Die Zauberflöte

C855   Cornelissen, Thilo. Die Zauberflöte von W. A. Mozart. Berlin, R. Lineau, 1963. 107 p. In German. Includes discography.

MUSSORGSKY, MODEST (Russian composer)

C856   Marnat, Marcel. Moussorgsky. Paris, Éditions du Seuil, 1962. 189 p. In French. Discography: pp. 182-186.

MUZIO, CLAUDIA (Italian soprano)

C857   Barnes, H. M. Discography [Claudia Muzio]. *The Record Collector*, XVII (#9-10, 1968), 224-37.

C858   Wile, Raymond R. The Edison legacy of Claudia Muzio. *American Record Guide*, XXVII (Apr. 1961), 634-37.

NASH, HEDDLE (English tenor)

C859   Heddle Nash: a discography. 78 RPM, June 1969, 3-10.

C860   Heddle Nash: the HMV records. 78 RPM, Sep. 1969. 7.

C861   Jarrett, J. Heddle Nash. *Record Advertiser*, July-Aug. 1973, 2-11; Sep.-Oct. 1973, 22.

NAZARETH, ERNESTO (Brazilian composer and pianist)

C862   Rio de Janeiro. Biblioteca Nacional. Exposiçao comemorativa do centenário do nascimento de Ernesto Nazareth, 1863-1934. Rio de Janeiro, Biblioteca Nacional, 1963. 66 p. In Portuguese. Discography: pp. 60-66.

NEVEU, GINETTE (French violinist)

C863   Ronze-Neveu, Marie-Jeanne. Ginette Neveu. London, Rockliff, 1957. 159 p. Discography: pp. 109-110.

NIELSEN, CARL (Danish composer)

C864   Fabricius-Bjerre, Claus. Carl Nielsen diskografi. København, Nationaldiskoteket, 1965. 22 p. In Danish.

Febricius-Bjerre, Claus. Carl Nielsen diskografi. 2d ed. København, Nationaldiskoteket, 1968. 44 p. In Danish.

NIKISCH, ARTUR (Hungarian conductor)

C865   Shawe-Taylor, D., and E. Hughes. Arthur Nikisch. *Recorded Sound*, #4 (Oct. 1961), 114-15.

C866   Stone, Ralph. Artur Nikisch. *Le Grand Baton*, May 1968, 17-21.

NONO, LUIGI (Italian composer)

C867   Works by Luigi Nono on records. *Recorded Sound*, #24 (Oct. 1966), 121.

NORDICA, LILLIAN (real name, LILLIAN NORTON; American soprano)

C868   Glackens, Ira. Yankee diva; Lillian Nordica and the golden days of opera. New York, Coleridge Press, 1963. 366 p. Discography: pp. 292-300.

NOVÁK, VÍTĚZSLAV (Czech composer)

C869   Budiš, Ratibor. Vítězslav Novák. Výběrová bibliografie. Praha, Kniha, 1967. 166 p. In Czech; summary in French, English, Russian, and German. Includes discography.

NOWOWIEJSKI, FELIKS (Polish composer)

C870 Nowowiejski, Feliks M., and Kazimierz Nowowiejski. Dookoła kompozytora; wspomnienia o ojcu. Poznań, Wydawn. Poznańskie, 1968. 303 p. In Polish. Includes discography.

NYSTROEM, GÖSTA (Swedish composer)

C871 Mörner, Carl-Gabriel Stellan. Gösta Nystroem paa skiva. En diskografi. *Biblioteksbladet*, LXII (#3-4, 1967), 290-93. In Swedish.

OFFENBACH, JACQUES (French composer)

C872 Folstein, Robert L., and Stephan Willis. A bibliography on Jacques Offenbach. *Current Musicology*, XII (Sep. 1971), 116-28. Discography: pp. 27-28.

OISTRAKH, DAVID (Russian violinist)

C873 Jampolski, Israel. David Oistrakh. Moskva, Muzyka, 1968. [Citation transliterated from the Russian.] 144 p. In Russian. Includes discography.

OLCOTT, CHAUNCEY (American composer)

C874 Kunstadt, L., and B. Colton. Chauncey Olcott discography. *Record Research*, #83 (Apr. 1967), 10.

OLDHAM, DEREK

C875 Recollections of Derek Oldham. *Record Advertiser*, Sep.-Oct. 1973, 19-22.

O'MARA, JOSEPH (Irish tenor)

C876 Potterton, R. Joseph O'Mara [includes discography]. *The Record Collector*, XIX (#1-2, 1970), 33-42.

ORFF, CARL (German composer)

C877 Carl Orff: Werk und Schallplatte. *Neue Zeitschrift für Musikwissenschaft*, CXXVI (July-Aug. 1965), 315-20. In German.

PACHMAN, VLADIMIR DE (Russian pianist)

C878 Vladimir de Pachman: a discography. 78 RPM, #1 (1968), 7-8.

PADEREWSKI, IGNACE JAN (Polish pianist and composer)

C879 Anderson, Harry L. Ignace Jan Paderewski—discography. *British Institute of Recorded Sound Bulletin*, #10 (1958), 2-7.

C880 Kanski, Jozef. Plytowe dokumenty sztuki Ignacego Paderewskiego. *Ruch Muzyczny*, XIV (July 1971), 5-6. In Polish.

PANDOLFINI, ANGELICA (Italian soprano)

C881 Henstock, Michael. Some notes on Angelica Pandolfini. *Recorded Sound*, #37 (Jan. 1970), 622-25.

PARETO, GRAZIELLA (Spanish soprano)

C882 Fraser, G. Graziella Pareto. *The Record Collector*, XVII (#4, 1967), 84-89.

PATZAK, JULIUS (Austrian tenor)

C883 Brew, D. Julius Patzak, discography. *The Record Collector*, XIX (#9-10, 1971), 209-22.

PEROSI, LORENZO (Italian composer)

C884 Rinaldi, Mario. Lorenzo Perosi. Roma, Edizioni de Santis, 1967. 617 p. In Italian. Discography: pp. 565-585.

PERSICHETTI, VINCENT (American composer)

C885 Evett, R. The music of Vincent Persichetti. *Juilliard Review*, Spring 1955, 15-30.

PETERSON, MAY (American soprano)

C886 Gardner, M. L. May Peterson. *Recorded Sound*, #32 (Oct. 1968), 344-46.

PETRI, EGON (German pianist)

C887 Egon Petri: a discography. *78 RPM*, Sep. 1969. 24-28.

PFITZNER, HANS (German composer)

C888 Moore, J. N. Hans Pfitzner discography. *Recorded Sound*, #45-46 (Jan.-Apr. 1972), 54-57.

C889 Weber, Jerome F. Pfitzner. (Weber discography series) Utica, N.Y., Jerome F. Weber, 1974. [Scheduled for publication.]

PHILADELPHIA ORCHESTRA

C890 Kupferberg, Herbert. Those fabulous Philadelphians: the life and times of a great orchestra. New York, C. Scribner's Sons, 1969; London, W. H. Allen, 1970. 259 p. "List of available recordings by the Philadelphia Orchestra on Columbia and RCA Labels": pp. 239-247.

PHILIPP, ISIDORE (French pianist)

C891 Isidore Philipp discography. *Recorded Sound*, I (#8, 1962), 248.

PIATIGORSKY, GREGOR (Russian cellist)

C892 Piatigorsky, Gregor. Mein Cello und ich. Tübingen, Wunderlich, 1968. 255 p. In German. Discography: p. 255.

PINZA, EZIO (Italian basso)

C893 Verducci, Pasquale. The first Pinza discography. New York, Verducci, 1957. 16 p.

PLANTÉ, FRANCIS (French pianist)

C894   Soall, T. A. Francis Planté discography. *Recorded Sound*, #35 (July 1969), 494.

PONSELLE, ROSA (American soprano)

C895   Villella, Tom, and Bill Park. Rosa Ponselle: a discography. *Le Grand Baton*, Feb.-May 1970, 5-14.

PORTER, COLE (American composer)

C896   Ewen, David. The Cole Porter story. New York, Holt, Rinehart and Winston, 1965. 192 p. Discography: pp. 182-185.

C897   Kreuger, M. The complete Cole Porter discography. *American Record Guide*, XXV (May 1959), 666.

POULENC, FRANCIS (French composer)

C898   Ardoin, J. Poulenciana [recordings]. *Musical America*, LXXXIII (Sep. 1963), 47-48.

C899   Discografía de Francis Poulenc. *Arte Musical*, XXIX (#20-22, 1963-1964), 471-72. In Portuguese.

C900   L'oeuvre de Poulenc et le disque [recordings]. *Musique et Radio*, LIII (July 1963), 238. In French.

C901   Roy, Jean. Francis Poulenc; l'homme et son oeuvre. Liste complète des oeuvres, discographie, illustrations. Paris, Seghers, 1964. 190 p. In French. Discography: pp. 175-183.

PREVIN, ANDRÉ (American pianist, conductor, and composer)

C902   Greenfield, Edward. André Previn. London, Ian Allen, 1973. 96 p. Discography by Malcolm Walker: pp. 93-96.

PRINTEMPS, YVONNE

C903   Liff, Vivian. Yvonne Printemps. *Recorded Sound*, #31 (July 1968), 309-314.

PROKOFIEV, SERGEY SERGEYEVITCH (Russian composer)

C904   Brockhaus, Heinz Alfred. Sergei Prokofjew. Leipzig, P. Reclam Jun., 1964. 249 p. In German. Discography: pp. 226-230.

C905   Frankenstein, A. Prokofiev on microgroove. *High Fidelity*, VI (Mar. 1956), 95-96.

C906   Hofmann, Rostislav. Serge Prokofiev; l'homme et son oeuvre. Paris, Seghers, 1963. 190 p. In French. Discography: pp. 182-188.

Operas

C907   Streller, F. Prokofjews Opern auf Schallplatten. *Musik und Gesellschaft*, XV (Sep. 1965), 631-32+ In German.

PUCCINI, GIACOMO (Italian composer)

C908   Amy, Dominique. Giacomo Puccini; l'homme et son oeuvre. Paris, Seghers, 1970. 186 p. In French. Discography: pp. 181-182.

C909   Discografía de Puccini (1858-1924). *Musica* (Madrid), III (Oct.-Dec. 1954), 52-58. In Spanish.

C910   Gauthier, André. Puccini. Bourges, Éditions du Seuil, 1961. 183 p. In French. Includes discography.

Operas

C911   Johnson, D. The Puccini operas on records. *High Fidelity*, VIII (Dec. 1958), 93-95.

Tosca

C912   Greenfield, E. Opera on the gramophone: "Tosca." *Opera* (England), XV (Jan. 1964), 6-15.

C913   A teacher's guide to Tosca. New York, Education Dept. of the Metropolitan Opera Guild, 1968. 45 p. Discography: p. 45.

Turandot

C914   Greenfield, E. Opera on the gramophone: "Turandot." *Opera* (England), XXII (Jan. 1971), 9-19.

PURCELL, HENRY (English composer)

C915   Mayer, G. L. The vocal works of Henry Purcell: a discography. *American Record Guide*, XXV (May 1959), 588-91.

RACHMANINOFF, SERGEY VASSILIEVITCH (Russian composer and pianist)

C916   Ericson, R. Rachmaninoff: a discography. *High Fidelity*, V (May 1955), 76.

C917   Smolian, Steven. Da capo [Sergei Rachmaninoff discography]. *American Record Guide*, XXXIII (Oct. 1966), 154-55+

Piano Concerti

C918   Rachmaninoff piano concerti. *The Saturday Review*, XXXVIII (Nov. 26, 1955), 46.

RADFORD, ROBERT (English basso)

C919   Kenyon, J. P. The records of Robert Radford. *The Record Collector*, XIV (#9-10, 1962), 212-30.

RAMEAU, JEAN PHILIPPE (French composer)

C920   Malignon, Jean. Rameau. Paris, Éditions du Seuil, 1960. 187 p. In French. Includes discography.

RAPPOLD, MARIE (German soprano)

C921   Wile, Raymond R. The recordings of Marie Rappold. *Hobbies*, LXXII (June 1967), 36+

RAVEL, MAURICE (French composer)

C922　Léon, Georges. Maurice Ravel; l'homme et son oeuvre. Paris, Seghers, 1964. 191 p. In French. Discography: pp. 183-188.

C923　Petit, Pierre Yves Marie Camille. Ravel. Paris, Hachette, 1970. 96 p. In French. Discography: pp. 94-95.

C924　Wybrana dyskografie utworow Ravela. *Ruch Muzyczny*, VI (#24, 1962), 7. In Polish.

Piano Works

C925　Perlemuter, Vlado, and Hélène Jourdan-Morhange. Ravel d'après Ravel: les oeuvres pour piano, les deux concertos. Lausanne, Éditions du Cervin, 1970. 92 p. In French. "Discographie sommaire": p. 90.

RAWSTHORNE, ALAN (English composer)

C926　Oxford University Press, London. Alan Rawsthorne: a catalogue of music. London, Oxford University Press, 1970. 12 p. "Complete list of gramophone recordings": pp. 11-12.

REGER, MAX (German composer)

C927　Pfluger, R. Diskographie der Werke von Max Reger. *Österreichische Musikzeitschrift*, XXVIII (Mar. 1973), 153-56. In German.

C928　Rockwell, John. Max Reger: windbag or prophet. *High Fidelity*, XXIV (#5, May 1974), 53-59.

C929　Weber, Jerome F. Reger discography. (Weber discography series) Utica, N.Y., Jerome F. Weber, 1974. [Scheduled for publication.]

Organ Works

C930　Herand, F. A Reger organ discography. *The Diapason* (U.S.A.), LXII (June 1971), 27.

REHKEMPER, HEINRICH (German baritone)

C931　Smolian, Steven. Da capo [Heinrich Rehkemper discography]. *American Record Guide*, XXVIII (July 1962), 899-901.

REINER, FRITZ (Hungarian conductor)

C932   Hart, P. Reiner in Chicago. *High Fidelity*, XIV (Apr. 1964), 45+

RICHTER, SVIATOSLAV TEOFILOVITCH (Russian pianist)

C933   Widmaier, K. Begegnung mit Svjatoslav Richter. *Phonoprisma*, VI (#4, 1963), 85. In German.

RIEGGER, WALLINGFORD (American composer)

C934   Gatwood, Dwight Dean, Jr. Wallingford Riegger: a biography and analysis of selected works. Nashville, Tenn., Photo-duplication Service of Joint University Libraries, 1970. 305 p. Discography: pp. 294-296.

C935   Goodfriend, J. Riegger recorded. *HiFi/Stereo Review,* XX (Apr. 1968), 66.

C936   Wallingford Riegger: list of works and discography. *Bulletin of the American Composers Alliance*, IX (#3, 1960), 19.

RODGERS, RICHARD (American composer)

C937   Richard Rodgers: fact book with supplement. New York, Lynn Farnol Group, 1968. 659 p. Discography: pp. 553-564.

ROLF, ERNST

C938   Liliedahl, Karleric. Ernst Rolf. (Nationalfonotekets diskografier 501) Stockholm, Kungliga biblioteket, 1970. 71 p. In Swedish.

ROSBAUD, HANS (Austrian conductor)

C939   Gerber, Leslie. Hans Rosbaud: a discography. *Association of Recorded Sound Collections Journal*, IV (#1-3, 1972), 47-53.

ROSENTHAL, MORIZ (Polish pianist)

C940   Anderson, H. L., and P. Saul. Moriz Rosenthal discography. *Recorded Sound*, I (#7, 1962), 217-20.

ROSSINI, GIOACCHINO (Italian composer)

C941   Caussou, Jean Louis. Gioacchino Rossini. Lausanne, La Guilde du livre, 1971. 193 p. In French. Discography: pp. 185-189.

C942   Caussou, Jean Louis. Gioacchino Rossini; l'homme et son oeuvre. Paris, Seghers, 1967. 192 p. In French. Discography: pp. 185-189.

C943   Pols, André M. Het leven van G. Rossini. Brussel, Reinaert Uitgaven, 1970. 48 p. In Flemish. Discography: pp. 44-48.

ROSTROPOVICH, MSTISLAV LEOPOLDOVITCH (Russian cellist)

C944   Brown, Than. The "unauthorized" Rostropovich [a discography of 'off-the air' and other non-commercial recordings]. *Le Grand Baton*, Aug. 1970, 3-8.

ROTHENBERGER, ANNELIESE (German soprano)

C945   Lewinski, Wolf-Eberhard von. Anneliese Rothenberger. Velber bei Hannover, Friedrich, 1968. 104 p. In German. Discography: pp.89-98.

C946   Rothenberger, Anneliese. Melodie meines Lebens; Selbsterlebtes, Selbsterzähltes. Mit einer Diskographie, einem Repertoire-Verzeichnis und einer Biographie in Datenform. 2. Aufl. München, Lichtenberg, 1972. 191 p. In German. Discography: pp. 176-180.

ROUSSEL, ALBERT (French composer)

C947   Deane, Basil. Albert Roussel. London, Barrie and Rockliff, 1961. 188 p. Discography by Eric Hughes: pp. 173-176.

C948   Manal, Georges. Albert Roussel (1869-1937). *Recorded Sound*, #38 (Apr. 1970), 621.

C949   Neill, Edward D. R. Albert Roussel. *Musicalia*, I (#1, Feb. 1970), 5-10. In Italian.

C950   Surchamp, Angelico. Albert Roussel, l'homme et son oeuvre. Paris, Seghers, 1967. 192 p. In French. Discography: pp. 186-189.

RUBINSTEIN, ARTUR (Polish pianist)

C951   Ashman, Mike. Rubinstein discography. *Records and Recordings*, Oct. 1973, 27-28.

SAMUEL, HAROLD (English pianist)

C952   Anderson, H. L. Harold Samuel discography. *Recorded Sound*, I (#6, 1962), 191-92.

SANDBERG, SVEN-OLOF

C953   Liliedahl, Karleric. Sven-Olof Sandberg. (Nationalfonotekets diskografier 503) Stockholm, Kungliga biblioteket, 1971. 72 p. In Swedish.

SANTLEY, CHARLES (English baritone)

C954   Sir Charles Santley: the record. *Record Advertiser*, Mar.-Apr. 1971, 4.

SARASATE, PABLO DE (Spanish violinist)

C955   Aahlén, Carl-Gunnar. Grammofonens veteraner: Pablo de Sarasate (1844-1908). *Musikrevy*, XXVI (#6, 1971), 364-65. In Swedish.

SATIE, ERIK (French composer)

C956   Templier, Pierre-Daniel. Erik Satie. Translated by Elena L. French and David S. French. Cambridge, Mass., Massachusetts Institute of Technology, 1971. 127 p. Discography: pp. 117-127.

SAUGUET, HENRI (French composer)

C957   Bril, France Yvonne. Henri Sauguet; l'homme et son oeuvre. Avec des écrits d'Henri Sauguet. Paris, Seghers, 1967. 192 p. In French. Discography: pp. 187-188.

SCHALK, FRANZ (Austrian conductor)

C958   Hughes, E. Franz Schalk discography. *Recorded Sound*, #38 (Apr. 1970), 605.

SCHIØTZ, AKSEL (Danish tenor)

C959   Rosenberg, Herbert. Aksel Schiøtz: a discography. København,
        Nationaldiskoteket, 1966. 48 p.

SCHNABEL, ARTUR (Austrian pianist)

C960   Stone, Ralph. An Artur Schnabel discography. *Le Grand Baton*, Aug.
        1972, 22-27.

SCHÖFFLER, PAUL (German baritone)

C961   Christian, Hans. Paul Schöffler. Versuch einer Würdigung. Wien,
        München, Österreichischer Bundesverlag, 1967. 40 p. In German.
        Discography: pp. 37-40.

SCHOENBERG, ARNOLD (Austrian composer)

C962   Cohn, Arthur. Music of Arnold Schoenberg: from Columbia, the
        first complete recorded edition. *American Record Guide*, XXX
        (Nov. 1963), 192-94.

C963   Leibowitz, René. Schoenberg. Paris, Éditions du Seuil, 1969. 192 p.
        In French. "Discographie, établie et commentée par Marcel Marnat":
        pp. 182-187.

C964   Romano, Jacobo. El otro Schoenberg. Buenos Aires, Editores Dos,
        1969. 181 p. In Spanish. Discography: pp. 173-178.

C965   Rufer, Josef. The works of Arnold Schoenberg. Translated by Dika
        Newlin. London, Faber and Faber, 1962; New York, Free Press of
        Glencoe, 1963. 214 p. Discography: pp. 189-190.

SCHÖNE, LOTTE (real name, CHARLOTTE BODENSTEIN; Austrian soprano)

C966   Lotte Schöne [includes discography]. *The Record Collector*, XX
        (#4, 1971), 77-89.

SCHORR, FRIEDRICH (Hungarian baritone)

C967   Dennis, J. Friedrich Schorr. *The Record Collector*, XIX (#11-12,
        1971), 262-74.

SCHUBERT, FRANZ (Austrian composer)

C968   Bruyr, José. Franz Schubert; l'homme et son oeuvre. Paris, Seghers, 1965. 191 p. In French. Discography: pp. 184-188.

Lieder

C969   Weber, Jerome F. Schubert Lieder. (Weber discography series, 1) Utica, N.Y., Jerome F. Weber, 1969.

Weber, Jerome F. Schubert Lieder. 2d ed. Utica, N.Y., Jerome F. Weber, 1970. 49 p.

Weber, Jerome F. Schubert Lieder. 3d ed. [In preparation.]

SCHÜTZ, HEINRICH (German composer)

C970   Blum, Klaus, and Martin Elste. Internationale Heinrich-Schütz-Diskographie 1928-1972. Bremen, K. Blum, 1972. 232 p. In German.

C971   Delalande, J. Heinrich Schütz—14.10.1585-6.11.1672 [includes discography]. *Hifi-Stereophonie*, XI (Nov. 1972), 1075-78+ In German.

C972   Heinrich Schütz. Verzeichnis der Schallaufnahmen. Frankfurt am Main, Deutsches Rundfunkarchiv, 1972. 175 p. In German.

C973   Moser, Hans Joachim. Heinrich Schütz: a short account of his life and works. Translated and edited by Derek McCulloch. London, Faber; New York, St. Martin's Press, 1967. 121 p. Discography: pp. 111-116.

C974   Tellart, Roger. Heinrich Schütz; l'homme et son oeuvre. Paris, Seghers, 1968. 192 p. In French. Discography: pp. 183-188.

C975   Zur Heinrich-Schütz-Discographie. *Phono*, IX (#6, 1963), 137-38. In German.

SCHUMANN, ROBERT (German composer)

C976   Buenzod, Emmanuel. Robert Schumann; l'homme et son oeuvre. Paris, Seghers, 1965. 192 p. In French. Discography: pp. 187-190.

C977   Lawrence, H. Schumann on LP. *The Saturday Review*, XXXIX (July 28, 1956), 36-37+

C978   Pirie, Peter J. A bibliography of Schumann records [available in England]. *Music Review*, XVII (Aug. 1956), 238-42.

C979   Schauffler, Robert Haven. Florestan; the life and work of Robert Schumann. New York, H. Holt, 1945; New York, Dover, 1963. 574 p. Discography: pp. 533-538.

Frauenliebe und -leben

C980   Schumann: "Frauenliebe und Leben"; eine vergleichende Discographie zum Liederzyklus Op. 42. *Phono*, X (#1, 1963), 20-21. In German.

Lieder

C981   Weber, Jerome F. Schumann Lieder. (Weber discography series, 3) Utica, N.Y., Jerome F. Weber, 1970. 20 p.

       Weber, Jerome F. Schumann Lieder. 2d ed. [In preparation.]

Orchestral and Chamber Music

C982   Schonberg, Harold C. Schumann—orchestral and chamber music. *High Fidelity*, VII (Dec. 1957), 103-112.

Piano Music

C983   Schonberg, Harold C. The piano music of Robert Schumann. *High Fidelity*, VI (Sep. 1956), 85-93.

Symphonies

C984   Vokurka, K. A. Widerstand des Geistes; die vier Symphonien Robert Schumanns auf Schallplatten. Eine vergleichende Discographie. *Phono*, XII (#4, 1966), 99-102. In German.

SCHUMANN-HEINK, ERNESTINE (Czech alto)

C985   Moran, W. R. The recordings of Ernestine Schumann-Heink. *The Record Collector*, XVII (#5-6, 1967), 118-44.

SCHWARZKOPF, ELISABETH (German soprano)

C986   Kesting, J. 'Die Zeit, die aendert doch nichts an den Sachen'; Elisabeth Schwarzkopf gab ihren Buehnenabschied [includes discography]. *Opern Welt*, Feb. 1972, 24-28. In German.

SCOTT, CYRIL MEIR (English composer)

C987   Cyril Scott: a discography [of his own recordings of his own piano works]. *78 RPM*, Nov. 1969, 56.

SCRIABIN, ALEXANDER NIKOLAYEVITCH (Russian composer)

C988   Forchert, Arno. Mystiker und Avantgardist. Zur Musik von Alexander Skrjabin. *Fono Forum*, IX (Sep. 1969), 564-69. In German.

C989   Skriabin Diskographie. *Hifi-Stereophonie*, XI (Jan. 1972), 16+ In German.

SEMBRICH, MARCELLA (Polish soprano)

C990   Moran, W. R. The recordings of Marcella Sembrich. *The Record Collector*, XVIII (#5-6, 1969), 110-36.

SHALIAPIN, FEODOR IVANOVITCH (Russian basso)

C991   Feschotte, Jacques. Ce géant, Féodor Chaliapine. Paris, la Table ronde, 1968. 229 p. In French. Discography: pp. 223-226.

C992   Goury, Jean. Fedor Chaliapine; iconographie, biographie, discographie. Paris, Société de diffusion d'art lyrique, 1969. 80 p. In French. Discography: pp. 65-74.

C993   Kelly, A. Fedor Ivanovich Chaliapin [discography]. *The Record Collector*, XX (#8-10, 1972), 180-230.

SHOSTAKOVITCH, DMITRI DMITRIEVITCH (Russian composer)

C994   Brockhaus, Heinz Alfred. Dmitri Schostakowitsch. Leipzig, Philipp Reclam Jun., 1962. 195 p. In German. Discography: pp. 172-175.

C995   Hofmann, Rostislav. Dimitri Chostakovitch; l'homme et son oeuvre. Paris, Seghers, 1963. 191 p. In French. Discography: pp. 183-187.

C996   Santomartino, P. Dimitri Shostakovich. *Musica e Dischi*, XIX (May 1963), 48. In Italian.

Symphonies

C997   Brown, R. S. Shostakovich's symphonies—an appraisal of the music and the recordings. *High Fidelity/Musical America*, XIX (Apr. 1969), 43-47+

SIBELIUS, JEAN (Finnish composer)

C998   Bauman, J. C. Sibelius on record. *Le Grand Baton*, Oct.-Dec. 1965, 1-25.

C999   Heininen, P. Dodecafonia Sibeliana. *Music Journal*, XX (Oct. 1962), 44+ In English.

C1000   Johnson, Harold Earle. Jean Sibelius; the recorded music. Helsinki, R. E. Westerlund, 1957. 31 p. In English, Swedish, and Finnish.

C1001   Krellmann, Hanspeter. Plädoyer für Sibelius. Mit einer vergleichenden Diskographie. *Musica*, XXIV (#5, Sep.-Oct.1970), 442-44. In German.

C1002   Sibelius on microgroove, a selective discography. *High Fidelity/ Musical America*,XV (Dec. 1965), 52-53+

C1003   Vignal, Marc. Jean Sibelius; l'homme et son oeuvre. Paris, Seghers, 1965. 192 p. In French. Discography: pp. 185-188.

C1004   Werke von Jean Sibelius auf Schallplatten. *Sibelius-Mitteilungen*, #1 (Mar. 1958), 13-15. In German.

Symphonies

C1005   Goldsmith, H. Sibelius' seven symphonies; a critic's view of the recordings. *High Fidelity/Musical America*, XIX (May 1969), 56-60.

SIMPSON, ROBERT (English composer)

C1006   Robert Simpson: fiftieth birthday essays. Ed. by Edward Johnson. London, Triad Press, 1971. 28 p. List of works and discography: pp. 27-28.

C1007   Simpson, Robert. Composer's anthology [includes list of recordings].
          Recorded Sound, #47 (July 1972), 79-84.

SLEZAK, LEO (Czech tenor)

C1008   Kaufman, T. G. Leo Slezak; discography. *The Record Collector*, XV
          (#9-10, 1964?), 208-35.

SLOBODSKAYA, ODA (Russian soprano)

C1009   Barnes, H. M., and S. Junge. Oda Slobodskaya discography. *Recorded
          Sound*, #35 (July 1969), 502-11.

SMETANA, BEDŘICH (Czech composer)

C1010   Karásek, Bohumil. Bedřich Smetana. Praha, Státní hudební
          vydavatelství, 1966. 123 p. In Czech. Discography: pp. 104-120.

SMETERLIN, JAN (Polish pianist)

C1011   Maciejewski, B. M., and Felix Aprahamian. Karol Szymanowski and
          Jan Smeterlin: correspondence and essays. London, Allegro Press,
          196? 160 p. "Jan Smeterlin's recordings": pp. 135-137.

SMIRNOFF, DMITRI (Russian tenor)

C1012   Stratton, J. Dmitri Smirnoff, tenor (1882-1944). *The Record Collec-
          tor*, XIV (#11-12, 1962), 245-77.

SOLTI, GEORG (Hungarian conductor)

C1013   Georg Solti on disc. *High Fidelity/Musical America*, XIX (Oct. 1969),
          71.

SOUSA BAND

C1014   Smart, James Robert. The Sousa Band; a discography. Washington,
          D.C., U.S. Govt. Print. Off., 1970. 123 p.

SPOHR, LUDWIG (German composer)

C1015 Powell, M. New appraisement of Spohr [includes discography]. *Music* (S.M.A.), IV (#1, 1970), 6-8.

STADER, MARIA (Hungarian soprano)

C1016 Stader, Maria. Soprano; Joh. Seb. Bach: St. Matthew's Passion; Aria: Aus Liebe will mein Heiland sterben. Translated by John Bell. Zürich, Panton Publishers; distributed in U.S.A. by C. F. Peters, 1968. 97 p. [A master lesson, this also includes a biography and discography of Maria Stader.]

STEVENSON, RONALD (English composer)

C1017 Recordings of Ronald Stevenson. *Recorded Sound*, #42-43 (Apr.-July 1971), 755.

STOCK, FREDERICK (German conductor)

C1018 Holmes, William A. Frederick Stock. *Le Grand Baton*, May 1969, 3-48. Discography by Joseph H. Hurka: pp. 5-11.

STOCKHAUSEN, KARL HEINZ (German composer)

C1019 Karlheinz Stockhausen diskografi. *Dansk Musiktidsskrift*, XLVII (#4, 1972), 120. In Danish.

C1020 Wörner, Karl Heinrich. Stockhausen: life and work. Introduction and translation by Bill Hopkins. London, Faber, 1973. 278 p. Discography: pp. 21-29.

STOKOWSKI, LEOPOLD (English conductor)

C1021 Stokowski: essays in analysis of his art. Ed. by Edward Johnson. London, Triad Press, 1973. ? p. Discography by Ivan Lund: pp. 85-114.

STOLZ, ROBERT (Austrian composer)

C1022   Brümmel, Wolf-Dietrich. Robert Stolz. Melodie eines Lebens. Hamburg, Schröder; Wien, Spiedel, 1967. 199 p. In German. Discography: pp. 191-198.

STRACCIARI, RICCARDO (Italian baritone)

C1023   Discografia di Stracciari. *Musica e Dischi*, XVIII (Feb. 1962), 72. In Italian.

STRAUBE, KARL (German organist)

C1024   Aahlén, Carl-Gunnar. Grammofonens veteraner: Karl Straube (1873-1950). *Musikrevy*, XXVII (#2, 1972), 101-03. In Swedish.

STRAUSS, EDUARD (Austrian composer and conductor)

C1025   Povey, Philip G. Recordings of music by the Strauss family, conducted by the late Eduard Strauss. Wembley, Middlesex, Johann Strauss Society of Great Britain, 1972.

STRAUSS, JOHANN, JR. (Austrian composer)

C1026   Grasberger, Franz. Die Wiener Philharmoniker bei Johann Strauss. Wien, Verlag Brüder Rosenbaum, 1963. 83 p. In German. Discography: pp. 82-83.

C1027   Pols, André M. Het leven van J. Strauss. Brussel, Reinaert Uitgaven, 1969. 48 p. In Flemish. Discography: pp. 44-48.

STRAUSS, RICHARD (German composer and conductor)

C1028   Aahlén, Carl-Gunnar. Grammofonens veteraner: Rickard Strauss [as performer]. *Musikrevy*, XXVI (#4, 1971), 217-19.

C1029   Del Mar, Norman René. Richard Strauss; a critical commentary on his life and works. London, Barrie and Jenkins; Philadelphia, Chilton Book Co., 1962-1972. 3v. Discography of Strauss as a performer: v. 3, pp. 507-509.

C1030   Glass, H. Richard Strauss on microgroove. *High Fidelity*, XII (Mar. 1962), 50-52+

C1031   Goléa, Antoine. Richard Strauss. Paris, Flammarion, 1965. 281 p. In French. Discography: p. 273.

C1032   Jameux, Dominique. Richard Strauss. Paris, Éditions du Seuil, 1971. 185 p. In French. Discography: pp. 184-185.

C1033   Richard Strauss: a centennial discography. *The Saturday Review*, XLVII (May 30, 1964), 62-63+

C1034   Rostand, Claude. Richard Strauss; l'homme et son oeuvre. Paris. Seghers, 1964. 189 p. In French. Discography: pp. 188-189.

C1035   Vienna. Nationalbibliothek. Richard-Strauss-Ausstellung zum 100. Geburtstag. Wien, Österreichisches Nationalbibliothek, 1964. 359 p. In German. Discography: pp. 324-332.

Arabella

C1036   Jefferson, A. Opera on the gramophone: "Arabella." *Opera* (England), XVIII (Jan. 1967), 25-28+

Ariadne auf Naxos

C1037   Jefferson, A. Opera on the gramophone: "Ariadne auf Naxos." *Opera* (England), XIX (Sep. 1968), 703-13.

Lieder

C1038   Morse, Peter. Strauss Lieder. (Weber discography series, 7) Utica, N.Y., Jerome F. Weber, 1970. 14 p.

Morse, Peter. Strauss Lieder. 2d ed. Utica, N.Y., Jerome F. Weber, 1973. 46 p.

Operas

C1039   Jefferson, A. Opera on the gramophone: Richard Strauss's other operas. *Opera* (England), XX (Oct. 1969), 844-55.

Der Rosenkavalier

C1040   Jefferson, A. More letters: "Così" and "Rosenkavalier" discographies. *Opera* (England), XIX (Sep. 1968), 772-73.

Salome

C1041   Mann, William. Opera on the gramophone: "Salome." *Opera*
(England), VIII (July 1957), 420-25.

STRAVINSKY, IGOR (Russian composer and conductor)

C1042   Boonin, J. M. Stravinsky records Stravinsky; Stravinsky in print.
Musical America, LXXXII (June 1962), 12-13.

C1043   Frankfurt am Main. Deutsches Rundfunkarchiv. Igor Strawinsky
(1882-1971) Phonographie. Seine Eigeninterpretation auf Schallplatten und in den europäischen Rundfunkanstalten, zusammen mit
einem Verzeichnis der in den deutschen Rundfunkanstalten
vorhandenen Rundfunkproduktionen und historischen Schall-
plattenaufnahmen von Strawinsky-Werken. Frankfurt am Main,
Deutsches Rundfunkarchiv, 1972. 216 p. Preface in English, French
and German.

C1044   Hamilton, David. Igor Stravinsky: a discography of the composer's
performances. *Perspectives of New Music*, IX (#2, 1971), 163-79.

C1045   Hart, P. Stravinsky—just for the record. *Music Magazine*, CLXIV
(June 1962), 42-47.

C1046   Odriozola, A. La discografía LP de Igor Strawinsky. *Musica* (Madrid),
IV (#14, 1955), 139-54. In Spanish.

C1047   Philippot, Michel. Igor Stravinsky; l'homme et son oeuvre. Paris,
Seghers, 1965. 188 p. In French. Discography: pp. 177-188.

C1048   Sopeña Ibáñez, Federico. Strawinsky; vida, obra y estilo. Madrid,
Sociedad de Estudios y Publicaciones, 1956. 270 p. In Spanish.
Discography: pp. 265-270.

C1049   Stravinsky. Par André Boucourechliev, Olivier Merlin, Michel
Philippot, Claude Rostand, [etc.]. Paris, Hachette, 1968. 280 p. In
French. Discography by Harry Halbreich: pp. 241-274.

C1050   A Stravinsky discography: performances with, or by, the composer.
The Saturday Review, XLV (May 12, 1962), 58-59.

C1051   Tintori, Giampiero. Stravinski. Milano, Nuova Accademia Editrice,
1964. 263 p. In Italian. Discography: pp. 245-252.

SULLIVAN, ARTHUR SEYMOUR (English composer)

C1052   Hardwick, John Michael Drinkrow. The Osprey guide to Gilbert and
         Sullivan. Reading, Osprey, 1972. 184 p. Discography: pp. 271-279.

SUPERVIA, CONCHITA (Spanish mezzo)

C1053   Newton, Ivor. Conchita Supervia. *Recorded Sound*, #52 (Oct. 1973),
         205-29.

SUTHERLAND, JOAN (Australian soprano)

C1054   Greenfield, Edward. Recordmasters: Joan Sutherland. Shepperton,
         Middlesex, Allan, 1972; New York, Drake, 1973. 64 p. Discography:
         pp. 59-64.

SZELL, GEORGE (Austrian conductor and pianist)

C1055   Marsh, Robert Charles. The Cleveland Orchestra. Cleveland, World
         Pub. Co., 1967. 205 p. Discography of the Cleveland Orchestra
         [with Szell and others conducting] : pp. 189-200. "A selected list
         of Szell recordings with groups other than the Cleveland Orchestra":
         pp. 201-202.

SZIGETI, JOSEPH (Hungarian violinist)

C1056   Szigeti, Joseph. With strings attached; reminiscences and reflections.
         2d ed., rev. and enlarged. New York, A. A. Knopf, 1967. 376 p.
         "The recordings of Joseph Szigeti": pp. 365-376.

SZYMANOWSKI, KAROL (Polish composer)

C1057   Crylinska, Teresa. Karol Szymanowski. Kraków, 1967. ? p. In Polish.
         Includes discography.

C1058   Kosmala, Jerzy S. String quartets of Karol Szymanowski. Unpub-
         lished D.M.A. dissertation, Indiana University, 1972. 58 p. Includes
         discography.

TAJO, ITALO (Italian basso)

C1059   Tajo discography. In prepartion by Joseph Chouinard, SUNYAB
         Music Library, Buffalo, N.Y. 14214, U.S.A.

TATE, PHYLLIS (English composer)

C1060   Oxford University Press, London. Phyllis Tate. London, Oxford
University Press, 1972. 12 p. Discography: p. 12.

TAUBER, RICHARD (Austrian tenor)

C1061   Abell, G. O., and L. E. Abell. A representative Tauber collection.
The Record Collector, XVIII (#11-12, 1969), 266-72.

C1062   Dennis, J. Richard Tauber discography. *The Record Collector*,
XVIII (#8-10, 1969), 171-239; XIX (#3-4, 1970), 81-85.

C1063   Korb, Willi. Richard Tauber. Biographie eines unvergessenen Sängers.
Wien, Europäischer Verlag, 1966. 171 p. In German. Discography:
pp. 149-171.

TCHAIKOVSKY, PIOTR ILYITCH (Russian composer)

C1064   Blasl, F. Werke von P. I. Tschaikowsky auf Langspielplatten.
Musikerziehung, XIV (Sep. 1960), 36-40. In German.

C1065   Briggs, John. The collector's Tchaikovsky and the Five [Mily
Alexeyevitch Balakirev, Alexander Porfirievitch Borodin, César
Antonovitch Cui, Modest Petrovitch Mussorgsky, and Nikolay
Andreyevitch Rimsky-Korsakov]. (Keystone books in music)
Philadelphia, Lippincott, 1959. 256 p.

C1066   Erismann,Guy. Piotr Illitch Tchaikovski; l'homme et son oeuvre.
Paris, Seghers, 1964. 191 p. In French. Discography: pp. 183-188.

C1067   Hofmann, Rostislav. Tchaikovsky. Translated by Angus Heriot.
London, J. Calder, 1962. 192 p. Discography: pp. 183-185.

Orchestral Suites, Chamber Music, and Operas

C1068   Indcox, J. F. Tchaikovsky recordings on microgroove: orchestral
suites, chamber music, opera. *High Fidelity*, V (May 1955), 85-89.

Symphonies

C1069   Hamburger, Povl. Tjajkovskij som symfoniker. Udg. af Folkeuniversi-
tetsforeningen i København. København, Rhodos, 1962. 89 p. In
Danish. Discography: p. 89.

C1070   Wienke, G. 15 [i.e., Fünfzehn] Dirigenten, 11 Orchester, 7 Nationen
[Tschaikowsky Symphonie Nr. 6: eine vergleichende Discographie].
Phono, IX (#2, 1962), 32-35. In German.

TEBALDI, RENATA (Italian soprano)

C1071   Seroff, Victor Ilyitch. Renata Tebaldi, the woman and the diva. New
York, Appleton-Century-Crofts, 1961; Freeport, N.Y., Books for
Libraries Press, 1970. 213 p. Discography of Renata Tebaldi record-
ings issued in the U.S. by George Jellinek: pp. 203-210.

TELEMANN, GEORG PHILIPP (German composer)

C1072   Grebe, Karl. Georg Philipp Telemann in Selbstzeugnissen und
Bilddokumenten. Reinbek bei Hamburg, Rowohlt, 1970. 157 p. In
German. Discography: pp. 139-144.

THEODORAKIS, MIKIS (Greek composer)

C1073   Giannaris, George. Mikis Theodorakis: music and social change.
New York, Praeger, 1972. 322 p. Discography: pp. 309-311.

THOMAS, JOHN CHARLES (American baritone)

C1074   Thomas discography. In preparation by Cam Denoncour, Haverhill,
Mass., U.S.A.

C1075   Thomas discography. In preparation by Edward Bridgewater, 10
Horbury Crescent, Notting Hill Gate, London W.11 3NF, England.

TOMKINS, THOMAS (English composer)

C1076   Stevens, Denis William. Thomas Tomkins, 1572-1656. New York,
Dover Publications, 1967. 214 p. Discography: p. 203.

TOSCANINI, ARTURO (Italian conductor)

C1077   Amico, Fedele d', and Rosanna Paumgartner, eds. La lezione di
Toscanini. Atti del Convegno di studi toscaniniani al XXX Maggio
musicale fiorentino. Firenze, Vallecchi, 1970. 387 p. In Italian.
Discography by Raffaele Vegeto: pp. 347-366.

C1078   Antek, Samuel. This was Toscanini. New York, Vanguard Press,
1963. 192 p. "The recorded repertoire of Arturo Toscanini":
pp. 186-192.

C1079   Discographie générale d'Arturo Toscanini. *Disques*, #89 (May-June 1957), 576-78. In French.

C1080   Haggin, Bernard H. Conversations with Toscanini. Garden City, N.Y., Doubleday, 1959. 261 p. Discography: pp. 165-249.

C1081   Hughes, Patrick Cairns. The Toscanini legacy; a critical study of Arturo Toscanini's performances of Beethoven, Verdi and other composers. London, Putnam, 1959. 346 p.

Hughes, Patrick Cairns. The Toscanini legacy; a critical study of Arturo Toscanini's performances of Beethoven, Verdi and other composers. 2d enl. ed. New York, Dover Publications; London, Constable, 1969. 399 p.

C1082   Toscanini, Walter. Arturo Toscanini; a complete discography. 2d ed. New York, Radio Corporation of America, RCA Victor Record Division, 1966. 64 p.

C1083   Toscanini et le disque. *Disques*, #88 (Apr. 1957), 453-56. In French.

VARÈSE, EDGAR (French composer)

C1084   Charbonnier, Georges. Entretiens avec Edgard Varèse. Suivis d'une étude de l'oeuvre par Harry Halbreich. Paris, P. Belfond, 1970. 169 p. In French. Discography: p. 169.

C1085   Edgard Varèse; a discography—published and recorded works. *Stereo Review*, XXVI (June 1971), 66.

C1086   Weber, Jerome F. An Edgar Varèse discography. *Association of Recorded Sound Collections Journal*, V (#1, 1973), 30-37.

VARNAY, ASTRID (Hungarian soprano)

C1087   Wessling, Berndt Wilhelm. Astrid Varnay. Bremen, Schünemann, 1965. 123 p. In German. Bibliography and discography: pp. 119-123.

VASILESCU, ION (Rumanian composer)

C1088   Frost, Ana. Ion Vasilescu. *Muzica*, XXI (#2, Feb. 1971), 42-44. In French.

VAUGHAN WILLIAMS, RALPH (English composer)

C1089   Clough, Francis F., and G. J. Cuming. [Ralph Vaughan Williams] discography 1964-71. *The Music Yearbook*, I (1972/73), 151-60.

C1090   Kennedy, Michael. The works of Ralph Vaughan Williams. London, New York, Oxford University Press, 1964. 776 p. Discography by Francis F. Clough and G. J. Cuming: pp. 725-746.

VERDI, GIUSEPPE (Italian composer)

C1091   Bachtík, Josef. Giuseppe Verdi; život a dílo. Praha, Státní hudební vydavatelství, 1963. 402 p. In Czech. Discography: pp. 384-387.

C1092   Baptista, J. A. Discografía seleccionada de Verdi e Wagner. *Arte Musical*, XXIX (#23, 1964), 623-40. In Portuguese.

C1093   De Schauensee, Maximilien. The collector's Verdi and Puccini. (Keystone books in music) Philadelphia, Lippincott, 1962. 156 p.

C1094   Gianoli, Luigi. Verdi, 2. ed. interamente riv. Brescia, La Scuola editrice, 1961. 262 p. In Italian. Discography: pp. 251-257.

C1095   Malraye, Jean. Giuseppe Verdi; l'homme et son oeuvre. Paris, Seghers, 1965. 192 p. In French. Discography: pp. 179-187.

C1096   Osborne, C. L. The collector's Verdi. *High Fidelity*, XIII (Oct. 1963), 37-38+; (Dec. 1963), 90+

C1097   Osborne, C. L. Verdi on microgroove. *High Fidelity*, X (Jan. 1960), 46-49.

C1098   Petit, Pierre Yves Marie Camille. Verdi. Translated from the French by Patrick Bowles. London, J. Calder, 1962. 192 p. Discography: pp. 185-190.

Un ballo in maschera

C1099   Harewood, Earl of. Opera on the gramophone: "Un ballo in maschera." *Opera* (England), XXII (Apr. 1971), 287-302.

Falstaff and Otello

C1100   Blyth, A. Verdi's "Otello" [includes discography]. *Opera* (England), XX (Feb. 1969), 101-12.

C1101 "Falstaff" discography. *Opera* (England), XXI (Aug. 1970), 727.

C1102 Rosenthal, H. Opera on the gramophone: Verdi's "Falstaff." *Opera* (England), XXI (May 1970), 384-94.

C1103 Schauensee, M. de. Discography: Verdi-Shakespeare. *Musical America*, LXXXIV (Jan. 1964), 14-15+

Simon Boccanegra

C1104 Harewood, Earl of. Opera on the gramophone: Verdi's "Simon Boccanegra." *Opera* (England), XVI (Dec. 1965), 855-62.

La Traviata

C1105 Jefferson, A. Opera on the gramophone: "La Traviata." *Opera* (England), XXIII (June 1972), 504-12; (Aug. 1972), 697-708.

VERLET, ALICE (American soprano)

C1106 Wile, Raymond R. The Edison disc recordings of Alice Verlet. *Association of Recorded Sound Collections Journal*, III (#2-3, Fall 1971), 53-56.

VIENNA PHILHARMONIC ORCHESTRA

C1107 Pfluger, Rolf. Diskographie der Wiener Philharmoniker. *Österreichische Musikzeitschrift*, XXII (#2-3. Feb.-Mar. 1967), 153-67. In German.

VIENNA SYMPHONY ORCHESTRA

C1108 Schreiber, Wolfgang. Die Wiener Symphoniker. *Musicalia*, L (#1, Sep. 1970), 30-43. In German.

VILLA-LOBOS, HEITOR (Brazilian composer)

C1109 França, Eurico Nogueira. Villa-Lobos; síntese crítica e biográfica. Rio de Janeiro, Museu Villa-Lobos, 1970. 179 p. In Portuguese. Discography: pp. 57-123.

C1110 Mariz, Vasco. Hector Villa Lobos; l'homme et son oeuvre. Paris, Seghers, 1967. 190 p. In French. Discography: pp. 175-182.

C1111   Mariz, Vasco. Heitor Villa-Lobos; life and work of the Brazilian composer. 2d rev. ed. Washington, D.C., Brazilian American Cultural Institute, 1970. 84 p. Discography: pp. 78-84.

C1112   Rio de Janeiro. Museu Villa-Lobos. Villa-Lobos: em discografía. Rio de Janeiro, Museu Villa-Lobos, 1965. 28 p. In Portuguese.

VIVALDI, ANTONIO (Italian composer)

C1113   Anderson, Nils. Vivaldi discography. (Weber discography series) Utica, N.Y., Jerome F. Weber, 1974. [Scheduled for publication.]

C1114   Berri, Pietro. Indice discografico vivaldiano. Milano, G. Ricordi, 1953. 35 p. In Italian.

C1115   Candé, Roland de. Vivaldi. Paris, Éditions du Seuil, 1967. 192 p. In French. Discography: pp. 185-186.

C1116   Gallois, Jean. Antonio Vivaldi. Lyon, Éditions et Impr. du Sud-Est, 1967. 116 p. In French. Discography: pp. 112-114.

C1117   Marnat, Marcel. Antonio Vivaldi; l'homme, son milieu et sa musique. Paris, Seghers, 1965. 189 p. In French. Discography: pp. 161-180.

C1118   Parkinson, Timothy. Discography of Antonio Vivaldi on long-playing records. Master's research paper, Kent State University School of Library Science, 1972. 175 p.

WAGNER, RICHARD (German composer)

C1119   Gallois, Jean. Richard Wagner. Lyon, Éditions et Impr. du Sud-Est, 1962. 123 p. In French. Discography: pp. 121-122.

C1120   Hinton, J. Wagner on microgroove. *High Fidelity*, V (Apr. 1955), 73-85; (Aug. 1955), 64-69.

C1121   Kanski, J. Wagner na plytach gramofonowych. *Ruch Muzyczny*, VII (#13, 1963), 18-19; (#14, 1963), 18; (#16, 1963), 19; (#19, 1963), 18. In Polish.

C1122   Marinelli, C. Discografia Wagneriana. *Rassegna Musicale*, XXXI (#3, 1961), 259-85. In Italian.

C1123   Matter, Jean. Wagner, l'enchanteur. Neuchâtel, Éditions de la Baconnière, 1968. 283 p. In French. Discography: pp. 272-281.

C1124   Richard Wagner. Paris, Hachette, 1962. 302 p. In French. "Catalogue complet et discographie des oeuvres de Richard Wagner, établis par Jean Witold": pp. 279-299.

C1125   Wagner's late works. *Nation*, Jan. 6, 1964, 37-39.

Operas

C1126   Glass, H. The Wagner operas on microgroove. *High Fidelity*, XI (Nov. 1961), 57-60.

C1127   Osborne, C. L. The Wagner operas on records—a discography. *High Fidelity/Musical America*, XVI (Nov. 1966), 78-82+; (Dec. 1966), 26+; XVII (Jan. 1967), 44+

C1128   Williamson, Audrey. Wagner opera. London, J. Calder, 1962. 192 p. Discography: pp. 184-192.

Der Ring des Nibelungen

C1129   Leyns, Bert. Richard Wagners Musickdrama *Der Ring des Nibelungen;* een inleiding tot de tetralogie. Leuven, De Monte, 1972. 105 p. In Flemish. Discography: pp. 104-105.

Siegfried

C1130   Osborne, C. L. For the first time on records, Siegfried in its entirety. *High Fidelity*, XIII (Apr. 1963), 71-72.

Die Walküre

C1131   Blyth, A. Opera on the gramophone: "Die Walküre." *Opera* (England), XXI (Sep. 1970), 826-36; (Oct. 1970), 922-30+; XXII (Feb. 1971), 160-62.

WAGNER, WIELAND (German opera producer)

C1132   Goléa, Antoine. Gespräche mit Wieland Wagner. Deutschsprachige Originalfassung des Autors. Salzburg, SN Verlag, Salzburger Nachrichten, 1968. 150 p. In German. Discography and bibliography: pp. 149-150.

WALKER, EDYTH (American mezzo)

C1133   Wile, Raymond R. The Edison disc recordings of Edyth Walker. *Association of Recorded Sound Collections Journal*, III (#2-3, Fall 1971), 57.

WALLNÖFER, ADOLF (Austrian tenor and composer)

C1134   Wimmer, W. Adolf Wallnöfer. *The Record Collector*, XIV (#11-12, 1962), 277-78.

WALTER, BRUNO (German conductor)

C1135   Bernheimer, Martin. Last recordings of Bruno Walter. *The Saturday Review*, XLVI (Dec. 28, 1963), 58-59.

C1136   Boonin, J. M. Bruno Walter: discography. *Musical America*, LXXXII (Apr. 1962), 20-21.

C1137   Frankfurt am Main. Deutsches Rundfunkarchiv. Bruno Walter. Schallplattenverzeichnis. Frankfurt am Main, Deutsches Rundfunkarchiv, 1972. 35 p. In German.

C1138   Marsh, R. C. The heritage of Bruno Walter: a discography. *High Fidelity*, XIV (Jan. 1964), 44-48+

C1139   Ricordo di Bruno Walter. *Musica e Dischi*, XVIII (Mar. 1962), 18. In Italian.

WALTON, WILLIAM TURNER (English composer)

C1140   Craggs, Stewart R. Sir William Walton. Unpublished FLA thesis, The Library Association, London, 1973. ? p. Discography: pp. 369-414.

C1141   Greenfield, E. Walton by Walton; a 70th birthday tribute. *Gramophone*, XLIX (May 1972), 1865-66.

C1142   Howes, Frank Stewart. The music of William Walton. London, New York, Oxford University Press, 1965. 234 p. Discography by Francis F. Clough and G. J. Cuming: pp. 219-228.

WARING, FRED M. (American conductor)

C1143   Gottlieb, R. E. Waring's Pennsylvanians—Victor record discography.
         Record Research, #119-120 (Dec.-Jan. 1972/73), 8-9.

WEBER, CARL MARIA VON (German composer)

C1144   Laux, Karl. Carl Maria von Weber. Leipzig, P. Reclam Jun., 1965.
         319 p. In German. Discography: pp. 291-293.

WEBERN, ANTON VON (Austrian composer)

C1145   Rostand, Claude. Anton Webern; l'homme et son oeuvre. Paris,
         Seghers, 1969. 192 p. In French. Discography: p. 189.

C1146   Wildgans, Friedrich. Anton Webern. Translated from the German by
         Edith Temple Roberts and Humphrey Searle. London, Calder &
         Boyars, 1966; New York, October House, 1967. 185 p. Discography:
         p. 182.

WHITMAN, WALT (American poet)

C1147   Neilson, Kenneth P. The world of Walt Whitman music: a biblio-
         graphical study. Hollis, N.Y., Neilson, 1963. 144 p. Includes
         discography.

WILSON, STEUART (English tenor)

C1148   Stewart, Margaret. English singer; the life of Steuart Wilson. London,
         Duckworth, 1970. 320 p. "List of Decca records": p. 287.

WOLF, HUGO (Austrian composer)

C1149   Blaukopf, K. Discographische Notizen zu Hugo Wolf. *Österreichische
         Musikzeitschrift*, XV (Feb. 1960), 110-11. In German.

C1150   Langevin, Gilbert. Hugo Wolf; l'oeuvre posthumé. *Musicalia*, I (#1,
         Sep. 1970), 45-53. In French.

C1151   Weber, Jerome F. Hugo Wolf complete works. (Weber discography
         series, 2) Utica, N.Y. Jerome F. Weber, 1970. 34 p.

Weber, Jerome F. Hugo Wolf complete works. 2d ed. Utica, N.Y., Jerome F. Weber, 1974. [Scheduled for publication.]

WOODHOUSE, VIOLET GORDON (English harpsichordist)

C1152 Hughes, E. A., and A. E. Cooban. Violet Gordon Woodhouse: a discography. *Recorded Sound*, #41 (Jan. 1971), 727-29.

XENAKIS, YANNIS (Greek composer)

C1153 Bois, Mario. Iannis Xenakis, the man and his music; a conversation with the composer and a description of his works. London, Boosey & Hawkes, 1967. 40 p. Discography: pp. 38-39.

C1154 Fleuret, M. Xenakis—a music for the future. *Music and Musicians*, XX (Apr. 1972), 20-27.

ZENATELLO, GIOVANNI (Italian tenor)

C1155 Hutchinson, T., and C. Williams. Giovanni Zenatello. *The Record Collector*, XIV (#5-6, 1961), 101-43.

PART II

JAZZ & BLUES

SECTION A

BLUES GENERAL GUIDES,
BUYERS' GUIDES, AND SUBJECTS

GENERAL GUIDES AND HISTORICAL SURVEYS

J1   Brack, R., and E. Paige. Chess and the blues: from the streets to the studio [history]. *Billboard*, LXXIX (June 24, 1967, supplement), 20-23.

J2   Carl Gregor, Duke of Mecklenburg, and Waldemar Scheck. Die Theorie des Blues im modernen Jazz. [1st ed.] Baden-Baden, Heitz, 1963. 131 p. In German. "Auswahldiskographie": p. 128.

Carl Gregor, Duke of Mecklenburg, and Waldemar Scheck. Die Theorie des Blues im modernen Jazz. 2d ed. Baden-Baden, Koerner, 1971. 131 p. In German. "Auswahldiskographie": p. 128.

J3   Dixon, Robert M. W., and John Godrich. Recording the blues. [An historical and discographical essay.] New York, Stein and Day, 1970. 109 p.

J4   Garland, Phyl. The sound of soul. Chicago, H. Regnery Co., 1969. 246 p. Discography: pp. 239-241.

J5   Jahn, Jahnheinz. Blues und Work Songs. Frankfurt, Hamburg, Fischer, 1964. 186 p. In German. Includes discography.

Jahn, Jahnheinz. Blues und Work Songs. 2d ed. Frankfurt, Hamburg, Fischer, 1967. 186 p. In German. Includes discography.

J6   McCutcheon, Lynn Ellis. Rhythm and blues; an experience and adventure in its origin and development. Arlington, Va., Beatty, 1971. 305 p. Includes discographies.

J7   Myrus, Donald. Ballads, blues and the big beat. New York, Macmillan, 1966. 136 p. "List of records": pp. 125-129.

J8   Oliver, Paul. Blues fell this morning; the meaning of the blues. London, Cassell; New York, Horizon, 1960. 355 p. "Discography of quoted blues": pp. 311-340.

J9   Oliver, Paul. Conversation with the blues. London, Cassell; New York, Horizon, 1965; London, Jazz book Club, 1967. 217 p. Includes discography.

J10   Oliver, Paul. The story of the blues. London, Barrie & Rockliff; Philadelphia, Chilton Book Co., 1969; Harmondsworth, Penguin, 1972. 176 p. Discography: pp. 172-174.

J11   Russell, Tony. Blacks, whites, and blues. London, Studio Vista; New York, Stein and Day, 1970. 112 p. Discography: pp. 105-109.

J12   Russell, Tony. Talking blues; the first bluesmen? *Jazz & Blues*, II (June 1972), 15.

J13   Shaw, Arnold. The world of soul; black America's contribution to the pop music scene. New York, Cowles Book Co., 1970. 306 p. Discography: pp. 295-300.

J14   Shirley, Kay, ed. The book of the blues. New York, Leeds Music Corp., 1963. 301 p. Includes discographies.

BUYERS' GUIDES

J15   Ackerman, P. Mother lode in the archives. *Billboard*, LXXIX (June 24, 1967, supplement), 71.

J16   Cream of the blues catalog. *Billboard*, LXXIX (June 24, 1967, supplement), 74-82+

J17   Démètre, J., and M. Chauvard. Pour une discothèque de blues. *Jazz Hot*, #183 (Jan. 1963), 24-25; #184 (Feb. 1963), 22-23. In French.

J18   Dixon, Robert M. W., and John Godrich. Blues and gospel singers (1902-1942). Hatch End, Middlesex, Rust, 1964. 765 p. [For second edition, see J20 below.]

J19   Glover, T. The groovy boom in R & B. *Sing Out*, XVI (#3, 1966), 37-43.

J20   Godrich, John, and Robert M. W. Dixon. Blues and gospel singers (1902-1942). 2d ed. [of J18 above.] London, Storyville, 1969. 912 p.

J21   Lambert, G. E. Some foreign blues re-issues. *Jazz Monthly*, VIII (Feb. 1963), 26-27.

J22   Tenot, F. Au carrefour du blues. *Jazz Magazine*, VIII (Dec. 1962), 26-35. In French.

SUBJECTS AND GENRES

Afro-American Blues

J23   Oliver, Paul. Savannah syncopators: African retentions in the blues. London, Studio Vista; New York, Stein and Day, 1970. 112 p. Discography: pp. 106-107.

J24   Wilgus, D. K. Record reviews: Afro-American tradition. *Journal of American Folklore*, LXXXIV (#332, 1971), 264-71.

Country Blues

J25   Charters, Samuel Barclay. Die Story vom Blues. Country Blues. Mit einer Diskographie. [Translation of *The country blues* (New York, Toronto, 1959) by Iris and Rolf Hellmut Foerster.] München, Nymphenberger, 1962. 280 p. In German. Includes discography.

J26   Country blues (the rural blues). *Musical America*, LXXXIV (Feb. 1964), 52-53.

J27   The country blues. *Jazz Monthly*, VIII (May 1962), 27-28.

J28   Grossman, Stefan, Stephen Calt, and Hal Grossman. Country blues songbook. New York, Oak Publications, 1973. 208 p. Discography: pp. 207-208.

J29   Oster, Harry. Living country blues. Detroit, Folklore Associates, 1969. 464 p. Discography: pp. 455-456.

J30   Owen, F., and L. Wright. The country blues; a survey of currently available LPs and EPs. *Storyville*, #9 (Feb. 1967), 14-16.

Folk Blues

J31   Folk song discography. *Western Folklore*, XXI (#3, 1962), 223-28.

J32   Silverman, Jerry, ed. The art of the folk-blues guitar; an instruction manual. New York, Oak Publications, 1964. 71 p. Discography: p. 71.

J33   Silverman, Jerry, ed. Folk blues; 110 American folk blues. New York, Macmillan, 1968. 297 p. Includes discographies.

Piano Blues

J34   Welding, P. Some recent piano blues collections. *Sing Out*, XII (#4, 1962), 55+

Race Records

J35   Armagnac, Perry, and Carl A. Kendziora, Jr. Perfect dance and race catalog (1922-1930). *Record Research*, #51-52 (May-June 1963), whole issue (48 p.).

J36   Doyle, J. Million selling 'race' records. *Alley Music*, I (#2, 1968), 14; (#3, 1968), 11.

Southern Blues

J37   Ferris, William R. Blues from the Delta. London, Studio Vista, 1970. 111 p. Discography: pp. 110-111.

J38   Ferris, William R. Mississippi black folklore; a research bibliography and discography. Hattiesburg, Miss., University and College Press of Mississippi, 1971. 61 p. Discography: pp. 49-60.

Texas Blues

J39   Strachwitz, Chris, ed. Texas blues. [Discographies of Lowell Fulson, Lil Son Jackson, and Andrew "Smokey" Hogg.] n.p. [Reprinted from *Jazz Report*], 1966.

SECTION B

BLUES RECORDINGS TREATED
CHRONOLOGICALLY AND BY LABEL

BLUES RECORDINGS TREATED CHRONOLOGICALLY

1902-1942

J40   Dixon, Robert M. W., and John Godrich. Blues and gospel records
       1902-1942. Hatch End, Middlesex, Rust, 1963. 765 p.

       Dixon, Robert M. W., and John Godrich. Blues and gospel records
       1902-1942. 2d ed. London, Storyville, 1969. 912 p.

J41   Additions to Blues and gospel records 1902-1942. *John Edwards
       Memorial Foundation Quarterly*, VII (#3, 1971), 142; VIII (#1,
       1972), 7.

1943-1966

J42   Leadbitter, Mike, and Neil Slaven. Blues records: January 1943 to
       December 1966. London, Hanover Books; New York, Oak Publica-
       tions, 1968. 381 p.

1949-1971

J43   Whitburn, Joel. Top rhythm & blues records, 1949-1971. Menomonee
       Falls, Wisc., Record Research, 1973. 184 p.

1950-1959

J44 Propes, Steve. Those oldies but goodies: a guide to 50's record collecting. New York, Macmillan, 1973. 192 p.

1950-1966

J45 Rhythm and blues discography [recordings that made Billboard's best selling rhythm and blues chart, 1950 through 1966] . *Billboard*, LXXIX (June 24, 1967, supplement), 83-88.

1951-1964

J46 Godrich, John. John Godrich's survey of pre-war blues artists reissued on EP and LP 1951-1964. Bexhill-on-Sea, Blues Unlimited, 1965. 16 p.

1955-1970

J47 Whitburn, Joel. Top pop records, 1955-1970; facts about 9800 recordings listed in Billboard's "Hot 100" charts, grouped under the names of the 2500 recording artists. Detroit, Gale Research Co., 1972. 1v. (unpaged).

1964

J48 Best R & B records & artists of 1964. *Cash Box*, XXVI (Dec. 26, 1964), 36.

1964-1965

J49 Slaven, Neil. American R & B/blues records 1964/1965. New York, Blue Horizon Records, 1965. 24 p.

1965

J50 Oliver, Paul. Blues '65. *Jazz*, IV (#7, 1965), 26-29.

1966-1970

J51 Von Tersch, G. Records: rhythm 'n' blues, volume 2. *Rolling Stone*, #66 (Sep. 17, 1970), 48.

1970

J52 Cullaz, M. Blues [seven recordings]. *Jazz Hot*, #264 (Sep. 1970), 37-38. In French.

J53 Guralnick, P. Records, blues: a survey of recent releases. *Rolling Stone*, #77 (Mar. 4, 1971), 56.

1971

J54 Lowry, P. Blues bleachings. *Blues Unlimited*, LXXXIV (Sep. 1971), 23.

BLUES LABEL DISCOGRAPHY

J55 Label discography. *Billboard*, LXXIX (June 24, 1967, supplement), 90.

Arhoolie Records

J56 Chauvard, M., and J. Démètre. Pour une discothèque de blues [Arhoolie label]. *Jazz Hot*, #180 (Oct. 1962), 13+ In French.

English Brunswick Records

J57 Dutton, Frank. Brunswick modern rhythm series. *Matrix*, #50 (Dec. 1963), 3-12.

Excello Records

J58 Chauvard, M., and J. Démètre. Down Excello way. [Reprinted from *Jazz Hot*.] *Jazz Monthly*, VIII (Nov. 1962), 3-6.

J59 Chauvard, M., and J. Démètre. Du côté de chez Excello. *Jazz Hot*, #175 (Apr. 1962), 14-17. In French.

Goldband Records

J60 Leadbitter, Mike, and Eddie Shuler. From the bayou; the story of Goldband Records. Bexhill-on-Sea, Blues Unlimited, 1969. 62 p.

Southern Folk Heritage Records

J61   Oliver, Paul. Blues on the 'Southern Folk Heritage' LPs. *Jazz Monthly*, VII (Feb. 1962), 21-25.

Yazoo Records

J62   Blues labels: Yazoo [includes discography]. *Jazz Podium*, XXI (Jan. 1972), 16-18.

SECTION C

JAZZ GENERAL GUIDES, BUYERS' GUIDES, AND SUBJECTS

GENERAL GUIDES AND HISTORICAL SURVEYS

J63   Augustín, José. La nueva música clásica. México, D.F., Instituto Nacional de la Juventud Mexicana, 1968. 81 p. In Spanish. "Discografía elemental": pp. 77-81.

J64   Belz, Carl. The story of rock. New York, Oxford University Press, 1969. 256 p. "Selected discography, 1953-1963": pp. 220-247.

       Belz, Carl. The story of rock. 2d ed. New York, Oxford University Press, 1972. 286 p. "Selected discography, 1953-1971": pp. 244-273.

J65   Berendt, Joachim Ernst. Variationen über Jazz. Aufsätze. 3d ed. München, Nymphenburger, 1963. 228 p. In German. Includes discography.

J66   Berendt, Joachim Ernst, ed. Le Jazz. Des origines à nos jours. [Translation of Das neue Jazzbuch (Frankfurt, 1959) by Christian Metz.] Paris, Payot, 1963. 352 p. In French. Includes discography.

J67   Berendt, Joachim Ernst, ed. Das Jazzbuch—von New Orleans bis Free Jazz. [Revised and enlarged edition of Das neue Jazzbuch.] Frankfurt, München, Fischer, 1968. 334 p. In German. Includes discography.

J68   Berendt, Joachim Ernst. Das neue Jazzbuch. Entwicklung und Bedeutung der Jazzmusik. [Revised edition of Das Jazzbuch (Frankfurt, 1953).] Frankfurt, München, Fischer, 1959. 318 p. In German. Includes discography.

J69   Berendt, Joachim Ernst, ed. The new jazz book; a history and guide. [Translation by Dan Morgenstern of *Das neue Jazzbuch* (Frankfurt, 1959).] New York, Hill & Wang, 1962. 314 p. Discography: pp. 285-300.

J70   Boon, Bob. De geschiedenis van de jazz. Antwerpen, De Garve, 1962. 78 p. In Flemish. Includes discographies.

J71   Burton, Jack. The blue book of Tin Pan Alley; a human interest encyclopedia of American popular music. Expanded new ed., including 1950-1965 supplement. Watkins Glen, N.Y., Century House, 1962, 1965. 2 v. (304 p., 528 p.) Includes discographies.

J72   Christiansen, Lars Boie. Avant garde jazz. *Bogens Verden*, II (1971), 133-39; III (1971), 210-15. In Danish. Includes discographies of John Coltrane, Pharaoh Sanders, Cecil Taylor, Ornette Coleman, Don Cherry, Albert Ayler, Archie Shepp, and Miles Davis.

J73   Clayton, Peter, and Peter Gammond. 14 miles on a clear night: an irreverent, sceptical, and affectionate book about jazz records. London, Owen, 1966. 128 p.

J74   Condon, Eddie. We called it music; a generation of jazz. [Reprint of the 1947 edition.] Westport, Conn., Greenwood Press, 1970. 341 p. Discography: pp. 309-328.

J75   Dankworth, Avril. Jazz; an introduction to its musical basis. London, New York, Oxford University Press, 1968. 92 p. Includes discography.

J76   Dauer, Alfons M. Der Jazz. Seine Ursprünge und seine Entwicklung. 2d ed. Kassel, Röth, 1962. 286 p. In German. Includes discography.

J77   Dexter, Dave. The jazz story, from the '90s to the '60s. Englewood Cliffs, N.J., Prentice-Hall, 1964. 176 p. Discography: pp. 165-167.

J78   Esquire. Esquire's world of jazz. New York, Esquire; distributed by Grosset & Dunlop, 1962. 224 p. Discography: pp. 209-221.

J79   Fayenz, Franco. Il Jazz dal mito all'avanguardia. [Discography.] Milano, Sapere Ed., 1970. 510 p. In Italian.

J80   Feather, Leonard. The encyclopedia of jazz in the sixties. New York, Horizon Press, 1966. 312 p. Discography: pp. 309-310.

J81   Feather, Leonard. The new edition of the encyclopedia of jazz. New York, Horizon Press, 1960. 527 p. Discography: pp. 500-504.

J82   Finkelstein, Sidney. Jazz: a people's music. [Reprint of the New
       York, 1948 edition.] London, Jazz Book Club, 1964. 278 p.
       Includes discography.

J83   Fox, Charles. Jazz in perspective. London, British Broadcasting
       Corporation, 1969. 88 p. "Bibliography and discography": pp. 81-88.

J84   Geysen, Jan. Jazz-musiek van onze tijd. Antwerpen, Standaard Boek-
       handel, 1964. 134 p. In Flemish. Includes discography.

J85   Gitler, Ira. Jazz masters of the forties. [History, discographical
       commentary, and record lists.] New York, Macmillan; London,
       Collier-Macmillan, 1966. 286 p. Includes record lists.

J86   Goldberg, Joe [Howard S.]. Jazz masters of the fifties. [Gerry
       Mulligan, Thelonius Monk, Art Blakey, Miles Davis, Sonny Rollins,
       Modern Jazz Quartet, Charles Mingus, Paul Desmond, Ray Charles,
       John Coltrane, Cecil Taylor, and Ornette Coleman. History, disco-
       graphical commentary, and record lists.] New York, Macmillan;
       London, Collier-Macmillan, 1965. 246 p. Includes record lists.

J87   Gonda, János. Jazz; történet, elmélet, gyakorlat. Budapest, Zene-
       mükiadó, 1965. 371 p. In Hungarian. Discographies: pp. 358-371.

J88   Hadlock, Richard. Jazz masters of the twenties. [Louis Armstrong,
       Earl Hines, Bix Beiderbecke, Chicagoans of the twenties, Fats
       Waller, James P. Johnson, Jack Teagarden, Fletcher Henderson, Don
       Redman, Bessie Smith, and Eddie Lang. History, discographical
       commentary, and record lists.] New York, Macmillan; London,
       Collier-Macmillan, 1965. 255 p. Includes record lists.

J89   Harris, Rex. Enjoying jazz. Rev. ed. London, Phoenix House, 1963.
       157 p. Includes discographies.

J90   Heuvelmans, Bernard. Blues, be-bop, cool . . . el jazz. [Translation of
       De la Bamboula au Be Bop—le jazz (Verviers, 1959) by Julio Mateu.]
       Barcelona, Bruguera, 1962. 148 p. In Spanish. Includes discography.

J91   Heuvelmans, Bernard. Dalla Bamboula al Be-Bop—tutto sul jazz.
       [Translation of *De la Bamboula au Be Bop—le jazz* (Verviers, 1959)
       by Carlo Sini, with some updating by Jean Tarse.] Milano, AMZ,
       1961, 1962, 1965. 140 p. In Italian. Includes discography.

J92   Heuvelmans, Bernard, Jean Tarse, and Carlos de Radzitzky. Do New
       Orleans ao jazz moderno—o jazz. [Translation of Heuvelmans' *De la
       Bamboula au Be Bop—le jazz* (Verviers, 1959) with additional up-
       dated material, by Maria Amélia Barcia.] Lisboa, Empresa Nacional
       de Publicidade, 1967. 158 p. In Portuguese. Includes discography.

J93   Jazzologie. *Le Point du Jazz,* #4 (Mar. 1971), 83-90; #5 (Sep. 1971), 105-19. In French.

J94   Jørgensen, Birger, Knud Sandvej, and others. Musikkens Hvem-Hvad-Hvor. Jazz. København, Politikens Forlag, 1969. 500 p. In Danish. Includes discography.

J95   Jones, LeRoi. Black music. New York, W. Morrow, 1967; London, MacGibbon & Kee, 1969. 223 p. Discography: pp. 213-214.

J96   Jones, Raymond Peter. Jazz. New York, Roy; Toronto, Ryerson; London, Methuen, 1963. 96 p. Includes discography.

J97   Knobel, Bruno. Jazzfibel. 4. Aufl. Solothurn, Schweizer Jugend-Verlag; Stuttgart, Eulen-Verlag, 1962. 55 p. In German. "Diskothek": pp. 47-55.

J98   Lee, Edward. Jazz: an introduction. London, Kahn and Averill, 1972. 188 p. Discography: pp. 155-159.

J99   McCarthy, Albert J. The dance band era: the dancing decades from ragtime to swing, 1910-1950. London, Studio Vista, 1971. 176 p. Discography: pp. 171-173.

J100   McRae, Barry. The jazz cataclysm. London, Dent; South Brunswick, N.Y., A. S. Barnes, 1967. 184 p. "Selected discography": pp. 173-178.

J101   Miller, William Robert. The world of pop music and jazz. Saint Louis, Concordia Pub. House, 1965. 112 p. Discography: pp. 110-112.

J102   Myrus, Donald. I like jazz. New York, Macmillan, 1964. 118 p. Discography: pp. 110-115.

J103   Panassié, Hugues. La bataille du jazz. Paris, Albin-Michel, 1965. 220 p. In French. Discography: pp. 193-215.

J104   Panassié, Hugues. Die Geschichte des echten Jazz. [Translation of *Histoire du vrai jazz* (Paris, 1959) by Johannes Piron.] Gütersloh, Signum, 1962. 188 p. In German. Includes discography.

J105   Panassié, Hugues. Hot jazz; the guide to swing music. [Translation by Lyle and Eleanor Dowling of *Le jazz hot;* reprint of the New York, 1936 edition.] Westport, Conn., Negro Universities Press, 1970. 363 p. Discography: pp. 297-356.

J106   Panassié, Hugues. The real jazz. [Translation of *Le jazz hot* (Paris, 1934) by Anne Sorelle Williams revised and enlarged since the first edition of the translation (New York, 1942).] New York, Barnes;

London, Yoseloff; Toronto, Smithers, 1960; London, Jazz Book Club, 1967. 286 p. Includes discography.

J107   Rauhe, Hermann. Musikerziehung durch Jazz. Wolfenbüttel, Möseler, 1962. 105 p. In German. Discography: pp. 103-105.

J108   Renaud, H., ed. Jazz classique. Tournai, Casterman, 1971. 259 p. In French. Includes discographies.

J109   Renaud, H., ed. Jazz moderne. Tournai, Casterman, 1971. 255 p. In French. Includes discographies.

J110   Roberts, John Storm. Black music of two worlds. New York, Praeger, 1972. 286 p. Discography: pp. 269-280.

J111   Schuller, Gunther. The history of jazz. New York, Oxford University Press. v. 1— . 1968— . Discography: v. 1, pp. 385-389.

J112   Schulz-Köhn, Dietrich. Jazz in der Schule. Wolfenbüttel, Möseler, 1959. 118 p. In German. "Grundbestand einer Jazz-Diskothek": pp. 113-118.

J113   Schulz-Köhn, Dietrich. Kleine Geschichte des Jazz. Gütersloh, Bertelsmann, 1963. 189 p. In German. Discography: p. 161.

J114   Shaw, Arnold. The rock revolution. New York, Crowell-Collier Press, 1969. 215 p. Discography: pp. 206-211.

J115   Stambler, Irwin, Vern Bushway, and others. Encyclopedia of popular music. New York, St. Martin's Press, 1965. 353 p. Discography: pp. 341-353.

J116   Stewart, Rex William. Jazz masters of the thirties. [History, discographical commentary, and record lists.] New York, Macmillan; London, Collier-Macmillan, 1972. 223 p. Includes record lists.

J117   Tanner, Paul, and Maurice Gerow. A study of jazz. Dubuque, La., W. C. Brown, 1964. 83 p. Includes discographies.

        Tanner, Paul, and Maurice Gerow. A study of jazz. 2d ed. Dubuque, Ia., W. C. Brown, 1973. 189 p. Discography: pp. 174-176.

J118   Terkel, Studs [Louis]. Giants of jazz. New York, Crowell, 1957; London, Jazz Book Club, 1966. 216 p. Includes discography.

J119   Williams, Martin T. Where's the melody? A listener's introduction to jazz. New York, Pantheon Books, 1966. 205 p. Includes discographies.

Williams, Martin T. Where's the melody? A listener's introduction to jazz. Rev. ed. New York, Pantheon Books, 1969. 206p. Includes discographies.

J120   Wilson, John Steuart. Jazz: the transition years, 1940-1960. New York, Appleton-Century-Crofts, 1966. 185 p. Discography: pp. 167-171

BUYERS' GUIDES

J121   Awamura, Masaaki. Jazu rekōdo bukku [i.e., Jazz record book]. Tokyo, Ongaku no Tomo, 1968. 208 p. [Citation Romanized from the Japanese.] In Japanese.

J122   Cerri, Livio. Jazz in microsolco. Pisa, Nistri-Lischi, 1963. 505 p. In Italian.

J123   Clouzet, J. Les éditions phonographiques aux États-Unis. *Jazz Magazine*, #176 (Mar. 1970), xxxiv-xxxix. In French.

J124   Cullaz, Maurice. Guide des disques de jazz. Paris, Buchet-Chastel, 1971. 347 p. In French.

J125   Delaunay, Charles. New hot discography; the standard directory of recorded jazz. [Reprint of the 3d ed. (New York, 1948).] New York, Criterion, 1963. 608 p.

J126   De Michael, D. Jazz on tape; a survey of the year's prerecorded stereo jazz tapes. *Down Beat*, XXXII (Dec. 2, 1965), 15-16+

J127   Dengler, J. M. Disco Dengler. *Record Research*, #84 (June 1967), 3-5.

J128   Elmenhorst, Gernot W., and Walter von Bebenburg.Die Jazz-Diskothek. Reinbek bei Hamburg, Rowohlt, 1961. 362 p. In German.

J129   Feather, Leonard. Jazz per le biblioteche. *Musica Jazz*, XIX (July-Aug. 1963), 39-40. In Italian.

J130   Fox, Charles, Peter Gammond, and Alun Morgan. Jazz on record: a critical guide. London, Arrow Books; London, Hutchinson, 1960. 352 p.

J131   Hoefer, G. Basic library of long playing jazz classics. *Jazz*, III (July-Aug. 1964), 48-49.

J132   McCarthy, Albert J., and others. Jazz on record. Garden City, N.Y., Hanover, 1972. 416 p.

J133   Palmer, B. Jazz: the classic on record. *Rolling Stone*, #76 (Feb. 18, 1971), 54+

J134   Retour aux sources [the world of traditional jazz]. *Jazz Magazine*, IX (June 1963), 18-19. In French.

J135   Russell, Peter, comp. The good noise. [A series of leaflets.] Plymouth, Eng., Peter Russell's Hot Record Store. #1− . 1968− .

J136   Rust, Brian A. L. More sounds of silence. *Storyville*, #21 (Feb.-Mar. 1969), 96-99.

J137   Scheffner, Manfred. Katalog der Jazzschallplatten. Bielefeld, Bielefelder Verlagsanstalt, 1967. 207 p. In German.

J138   Selection discographique. *Jazz Hot*, #263 (summer 1970), 26-27. In French.

J139   Sullivan, P. J. Beating the squeeze [a guide to cheap label jazz issued between January 1966 and June 1967]. *Jazz Journal*, XX (Dec. 1967), 43.

J140   Sullivan, P. J. Beating the squeeze; a recap on bargain jazz. *Jazz Journal*, XXI (Mar. 1968), 25+

J141   Wedgeworth, Robert. Jazz. *Library Journal*, LXXXVII (May 1, 1963), 1830-32.

J142   Williams, Martin T. A basic LP jazz library. *The American Record Guide*, XXX (May 1964), 890-91.

Reissued Recordings

J143   Barbrook, A. T. Archive [jazz reissues]. *Pieces of Jazz*, #7 (1969), 7-10.

J144   Gardner, M. A desirable dozen; some recent American reissues. *Jazz Journal*, XXI (June 1968), 31-33.

J145   Godrich, John. Jazz information; a listing of the reissues. *Matrix*, #82 (Apr. 1969), 3.

J146   McCarthy, Albert J. Recent reissues. *Jazz Monthly*, XIII (Feb. 1968), 2-4; XIV (June 1968), 22-26; (Aug. 1968), 19-21.

J147   Morgenstern, Dan. Reissues: jazz's rich legacy. *Down Beat*, XXXVI (Jan. 23, 1969), 16-17+

J148   Reissue series. *Jazz Monthly*, XIV (June 1968), 27-28.

J149   Smith, C. E. The name of the game was jazz [historical reissues].
        Jazz & Pop, VII (Sep. 1968), 51-54.

SUBJECTS AND GENRES

American Jazz

J150   Mellers, Wilfrid Howard. Music in a new found land. New York,
        A. A. Knopf; London, Barrie and Rockliff, 1964. 543 p. Discography
        by Kenneth W. Dommett [jazz and blues portion]: pp. 479-510.

Australian Jazz

J151   Burgis, P. Recent Australian jazz artist recordings in the New Orleans/
        traditional idiom. *Jazz Report*, V (#4, 1966), 5-7.

J152   Mitchell, Jack. Australian discography. 2d ed. Lithgow, Mitchell,
        1960. 77 p. [See also corrections to this in J153 below.]

J153   Mitchell, Jack. Jazz Australia [corrections to Australian discography,
        2d ed., J152 above]. *Matrix*, #43 (Oct. 1962), 16-17.

Austrian Jazz

J154   Kraner, Dietrich Heinz, and Klaus Schulz. Jazz in Austria; a brief
        history and a discography of all jazz and jazz-like recordings made
        in Austria. Graz, The Authors, 1969. 40 p.

Bebop

J155   Porter, B. One sweet letter from you: bebopdiscography. *Jazz
        Journal*, XXII (Jan. 1969), 16.

Belgian Jazz

J156   Pernet, Robert. Jazz in little Belgium: history (1881-1966); discog-
        raphy (1895-1966). Bruxelles, Sigma, 1967. 518 p.

Bossa Nova

J157   Williams, Martin T. Bossa from both sides of the border. *The Saturday Review*, XLVI (Feb. 23, 1963), 57.

Clarinet

J158   McDonough, J. Old wine—new bottles [jazz clarinet]. *Down Beat*, XXXVIII (June 24, 1971), 24.

Czechoslovakian Jazz

J159   Dorůžka, Lubomír. 'Singly.' *Hudební Rozhledy*, XX (#21-22, 1967), 666-68. In Czech.

J160   Dorůžka, Lubomír. Zvuková historie našeho jazzu. *Hudební Rozhledy*, XIX (#5, 1966), 140-41. In Czech.

J161   Dorůžka, Lubomír, and Ivan Poledňák. Československý jazz. Minulost a přítomnost. Praha, Bratislava, Supraphon, 1967. 309 p. In Czech; summary in English. Includes discography.

J162   Matzner, Antonín. Československý jazz 1965 na desce. *Hudební Rozhledy*, XIX (#3, 1966), 88. In Czech.

J163   Matzner, Antonín. Jazzové profily. Praha, Supraphon, 1970. 406 p. In Czech. Includes discography.

J164   Poledňák, Ivan. Jazzová deska. *Hudební Rozhledy*, XV (#3, 1962), 127. In Czech.

Danish Jazz

J165   Nationaldiskoteket, København. Dansk jazz. Ordrup, Nationalmuseet, 1961. 4v. (102 p. total) In Danish.

English Jazz

J166   Walker, Edward Samuel. Early English jazz. *Jazz Journal*, XXI (July 1968), 18-19+

J167   Walker, Edward Samuel, and Steven Walker. English ragtime; a discography. Woodthorpe, Edward S. Walker, 1971. 104 p.

Free Jazz

J168   Raben, Erik. A discography of free jazz. [Albert Ayler, Don Cherry, Ornette Coleman, Pharaoh Sanders, Archie Shepp, and Cecil Taylor.] København, Knudsen, 1969. 38 p.

French Jazz

J169   Discographie française. *Jazz Hot*, #263 (Summer 1970), 28. In French.

J170   Ioakimidis, D. Pour une discothèque du middle jazz contemporain. *Jazz Hot*, #174 (Mar. 1962), 10-13+ In French.

German Jazz

J171   Lange, Horst Heinz. Die deutsche '78er' Discographie der Jazz- und Hot-Dance-Musik 1903-1958. Berlin, Colloquium, 1966. 775 p. In German.

J172   Lange, Horst Heinz. Jazz in Deutschland. Die deutsche Jazz-Chronik 1900-1960. Berlin, Colloquium, 1966. 210 p. In German. Discography: pp. 183-201.

Guitar

J173   Peynet, M. Discographie [guitar]. *Jazz Hot*, #283 (May 1972), 63. In French.

Italian Jazz

J174   Barazzetta, G. Discografia italiana: la serie "Italian jazz stars." *Musica Jazz*, XX (Feb. 1964), 44-45. In Italian.

J175   Mazzoletti, Adriano, and others. 40 [i.e., Quarant'] anni di jazz in Italia. Milano, Dischi Ricordi, 1964. 32 p. In Italian. Includes discography.

Japanese Jazz

J176   Close, A. B. Japanese jazz discography [1948-1953]. *Record Research*, #76 (May 1966), 8+

Jazz and Drugs

J177   Winick, C. Some jazz records dealing with drugs. *Jazz Monthly*, VIII (Oct. 1962), 11; (Nov. 1962), 10-12.

Jazz and Exotic Instruments

J178   Laade, Wolfgang. Globe unity—jazz meets the world. *Jazzforschung*, II (1970), 138-46. In German.

New Orleans Jazz

J179   Dorigné, Michel. Jazz 1, [i.e., un], les origines du jazz, le style Nouvelle Orléans et ses prolongements. Paris, l'École des loisirs, 1968. 160 p. In French. Includes discographies.

J180   The sound of New Orleans [recording Jazz Odyssey]. *Jazz Monthly*, X (Nov. 1964), 21-23.

J181   Williams, Martin T. Jazz masters of New Orleans. [Buddy Bolden, Original Dixieland Jazz Band, Jelly Roll Morton, King Oliver, New Orleans Rhythm Kings, Sidney Bechet, Louis Armstrong, Zutty Singleton, Kid Ory, Bunk Johnson, and Red Allen. History, discographical commentary, and record lists.] New York, Macmillan; London, Collier-Macmillan, 1967. 287 p. Includes record lists.

J182   Wilson, J. S. A real New Orleans sound; the story of Preservation Hall and its ancient jazzmen. *High Fidelity*, XIII (Sep. 1963), 59-63.

New York Jazz

J183   Charters, Samuel Barclay, and Leonard Kunstadt. A história do jazz nos palcos de Nova York. [Translation of *Jazz: a history of the New York scene* (Garden City, 1962) by Hersilia Teixeira and Leite Vasconcellos.] Rio de Janeiro, Lidador, 1962. 334 p. In Portuguese. Includes discography.

Norwegian Jazz

J184   Bergh, Johs. The Big Chief Jazz-Club 1953-63. Avsnittet om metropol ved Syver Reff. Oslo, Tengs, 1963. 32 p. In Norwegian. Includes discography.

Piano

J185   Edwards, Ernie, George Hall, and Bill Korst. Modern jazz piano 1. [Joe Albany, Gene Dinovi, Al Haig, Sadik Hakim.] Whittier, Calif., Erngeobil, 1966. 30 p.

J186   Feather, Leonard. Jazz piano; soul, skill and serenity. *Show*, III (July 1963), 34-35.

J187   Hot pianos 1926-1940. *Jazz Monthly*, #171 (June 1969), 25-26.

J188   Walker, Edward Samuel. Piano rolls on the phonograph. *Jazz Report*, VI (#5, 1968), 9-13; (#6, 1969), 11-12.

J189   Williams, Martin T. Jazz pianists, and Brubeck. *The Saturday Review*, XLVI (Sep. 28, 1963), 78.

Polish Jazz

J190   Radliński, Jerzy. Obywatel jazz [Citizen jazz] . Przedmowa Stefana Kisielewskiego. Warszawa, Polskie Wydawnictwo Muzyczne, 1967. 259 p. In Polish. Discography: pp. 233-252.

Ragtime

J191   Blesh, Rudi, and Harriet Janis. They all played ragtime. Revised and with new additional material. New York, Oak Publications, 1966. 347 p. "A selected list of phonograph records": pp. 338-347.

J192   Jasen, David A. Recorded ragtime, 1897-1958. Hamden, Conn., Archon Books, 1973. 155 p.

Swedish Jazz

J193   European recorded jazz: Sweden. *Jazz Monthly*, XI (July 1965), 24-27.

Swing

J194   Delaunay, Charles. Swing: aux USA en 1946. *Le Point du Jazz*, #5 (Sep. 1971), 14-18. In French.

J195   Frésart, Iwan. 78 rpm swing label discography. Brussels, Frésart, 1965. 16 p.

Swiss Jazz

J196   Hippenmeyer, Jean Roland. Le jazz en Suisse, 1930-1970. Yverdon, Éditions de la Thièle, 1971. 245 p. In French. Includes discographies.

Tenor Saxophone

J197   Evensmo, J. The tenor saxophonists, 1930-1942, volume 1. [Leon Chu Berry, Herschel Evans, Coleman Hawkins, Ben Webster, Lester Young.] Oslo, Norwegian Computing Center, 1970. 152 p.

SECTION D

JAZZ RECORDINGS TREATED
CHRONOLOGICALLY AND BY LABEL

GENERAL SOURCES

J198   Heider, Wally. Transcography; a discography of jazz and pop music
       issued on 16" transcriptions. San Francisco, The Author, 1970. 96 p.

J199   Now on hand at your Jazz Museum [complete record inventory].
       The Second Line, XXIII (Sep.-Oct. 1970), 398-410.

JAZZ RECORDINGS TREATED CHRONOLOGICALLY

1897-1931

J200   Rust, Brian A. L. Jazz records A-Z 1897-1931. Hatch End, Middlesex,
       The Author, 1961. 884 p.

       Rust, Brian A. L. Jazz records A-Z 1897-1931. 2d ed. Hatch End,
       Middlesex, Rust's Rare Records, 1962. 736 p. [For index see
       Grandorge, J201 below. For corrections and additions, see Kendziora,
       J202 below.]

       Rust, Brian A. L. Jazz records A-Z 1897-1931. 3d ed. Hatch End,
       Middlesex, Rust's Rare Records, 1965. 680 p.

J201   Grandorge, Richard. Jazz records A-Z 1897-1931: index. Hatch End,
       Middlesex, Rust's Rare Records, 1963. 62 p. [An index to the
       second edition (1962) of Rust, J200 above.]

J202   Kendziora, Carl A. Behind the cobwebs [corrections and additions
       to Brian Rust's Jazz records A-Z 1897-1931, 2d ed., 1962 (J200

above)] . *Record Research*, #70 (Aug. 1965), 5; #72 (Nov. 1965), 6+

1897-1942

J203   Rust, Brian A. L. The complete entertainment discography from the mid-1890s to 1942. New Rochelle, N.Y., Arlington House, 1973.

J204   Rust, Brian A. L. Jazz records 1897-1942. London, Storyville, 1970. 2v. (928 p., 1040 p.) [For corrections and additions, see Fonteyne, J205 below.]

J205   Fonteyne, A. Brian Rust, 'Jazz records 1897-1942': quelques corrections et additions. *Le Point du Jazz*, #6 (Mar. 1972), 106-10. In French. [Additions and corrections to J204 above.]

1903-1966

J206   Murrells, Joseph. Daily Mail book of golden discs: the story of every million selling disc in the world since 1903. Ed. by Norris & Ross McWhirter. London, McWhirter Twins on behalf of the Daily Mail, 1966. 374 p.

1917-1967

J207   Bruyninckx, Walter, ed. 50 years of recorded jazz 1917-1967. Mechelen, Belgium, The Author, 1968. 1000 p.

J208   McCarthy, Albert J., Alun Morgan, Paul Oliver, and Max Harrison. Jazz on record: a critical guide to the first fifty years, 1917-1967, London, Hanover; New York, Oak Publications, 1968. 416 p.

J209   Sterrenburg, F. A. S. Vijftig jaar jazz op platen. Amsterdam, I. V. I. O., 1967. 16 p. In Dutch.

1920-1929

J210   Dance, Stanley. Jazz in the twenties. *The Saturday Review*, XLVIII (Mar. 13, 1965), 136.

J211   Jazz sounds of the twenties. *Jazz Monthly*, VIII (June 1962), 22-25.

J212   Wilson, J. S. Treasure of the twenties. *High Fidelity*, XIV (Mar. 1964), 207.

1932-1942

J213   Rust, Brian A. L. Jazz records A-Z 1932-1942. Hatch End, Middle-
        sex, The Author, 1964. 680 p.

1940-1949

J214   Morgan, Alun. Sounds of the forties. *Jazz Monthly*, X (June 1964),
        4-5; (Sep. 1964), 2-3.

1942-1962

J215   Jepsen, Jørgen Grunnet. Jazz records 1942-1962, volume 5: M-N.
        København, Nordisk Tidsskrift, 1963. 379 p.

        Jepsen, Jørgen Grunnet. Jazz records 1942-1962, volume 5: M-N.
        2d ed. Holte, Knudsen, 1967. 379 p.

        Jepsen, Jørgen Grunnet. Jazz records 1942-1962, volume 5: M-N.
        Rev. ed. Holte, Knudsen, 1970. 379 p.

J216   Jepsen, Jørgen Grunnet. Jazz records 1942-1962, volume 6: O-R.
        Holte, Knudsen, 1964. 361 p.

        Jepsen, Jørgen Grunnet. Jazz records 1942-1962, volume 6: O-R.
        2d ed. Holte, Knudsen, 1967. 361 p.

        Jepsen, Jørgen Grunnet. Jazz records 1942-1962, volume 6: O-R.
        Rev. ed. Holte, Knudsen, 1970. 361 p.

J217   Jepsen, Jørgen Grunnet. Jazz records 1942-1962, volume 7: S-Te.
        Holte, Knudsen, 1965. 370 p.

        Jepsen, Jørgen Grunnet. Jazz records 1942-1962, volume 7: S-Te.
        Rev. ed. Holte, Knudsen, 1970. 370 p.

J218   Jepsen, Jørgen Grunnet. Jazz records 1942-1962, volume 8: Te-Z.
        Holte, Knudsen, 1965. 420 p.

        Jepsen, Jørgen Grunnet. Jazz records 1942-1962, volume 8: Te-Z.
        Rev. ed. Holte, Knudsen, 1970. 420 p.

1942-1965

J219   Jepsen, Jørgen Grunnet. Jazz records 1942-1965, volume 1: A-Bl.
       Holte, Knudsen, 1967. 397 p.

J220   Jepsen, Jørgen Grunnet. Jazz records 1942-1965, volume 2: Bl-Co.
       Holte, Knudsen, 1966. 399 p.

J221   Jepsen, Jørgen Grunnet. Jazz records 1942-1965, volume 3: Co-Ell.
       Holte, Knudsen, 1967. 464 p.

1942-1967

J222   Jepsen, Jørgen Grunnet. Jazz records 1942-1967, volume 4a: Ell-Goo.
       København, Knudsen, 1969. 389 p.

J223   Jepsen, Jørgen Grunnet. Jazz records 1942-1967, volume 4b: Goo-Iwr.
       København, Knudsen, 1969. 425 p.

1942-1968

J224   Jepsen, Jørgen Grunnet. Jazz records 1942-1968, volume 4c: J-Ki.
       København, Knudsen, 1970. 369 p.

1942-1969

J225   Jepsen, Jørgen Grunnet. Jazz records 1942-1969, volume 4d: Kl-L.
       København, Knudsen, 1970. 375 p.

1956-1959

J226   Traill, Sinclair, and Gerald D. Lascelles. Just jazz. London, Davies;
       [etc.; imprint varies.] v. 1-4. 1957-1960.

1956-1963

J227   Down Beat's jazz record review. [Title varies.] Chicago, Maher.
       v. 1-8. 1957-1964.

1957-1969

J228   Williams, Martin T. Jazz masters in transition 1957-69. [Selected record reviews and discographical essays from Saturday Review and other periodicals.] New York, Macmillan; London, Collier-Macmillan, 1970. 288 p.

1958

J229   McCarthy, Albert J. Jazz discography 1958: an international discography of recorded jazz including blues, gospel, and rhythm-and-blues. New releases and reissues 1958. London, Cassell, 1960, 1968. 272 p.

1960—

J230   Jazz catalogue. [Various editors.] London, Jazz Journal. v. 1— . 1960— . [annual]

1961-1968

J231   Larkin, Philip. All what jazz: a record diary 1961-68. London, Faber; New York, St. Martin's, 1970. 272 p. Discographical commentary.

1963—

J232   Dance, Stanley. The year in jazz. *Music Journal*. [Appears in annual issues.]

1967—

J233   A dozen of the best. *Melody Maker*. [Appears annually in an issue about December 1.]

1969

J234   Borretti, Raffaele. Collector's catalog 1969. Cosenza, Collector, 1969. 98 p.

1970

J235   Gray, Bartholomew. Jazz 70. Stockholm, Polydor, 1970. 36 p.

1972–

J236   Armitage, Andrew D. Annual index to popular music record reviews. Metuchen, N.J., Scarecrow. v. 1– . 1973– . [annual]

JAZZ LABEL DISCOGRAPHY

Columbia Records

J237   Mahony, Dan. Columbia 13/14000-D series; a numerical listing. Stanhope, N.J., Allen, 1961. 80 p.

Mahony, Dan. Columbia 13/14000-D series; a numerical listing. 2d ed. Stanhope, N.J., Allen, 1966. 80 p.

Decca Records

J238   A dip into Decca's jazz archives. *High Fidelity/Musical America*, XVIII (Feb. 1968), 118-19.

J239   Hentoff, Nat. The Decca Jazz Heritage Series. *HiFi/Stereo Review*, XX (Feb. 1968), 132.

Dutch Capitol Records

J240   Morgan, Alun. Classics on [Dutch] Capitol. *Jazz & Blues*, II (Aug. 1972), 22-24.

English Brunswick Records

J241   Hayes, Jim. English Brunswick artist catalogue 02000 series (02000 to 02999). Liverpool, Hayes, 1969. 30 p.

J242   Hayes, Jim, Barbara Luxton, and Desmond Luxton. Numerical catalogue listings number E1. English Brunswick 78/45 RPM (0)1000 series. Part 1: 1000 to 02000 (Dec. 1930 to May 1935). Millbrook, Southampton, Hayes, 1967. 50 p.

Hayes, Jim, Barbara Luxton, and Desmond Luxton. Numerical catalogue listings number E1. English Brunswick 78/45 RPM (0)1000 series. Part 1: 1000 to 02000 (Dec. 1930 to May 1935). [2d ed.] Liverpool, Hayes, 1969. 50 p.

English Columbia Records

J243   Hayes, Jim. English Columbia CBI series; artist alphabetical listing. Liverpool, Hayes, 1969. 44 p.

J244   Hayes, Jim. English Columbia discographical artist catalogue (CB 1 to 819). Liverpool, Hayes, 1969. 44 p. [Different issue of J243 above.]

J245   Hayes, Jim. English Columbia FB 1000 series (FB 1000 to 1999). Liverpool, Hayes, 1969. 26 p.

English H.M.V. Records

J246   Hayes, Jim. English H.M.V. BD 5000 series (BD 5000 to 6204). Liverpool, Hayes, 1969. 28 p.

English Parlophone Records

J247   Hayes, Jim. English Parlophone F 100 series (F 100 to 999). Liverpool, Hayes, 1969. 24 p.

English Regal and Regal Zonophone Records

J248   Hayes, Jim. English Regal/Regal Zonophone MR 1 series (MR 1 to 999). Liverpool, Hayes, 1969. 28 p.

German RCA Records

J249   McCarthy, Albert J. German RCA "jazz star" series. *Jazz Monthly*, XIII (June 1967), 13-16.

Imperial Records

J250   Horlick, Dick. Imperial records. New York, Imperial Records, 1968. 24 p.

King Records

J251   Rotante, A., and K. Mohr. The 'King' catalog; a listing in the growth of recorded popular music Americana. *Record Research*, #87 (Dec. 1967), 6-7; #90 (May 1968), 8; #91 (July 1968), 8; #93 (Nov. 1968), 7.

Paramount Records

J252   Vreede, M. E. The Paramount 12000-13000 series. *Storyville*, #11 (June-July 1967), 31-36.

Rex Records

J253   Hayes, Jim. Rex artist catalogue. 8001 to 8999. Liverpool, Hayes, 1969. 26 p.

Scala Records

J254   Elfström, Mats. Scala [complete discography]. (Nationalfonotekets diskografier 2) Stockholm, Kungliga Biblioteket, 1967. 79 p. In Swedish.

Sonora Records

J255   Englund, Björn. Sonora I. 8000-serien. (Nationalfonotekets diskografier 4) Stockholm, Kungliga Biblioteket, 1968. 15 p. In Swedish. Contains some jazz but mainly popular music.

J256   Englund, Björn. Sonora II. Swing-serien. (Nationalfonotekets diskografier 5) Stockholm, Kungliga Biblioteket, 1968. 38 p. In Swedish.

J257   Englund, Björn. Sonora III. 1000-serien. (Nationalfonotekets diskografier 6) Stockholm, Kungliga Biblioteket, 1968. 79 p. In Swedish. Contains some jazz but mainly popular and semi-classical music.

J258   Englund, Björn. Sonora IV. E 5000-serien, 6000-serien, 9000-serien, K 9500-serien. (Nationalfonotekets diskografier 8) Stockholm, Kungliga Biblioteket, 1968. 35 p. In Swedish. Contains some jazz but mainly popular music.

Strand Records

J259   Jazz on the Strand label. *Matrix*, #75 (Feb. 1968), 6.

Superior Records

J260   Kay, G. W. The Superior catalog. *Record Research*, #38 (Oct. 1961), 10-11; #39 (Nov. 1961), 19; #41 (Feb. 1962), 11; #47 (Nov. 1962), 19.

Tempo Records

J261   The Tempo label. *Matrix*, #45 (Feb. 1963), 11-14; #46 (Apr. 1963), 15-20.

Ultraphon Records

J262   Elfström, Mats. Ultraphon. (Nationalfonotekets diskografier 3) Stockholm, Kungliga Biblioteket, 1968. 15 p. In Swedish. Contains very little jazz.

Victor Records

J263   Rust, Brian A. L. The Victor master book, volume 2: 1925-1936. Hatch End, Middlesex,The Author, 1969; Stanhope, N.J., Walter C. Allen, 1970. 776 p.

Vocalion Records

J264   Cox, A. G. Discography of the Vocalion swing series, 1936 to 1940. *Jazz Journal*, XIX (Mar. 1966), 22-23; (Apr. 1966), 17-18; (May 1966), 25-26; (June 1966), 38-39.

J265   Hayes, Jim. Vocalion discographical artist catalogue. (S) 1.5000 C 0001, V 1000 series. Liverpool, Hayes, 1969.

World Records

J266   Kressley, D. Catalog of World transcriptions (1933 to 1963). *Record Research*, #89 (Mar. 1968), 1-8; #90 (May 1968), 6-7; #91 (July 1968), 5; #92 (Sep. 1968), 5; #93 (Nov. 1968), 8-10.

SECTION E

JAZZ AND BLUES PERFORMER DISCOGRAPHY

ADDERLEY, "CANNONBALL" (JULIAN EDWIN; alto sax, tenor sax, trumpet, clarinet, flute)

J267   Jepsen, Jørgen Grunnet. Discography of Cannonball Adderley/John Coltrane. Brande, Debut Records, 1959. 32 p.

ADDISON, BERNARD (guitar)

J268   Eyle, Willem Frederik van. Discography of Bernard Addison. Zaandam, van Eyle, 1966. 7 p.

ALLEN, ED (EDWARD; trumpet)

J269   Eyle, Willem Frederik van. Discography of Ed Allen. Zaandam, van Eyle, 1966. 9 p.

ALLEN, "RED" (HENRY, JR.; trumpet, singer)

J270   Eyle, Willem Frederik van. Discography of Henry Red Allen. Zaandam, van Eyle, 1966. 24 p.

ALVIS, HAYES (bass)

J271   Eyle, Willem Frederik van. Discography of Hayes Alvis. Zaandam, van Eyle, 1966. 11 p.

AMBROSE, BERT (leader)

J272   Rust, Brian A. L. Bert Ambrose: a discography. *Recorded Sound*,
        #21 (Jan. 1966), 26-29; #22-23 (Apr.-July 1966), 79-87.

AMMONS, ALBERT (piano)

J273   Eyle, Willem Frederik van. Discography of Albert Ammons. Zaandam,
        van Eyle, 1966. 4 p.

ANDERSON, CAT (WILLIAM ALONZO; trumpet)

J274   Bakalas, A. 'Cat' Anderson. *Le Point du Jazz*, #6 (Mar. 1972), 65-70.
        In French.

J275   Eyle, Willem Frederik van. Discography of Cat Anderson. Zaandam,
        van Eyle, 1966. 17 p.

        Eyle, Willem Frederik van. Discography of Cat Anderson. Rev. ed.
        Zaandam, van Eyle, 1966. 17 p.

ANDERSON, IVIE (or IVY; singer)

J276   Eyle, Willem Frederik van. Discography of Ivy Anderson. Zaandam,
        van Eyle, 1966. 4 p.

ARCHEY, JIMMY (JAMES; trombone)

J277   Eyle, Willem Frederik van. Discography of Jimmy Archey. Zaandam,
        van Eyle, 1966. 14 p.

ARMSTRONG, LOUIS "SATCHMO" (DANIEL LOUIS; trumpet, singer, leader)

J278   Eyle, Willem Frederik van. Discography of Louis Armstrong 1930-
        1947. Zaandam, van Eyle, 1966. 13 p.

J279   Jepsen, Jørgen Grunnet. Discography of Louis Armstrong. [Three
        volumes cover respectively 1923-1931, 1932-1946, and 1947-1960.]
        Brande, Debut Records, 1959. 3 v. (26 p., 19 p., 24 p.)

        Jepsen, Jørgen Grunnet. Discography of Louis Armstrong. 2d rev. ed.
        Brande, Debut Records, 1960. 3v. (27 p., 20 p., 25 p.)

        Jepsen, Jørgen Grunnet. New rev. ed. Holte, Knudsen, 196– ?

J280   Jones, Max, and John Chilton. Louis; the Louis Armstrong story, 1900-1971. London, Studio Vista; Boston, Little, Brown, 1971. 256 p. "Louis on record" [discographical essay by John Chilton]: pp. 221-247.

J281   Jones, Max, John Chilton, and Leonard Feather. Salute to Satchmo. London, I. P. C. Specialist & Professional Press, 1970. 155 p. Includes discography.

J282   Louis Satchmo Armstrong—jazz. Brussels, Siemens, ca. 1964. 9 p. Includes discography.

J283   Panassié, Hugues. Louis Armstrong. Paris, Nouvelles éditions latines, 1969. 224 p. In French. Includes discography.

J284   Satchmo, a musical autobiography of Louis Armstrong. Decca DXM 155 (DL 8604-8607), 1963. 4 records with notes. Discographical notes (11 p.) bound in container.

ARNOLD, KOKOMO (singer, guitar)

J285   Oliver, Paul, and J. H. Parsons. Kokomo Arnold discography. *Jazz Monthly*, VIII (May 1962), 15; (June 1962), 7.

ASMUSSEN, SVEND (violin)

J286   Henius, Bent. Svend Asmussen. København, Erichsen, 1962. 80 p. In Danish. Includes discography.

AUSTRIAN ALL STARS

J287   Kraner, Dietrich Heinz. The Austrian All Stars. A brief history and a short, but complete discography. *Jazz Studies*, I (#1, 1967), 8-9.

BAKER, CHET (CHESNEY H.; trumpet, singer)

J288   Morgan, Alun. A Chet Baker discography. *Jazz Monthly*, IX (May 1963), 24-27.

BARBIERI, GATO (LEANDRO; tenor sax)

J289   Vincent, B. Gato Barbieri, discographie. *Jazz Hot*, #242 (Aug.-Sep. 1968), 20. In French.

BARNES, ÉMILE (clarinet)

J290   Stenbeck, L. Émile Barnes diskografi. *Orkester Journalen*, XXXI
(Jan. 1963), 34. In Swedish.

BARNET, CHARLIE (CHARLES DALY; alto sax, tenor sax, soprano sax, leader)

J291   Edwards, Ernie, George Hall, and Bill Korst. Charlie Barnet and his
orchestra. Whittier, Calif., Erngeobil, 1965. 36 p.

Edwards, Ernie, George Hall, and Bill Korst. Charlie Barnet and his
orchestra. Rev. ed. Whittier, Calif., Erngeobil, 1967. 40 p.

J292   Hall, George. Charlie Barnet and his corhestra. Rev. ed. Maryland,
Jazz Discographies Unlimited, 1971. 52 p.

BASIE, COUNT (WILLIAM; leader, piano, organ, composer)

J293   Gelly, D. The Count Basie Octet. *Jazz Monthly*, IX (July 1963),
9-11.

J294   Jepsen, Jørgen Grunnet. A discography of Count Basie, vol. 2:
1951-1968. [New ed.] København, Knudsen, 1969. 44 p.

J295   Scherman, Bo, and Carl A. Haellstroem. A discography of Count
Basie, vol. 1: 1929-1950. København, Knudsen, 1969. 52 p.

BAUER, BILLY (WILLIAM HENRY; guitar)

J296   Eyle, Willem Frederik van. Discography of Billy Bauer. Zaandam,
van Eyle, 1966. 19 p.

BEATLES

J297   DiLello, Richard. The longest cocktail party; an insider's diary of
the Beatles, their million-dollar Apple empire, and its wild rise and
fall. Chicago, Playboy Press, 1972. 325 p. Discography: pp. 309-322.

J298   Hansen, Jeppe. Beatles-diskografi 1961-1972. Slagelse, Slagelse
Centralbibliotek, 1973. 33 p. In Danish.

BECHET, SIDNEY (soprano sax, clarinet)

J299   Bechet, Sidney. Treat it gentle; an autobiography. London, Transworld, 1964. 256 p. Discography by David Mylne: pp. 221-240.

J300   Berg, Arne. Sidney Bechet. Stockholm, Berg, 196–?

J301   Eyle, Willem Frederik van. Discography of Sidney Bechet. Zaandam, van Eyle, 1966. 26 p.

J302   Jepsen, Jørgen Grunnet. Sidney Bechet Discography. Lübbecke, Uhle & Kleimann, 1962. 38 p.

J303   Mauerer, Hans J. Sidney Bechet discography. New rev. ed. København, Knudsen, 1970. 86 p.

BEIDERBECKE, BIX (LEON BISMARCK; cornet, piano, composer)

J304   Evans, Phil. Bio-discography of Bix Beiderbecke. [Precise title and details of this work not found.]

J305   Eyle, Willem Frederik van. Discography of Bix Beiderbecke. Zaandam, van Eyle, 1966. 10 p.

J306   Martin, T. E. Playback; BBB & Co. *Jazz Monthly*, X (Oct. 1964), 9.

BENEKE, "TEX" (GORDON; tenor sax, leader)

J307   Edwards, Ernie, George Hall, and Bill Korst. Tex Beneke discography. Whittier, Calif., Erngeobil, 196–? 16 p.

BERMAN, "SONNY" (SAUL; trumpet)

J308   Eyle, Willem Frederik van. Discography of Sonny Berman. Zaandam, van Eyle, 1966. 6 p.

       Eyle, Willem Frederik van. Discography of Sonny Berman. Rev. ed. Zaandam, van Eyle, 1966. 6 p.

BERRY, "CHU" (LEON; tenor sax)

J309   Eyle, Willem Frederik van. Discography of Chu Berry. Zaandam, van Eyle, 1966. 12 p.

BIG BANDS

J310   Edwards, Ernie, George Hall, and Bill Korst. Big bands discography.
        Whittier, Calif., Erngeobil, 1965-69. 7 v. [Contents of the volumes
        analyzed individually in J311-J317 below.]

J311   Edwards, Ernie, George Hall, and Bill Korst. Big bands discography.
        [Volume I: Buddy De Franco, Herbie Fields, Bob Keene, Bunny
        Berigan, Jack Jenny, Eddie Miller, Vido Musso, Charlie Ventura,
        Will Bradley, Big Eighteen, Lee Castle, Fred Dale, Jerry Gray.]
        Whittier Calif., Erngeobil, 1965. 42 p.

J312   Edwards, Ernie, George Hall, and Bill Korst, Big bands discography.
        [Volume II: Tex Beneke, Randy Brooks, Bernie Mann, Urbie Green,
        Dan Terry, Jerry Gray, Jimmy Zito.] Whittier, Calif., Erngeobil,
        1965. 30 p.

J313   Edwards, Ernie, George Hall, and Bill Korst. Big bands discography.
        [Volume III: Tommy Alexander, Georgie Auld, Danny Belloc,
        Randy Brooks, Ike Carpenter, Commanders, Willis Conover, Jimmy
        Cook, Sonny Dunham, Herbie Fields, Jack Kane, Bob Keene, Bernie
        Mann, Billie Rogers, Bob Rogers, Buddy Ryland, Roy Stevens,
        Jerry Wald, Gene Williams, Keith Williams, Gerald Wilson.] Whittier,
        Calif., Erngeobil, 1965. 35 p.

J314   Edwards, Ernie, George Hall, and Bill Korst. Big bands discography.
        [Volume IV: Bunny Berigan, Gus Bivona, Will Bradley, Sonny Burke,
        Al Cooper, Buddy De Franco, Roy Eldridge, Bob Florence, Ken
        Hana, Jack Jenny, Vido Musso, Buddy Rich, Shorty Sherock, Clark
        Terry, Charlie Ventura, Jimmy Zito, and several miscellaneous listings.]
        Whittier, Calif., Erngeobil, 1966. 50 p.

J315   Edwards, Ernie, George Hall, and Bill Korst. Big bands discography.
        [Volume V: Ike Carpenter, Warren Covington, Sam Donahue, Urbie
        Green, Erskine Hawkins, Elliot Lawrence, Bernie Mann, Hal McIntyre,
        Eddie Miller, Teddy Powell, Sal Salvador, Gene Williams, and
        miscellaneous listings.] Whittier, Calif., Erngeobil, 1967. 65 p.

J316   Edwards, Ernie, George Hall, and Bill Korst. Big bands discography.
        [Volume VI: Danny Belloc and His Orchestra, The Sauter-Finegan
        Orchestra, The Commanders, Freddie Slack and His Orchestra,
        Ralph Flanagan and His Orchestra, Larry Sonn and His Orchestra,
        Terry Gibbs Big Band, Earle Spencer and His Orchestra, Buddy
        Morrow and His Orchestra, and other miscellaneous listings.]
        Whitter, Calif., Erngeobil, 1968. 60 p.

J317   Edwards, Ernie, George Hall, and Bill Korst. Big bands discography. [Volume VII: Bob Chester, Larry Clinton, Sonny Dunham, Hudson-Delange, Will Hudson, Eddie Delange, and Teddy Powell.] Whittier, Calif., Erngeobil, 1969.

J318   Jazz Statistics/Jazz Publications, ed. Discography of big bands from the twenties. [Volume I: Oliver Cobb, Lloyd Hunter, Neal Montgomery, Grant Moore, Curtis Mosby, Dave Nelson, Plantation Orchestra, Jimmy Powell, Alonzo Ross, Savoy Bearcats, Seminole Syncopators, Charlie Skeete, Six Scrambled Eggs, Leroy Smith, Reb Spikes.] Basel, Jazz Statistics/Jazz Publications, 196– ? 8 p. [This was a special publication for subscribers of *Swiss Jazz Notes*.]

J319   Jazz Statistics/Jazz Publications, ed. Discography of big bands from the twenties. [Volume II: Joe Steele, Sammy Stewart, Jesse Stone, Alphonse Trent, Speed Webb, Zack White, Russell Wooding, Sam Wooding.] Basel, Jazz Statistics/Jazz Publications, 196– ? 8 p. [This was a special publication for subscribers of *Swiss Jazz Notes*.]

BISHOP, WALTER, JR. (piano)

J320   Gardner, M., and F. Gibson. Walter Bishop Junior discography. *Jazz Journal*, XVII (Oct. 1964), 29; (Nov. 1964), 24+

BLANTON, JIMMY (bass)

J321   Eyle, Willem Frederik van. Discography of Jimmy Blanton. Zaandam, van Eyle, 1966. 4 p.

J322   Hoefer, G. Hot box [discography of Jimmy Blanton]. *Down Beat*, XXIX (Feb. 1, 1962), 36-37.

BLUE MOUNTAINEERS

J323   Badrock, A., and T. Lamont. The Blue Mountaineers. *Matrix*, #50 (Dec. 1963), 15-17.

BLYTHE, JIMMY (piano)

J324   Berg, Arne. Jimmy Blythe including piano-rollography, Earl Bostic, Graeme Bell, Dave Brubeck. Stockholm, Berg, 196– ?

J325   Eyle, Willem Frederik van. Discography of Jimmy Blythe. Zaandam, van Eyle, 1966. 8 p.

BOTHWELL, JOHNNY (alto sax)

J326   Edwards, Ernie. Johnny Bothwell, a discography. *Matrix*, #62 (Dec. 1965), 9-11.

BRADLEY, WILL (real name, WILBUR SCHWICHTENBERG; trombone, composer, leader)

J327   Edwards, Ernie. Will Bradley discography. Whittier, Calif., Erngeobil, 196– ? 12 p.

BRADSHAW, "TINY" (MYRON; cello, leader)

J328   Mohr, Kurt. Discography of Tiny Bradshaw. Reinach, Jazz Publications, 1961. 16 p.

BRAFF, RUBY (REUBEN; trumpet)

J329   Hall, George. A discography of Reuben "Ruby" Braff. *Matrix*, #54 (Aug. 1964), 3-12.

J330   Hall, George. Ruby Braff. Whittier, Calif., Erngeobil, 1965. 14 p.

BROONZY, "BIG BILL" (WILLIAM LEE CONLEY; singer, guitar)

J331   Broonzy, William. Big Bill blues; William Broonzy's story as told to Yannick Bruynoghe. New York, Oak Publications, 1964. 176 p. [First published in 1955.] Discography by Albert J. McCarthy: pp. 153-173.

BROWN, BOYCE (alto sax)

J332   Eyle, Willem Frederik van. Discography of Boyce Brown. Zaandam, van Eyle, 1966. 2 p.

BROWN, CLIFFORD (trumpet)

J333   Eyle, Willem Frederik van. Discography of Clifford Brown. Zaandam, van Eyle, 1966. 6 p.

J334   Jepsen, Jørgen Grunnet. Clifford Brown: a discography. København, Jepsen, 1957. 9 p.

J335   Jepsen, Jørgen Grunnet. Discography of Fats Navarro/Clifford Brown. Brande, Debut Records, 1960. 14 p., 12 p.

J336   Montalbano, Pierre. Biographie discographie Clifford Brown. Marseilles, Jazz Club Aix-Marseille, 1969. 13 p. In French.

BROWN, LES (LESTER RAYMOND; leader)

J337   Edwards, Ernie, George Hall, and Bill Korst. Les Brown and His Band of Renown. Whittier, Calif., Erngeobil, 1966. 53 p.

J338   Edwards, Ernie, George Hall, and Bill Korst. Les Brown discography 1936-1964. Whittier, Calif., Erngeobil, 1965. 52 p.

Edwards, Ernie, George Hall, and Bill Korst. Les Brown discography 1936-1964. 2d ed. Whittier, Calif., Erngeobil, 1965. 52 p.

Edwards, Ernie, George Hall, and Bill Korst. Les Brown discography 1936-1964. 3d ed. Whittier, Calif., Erngeobil, 1965. 52 p.

BROWN, MARION, JR. (alto sax)

J339   Tepperman, B. Marion Brown discography. *Jazz Monthly*, #187 (Sep. 1970), 19-21.

BROWN, PETE (JAMES OSTEND; alto sax, tenor sax)

J340   Eyle, Willem Frederik van. Discography of Pete Brown. Zaandam, van Eyle, 1966. 7 p.

BRUBECK, DAVE (DAVID W.; piano, composer, leader)

J341   Jepsen, Jørgen Grunnet. Dave Brubeck: a discography. København, Jepsen, 1957. 8 p.

BUNN, TEDDY (THEODORE; guitar)

J342   Tanner, P. A discography of Teddy Bunn. *Jazz Journal*, XXIV (Dec. 1971), 28-29.

BUTTERFIELD, BILLY (CHARLES WILLIAM; trumpet)

J343   Edwards, Ernie. Billy Butterfield, a name listing. *Matrix*, #53 (June 1964), 3-13.

BYAS, DON (CARLOS WESLEY; tenor sax)

J344   Eyle, Willem Frederik van. Discography of Don Byas. Zaandam, van Eyle, 1966. 25 p.

BYRD, DONALD (trumpet)

J345   Jepsen, Jørgen Grunnet. Donald Byrd: a discography. København, Jepsen, 1957. 13 p.

CARR, IAN (trumpet, fluegelhorn)

J346   Priestley, B. Ian Carr. *Jazz Monthly*, XII (Oct. 1966), 2-5.

CELESTIN, "PAPA" (OSCAR; cornet, leader)

J347   Eyle, Willem Frederik van. Discography of (Oscar) Papa Celestin. Zaandam, van Eyle, 1966. 2 p.

Eyle, Willem Frederik van. Discography of (Oscar) Papa Celestin. Rev. ed. Zaandam, van Eyle, 1966. 2 p.

CHALOFF, SERGE (baritone sax)

J348   Eyle, Willem Frederik van. Discography of Serge Chaloff. Zaandam, van Eyle, 1966. 7 p.

Eyle, Willem Frederik van. Discography of Serge Chaloff. Rev. ed. Zaandam, van Eyle, 1966. 7 p.

CHARLES, RAY (piano, singer, composer, sax)

J349   Mohr, K., and M. Chauvard. Discographie complète de Ray Charles. *Jazz Hot*, #176 (May 1962), 8-9; #177 (June 1962), 37; #178 (July-Aug. 1962), 44. In French.

J350   Ray Charles discography. *Billboard*, LXXVIII (Oct. 15, 1966), RC10.

CHITTISON, HERMAN (piano)

J351   Eyle, Willem Frederik van. Discography of Herman Chittison. Zaandam, van Eyle, 1966. 5 p.

CHRISTIAN, CHARLIE (CHARLES; guitar)

J352   Eyle, Willem Frederik van. Discography of Charlie Christian. Zaandam, van Eyle, 1966. 7 p.

J353   Jepsen, Jørgen Grunnet. Charlie Christian. København, Jepsen, 1957. 9 p.

CLAYTON, "BUCK" (WILBUR; trumpet, composer)

J354   Jepsen, Jørgen Grunnet. Buck Clayton 1949-1957. København, Jepsen, 1957. 15 p.

COBB, ARNETT CLEOPHUS (tenor sax)

J355   Demeusy, Bertrand, and Otto Flückiger. Arnett Cobb, with discography; the wild man of the tenor sax. Basel, Jazz Publications, 1962. 22 p.

COBB, JUNIE C. (piano, leader)

J356   Dürr, C. U. Junie Cobb; a discography. *Matrix*, #56 (Dec. 1964), 10-12.

J357   Dürr, C. U. Junie C. Cobb. *Record Research*, #75 (Apr. 1966), 4-5.

COLE, NAT "KING" (real name, NATHANIEL COLES; singer, piano, leader)

J358   Cole, Maria, and Louie Robinson. Nat King Cole; an intimate biography. New York, W. Morrow, 1971. 184 p. Discography: pp. 163-184.

J359   Hall, George. Nat "King" Cole Trio. Whittier, Calif., Erngeobil, 1965. 18 p.

J360   Teubig, Klaus. Nat "King" Cole Discographie 1963-1953. Hamburg, Teubig, 1964. 16 p. In German.

COLEMAN, BILL (WILLIAM JOHNSON; trumpet)

J361   Chilton, John. Bill Coleman on record. London, Lane, 1966. 18 p.

COLEMAN, ORNETTE (alto sax, composer)

J362   Walker, M. Ornette Coleman. *Jazz Monthly*, XII (May 1966), 24-25.

COLTRANE, JOHN WILLIAM (tenor sax)

J363   Fresia, E. Discografia [John Coltrane and Oscar Peterson 1961-1963]. *Musica Jazz*, XX (Feb. 1964), 42-43. In Italian.

J364   Jepsen, Jørgen Grunnet. A discography of John Coltrane. Rev. ed. København, Knudsen, 1969. 35 p.

J365   Kofsky, Frank, Bob Thiele, and John Norris. John Coltrane memorial. Toronto, Coda, 1968. Includes discography.

J366   Swoboda, Hubert. The John Coltrane Discographie 1949-1967. Stuttgart, Modern Jazz Series, 1968. 40 p. In German.

J367   Walker, M., and E. Raben. John Coltrane. *Jazz Monthly*, XII (Aug. 1966), 11-13; (Sep. 1966), 30-31; (Oct. 1966), 23-24; (Nov. 1966), 29-31.

CONNOLLY, DOLLY

J368   Kunstadt, L., and B. Colton. Dolly Connolly discography. *Record Research*, #84 (June 1967), 7.

COON-SANDERS ORCHESTRA (led by Carlton Coon and Joe "Red" Sanders)

J369   Rettburg, H. Coon-Sanders discography. *Second Line*, XIII (#3-4, 1962), 20+

CRISS, SONNY (WILLIAM; alto sax)

J370   Gardner, M. Sonny Criss discography. *Discographical Forum*, #16 (Jan. 1970), 9-12.

CROSBY, BOB (GEORGE ROBERT; singer, leader)

J371　Eyle, Willem Frederik van. Discography of Bob Crosby. Zaandam, van Eyle, 1966. 22 p.

CRUDUP, ARTHUR "BIG BOY" (guitar, singer)

J372　Coller, D. Arthur "Big Boy" Crudup. *Matrix*, #51 (Feb. 1964), 3-6.

DAMERON, TADD (TADLEY EWING; piano, composer)

J373　Eyle, Willem Frederik van. Discography of Tad [sic] Dameron. Zaandam, van Eyle, 1966. 9 p.

J374　Jazz Publications, ed. Discography of Tadd Dameron. Basel, Jazz Publications, 1962. 8 p.

J375　Morgan, Alun. The Tadd Dameron Band. *Jazz Monthly*, VIII (Apr. 1962), 3-6.

DANKWORTH, JOHNNY (alto sax)

J376　A Johnny Dankworth discography. *Jazz Monthly*, IX (Feb. 1964), 3-4; (Mar. 1964), 3-5.

DASH, JULIAN (ST. JULIAN BENNETT; tenor sax)

J377　Demeusy, B. The Julian Dash story. *Jazz Journal*, XVII (Apr. 1964), 12-13.

DAVENPORT, CHARLES "COW COW" (piano, singer)

J378　Eyle, Willem Frederik van. Discography of Cow Cow Davenport. Zaandam, van Eyle, 1966. 4 p.

Eyle, Willem Frederik van. Discography of Cow Cow Davenport. Rev. ed. Zaandam, van Eyle, 1966. 4 p.

DAVIS, MILES DEWEY, JR. (trumpet, fluegelhorn, composer, leader)

J379   Jepsen, Jørgen Grunnet. A discography of Miles Davis. Rev. ed. København, Knudsen, 1969. 40 p.

DAVISON, WILD BILL (WILLIAM; cornet, leader)

J380   Eyle, Willem Frederik van. Discography of Wild Bill Davison. Zaandam, van Eyle, 1966. 12 p.

DE ARANGO, BILL (WILLIAM; guitar)

J381   Eyle, Willem Frederik van. Discography of Bill de Arango. Zaandam, van Eyle, 1966. 3 p.

DODDS, "BABY" (WARREN; drums)

J382   Eyle, Willem Frederik van. Discography of Baby Dodds. Zaandam, van Eyle, 1966. 13 p.

Eyle, Willem Frederik van. Discography of Baby Dodds. Rev. ed. Zaandam, van Eyle, 1966. 13 p.

DODDS, JOHNNY (clarinet)

J383   Arx, R. von. Johnny Dodds. *Matrix*, #72-73 (Sep. 1967), 3-37.

J384   Eyle, Willem Frederik van. Discography of Johnny Dodds. Zaandam, van Eyle, 1966. 11 p.

Eyle, Willem Frederik van. Discography of Johnny Dodds. Rev. ed. Zaandam, van Eyle, 1966. 11 p.

DOLPHY, ERIC ALLAN (alto sax, clarinet, flute, bass clarinet)

J385   Kraner, Dietrich Heinz. The Eric Dolphy discography 1958-1964. Graz, Kraner, 1967. 14 p.

J386   Raben, E. Erich Dolphy. *Musica Jazz*, XXI (Nov. 1965), 36-37. In Italian.

J387   Walker, M. Eric Dolphy [discography]. *Jazz Monthly*, XI (Jan. 1966), 30-31; (Feb. 1966), 30-31; (Mar. 1966), 29.

DOMINQUE, NATTY (ANATIE; trumpet)

J388   Eyle, Willem Frederik van. Discography of Natty Dominique. Zaandam, van Eyle, 1966. 3 p.

Eyle, Willem Frederik van. Discography of Natty Dominique. Rev. ed. Zaandam, van Eyle, 1966. 3 p.

DORSEY, JIMMY (JAMES; clarinet, alto sax, leader)

J389   Edwards, Ernie, George Hall, and Bill Korst. Jimmy Dorsey and His Orchestra; a complete discography 1953-1957. Whittier, Calif., Erngeobil, 1966. 30 p.

DUNN, JOHNNY (trumpet)

J390   Eyle, Willem Frederik van. Discography of Johnny Dunn. Zaandam, van Eyle, 1966. 5 p.

DUPREE, CHAMPION JACK (piano, singer)

J391   Jazz Publications, ed. Discography of Champion Jack Dupree. Basel, Jazz Publications, 1961. 10 p.

EICHWALD, HAAKAN VON

J392   Englund, Björn. A discography of Haakan von Eichwald. *Matrix*, #50 (Dec. 1963), 13-14.

ELLINGTON, "DUKE" (EDWARD KENNEDY; composer, leader, piano)

J393   Connor, Donald Russell, and others. Twenty years of the Duke. Part 1: 1933-1955. Carnegie, Penn., Pope's Records Unlimited, 1966. 12 p.

J394   Dance, Stanley. The world of Duke Ellington. New York, C. Scribner's Sons, 1970. 311 p. Discography: pp. 293-294.

J395   Fresia, E. Discografia [Duke Ellington]. *Musica Jazz*, XIX (Oct. 1963), 50-51. In Italian.

J396   Jepsen, Jørgen Grunnet. Discography of Duke Ellington. [Three volumes covering respectively 1925-1936, 1937-1946, and 1947-1960.] Brande, Debut Records, 1959-1960. 3v. (24 p., 25 p., 27 p.)

J397   Lambert, G. E. Microgroove re-issues of rare early Ellington recordings. *Jazz Monthly*, XIII (Nov. 1967), 29-30.

J398   Massagli, Luciano, Liborio Pusateri, and Giovanni M. Volonté. Duke
Ellington's story on records, vol. 1: 1925-1931. Milano, L. Pusateri,
1966. 66 p.

J399   Massagli, Luciano, Liborio Pusateri, and Giovanni M. Volonté. Duke
Ellington's story on records, vol. 2: 1932-1938. Milano, Musica Jazz;
London, P. Seago, 1966. 78 p.

J400   Massagli, Luciano, Liborio Pusateri, and Giovanni M. Volonté. Duke
Ellington's story on records, vol. 3: 1939-1942. Milano, Musica Jazz;
London, P. Seago, 1967. 68 p.

J401   Massagli, Luciano, Liborio Pusateri, and Giovanni M. Volonté. Duke
Ellington's story on records, vol. 4: 1943-1944. Milano, Musica Jazz,
1968. 71 p.

J402   Massagli, Luciano, Liborio Pusateri, and Giovanni M. Volonté. Duke
Ellington's story on records, vol. 5: 1945. Milano, Musica Jazz, 1968.
93 p.

J403   Massagli, Luciano, Liborio Pusateri, and Giovanni M. Volonté. Duke
Ellington's story on records, vol. 6: 1946. London, P. Seago, 1971.

J404   Pope's Records, ed. Duke Ellington discography. Carnegie, Penn.,
Pope's Records, ca. 1967. 24 p.

J405   Reid, John D. Duke Ellington discography on Victor and Bluebird
records. [No imprint.] 23 p.

J406   Sanfilippo, Luigi. General catalog of Duke Ellington's recorded
music. Palermo, New Jazz Society, 1964. 70 p.

Sanfilippo, Luigi. General catalog of Duke Ellington's recorded
music. 2d ed. Palermo, New Jazz Society, 1966. 112 p.

J407   Tollara, G., and L. Massagli. Discografia [Duke Ellington's Orchestra
1939-1943]. *Musica Jazz*, XVIII (June 1962), 42-44. In Italian.

EVANS, BILL (WILLIAM J.; piano, composer)

J408   Walker, M. Bill Evans. *Jazz Monthly*, XI (June 1965), 20-22;
(July 1965), 30-31; (Aug. 1965), 24-25; (Sep. 1965), 18-19.

EVANS, HERSCHEL (tenor sax)

J409   Eyle, Willem Frederik van. Discography of Herschel Evans. Zaandam, van Eyle, 1966. 7 p.

EVANS, "STOMP"

J410   Eyle, Willem Frederik van. Discography of Stomp Evans. Zaandam, van Eyle, 1966. 3 p.

FOSTER, "POPS" (GEORGE MURPHY; bass)

J411   Foster, George Murphy. Pops Foster; the autobiography of a New Orleans jazzman as told to Tom Stoddard. Berkeley, University of California Press, 1971. 208 p. "Pops Foster discography, 1924-1940" (by Brian Rust): pp. 182-197.

FREDRIKSSON, BÖRJE (tenor sax, leader)

J412   Hansson, L. Börje Fredriksson diskografi. *Orkester Journalen*, XXXVI (Nov. 1968), 30. In Swedish.

GETZ, STAN (STANLEY; tenor sax)

J413   Edwards, Ernie. Stan Getz. *Jazz Monthly*, X (Aug. 1964), 8-9; (Oct. 1964), 23-27.

J414   Walker, Malcolm. Stan Getz: a discography 1944-1955. London, Walker, 1957. 20 p.

GIBBS, TERRY (real name, JULIUS GUBENKO; vibes, piano, drums)

J415   Morgan, Alun. Terry Gibbs. *Jazz Monthly*, XI (July 1965), 12-18.

GILLESPIE, "DIZZY" (JOHN BIRKS; trumpet, composer, singer, leader)

J416   Edwards, Ernie, George Hall, and Bill Korst. Dizzy Gillespie big bands 1945-1950, 1955-1957. Whittier, Calif., Erngeobil, 1966. 10 p.

Edwards, Ernie, George Hall, and Bill Korst. Dizzy Gillespie big bands 1945-1950, 1955-1957. Rev. ed. Whittier, Calif., Erngeobil, 1966. 10 p.

J417   Eyle, Willem Frederik van. Discography of Dizzy Gillespie. Zaandam, van Eyle, 1966. 28 p.

J418   Jepsen, Jørgen Grunnet. A discography of Dizzy Gillespie. [Two volumes covering respectively 1937-1952 and 1953-1968.] København, Knudsen, 1969. 2v. (39 p., 30 p.)

GILLHAM, ART (piano)

J419   Backensto, W. Art Gillham the whispering pianist. *Record Research*, #49 (Mar. 1963), 3-5.

GLENN, LLOYD (piano)

J420   Demeusy, B. Lloyd Glenn, Texas pianist. *Jazz Journal*, XVIII (Oct. 1965), 12-13.

GOODMAN, BENNY (BENJAMIN DAVID; clarinet, leader)

J421   Connor, Donald Russell, and Warren W. Hicks. BG on the record; a bio-discography of Benny Goodman. New Rochelle, N.Y., Arlington House, 1969. 691 p. Biography with discographical commentary.

J422   Teubig, Klaus. Discographie of Benny Goodman's Music Festival Concerts [AFRS radio transcriptions 1946-1947]. Hamburg, Teubig, 1963. 6 p.

GRAY, JERRY (composer, leader)

J423   Edwards, Ernie, George Hall, and Bill Korst. Jerry Gray discography. Whittier, Calif., Erngeobil, 196– ? 14 p.

GRAY, WARDELL (tenor sax)

J424   Eyle, Willem Frederik van. Discography of Wardell Gray. Zaandam, van Eyle, 1966. 10 p.

J425   Jepsen, Jørgen Grunnet. Wardell Gray: a discography. København, Jepsen, 1957. 10 p.

GULDA, FRIEDRICH (piano)

J426   Kraner, Dietrich Heinz. Friedrich Gulda jazz discography. [Part I; the records; part II: broadcast and television recordings.] *Jazz Studies*, I (#2, 1967), 5-9; (#4, 1967), 2-6.

GULLIN, LARS (baritone sax, composer)

J427   Jepsen, Jørgen Grunnet. Lars Gullin. København, Jepsen, 1957.

J428   Jepsen, Jørgen Grunnet, and L. Hansson. Lars Gullin diskografi. *Orkester Journalen*, XXXIII (Apr. 1965), 16; (May 1965), 34; (June 1965), 30; (July-Aug. 1965), 29; (Oct. 1965), 33; (Nov. 1965), 33; (Dec. 1965), 44. In Swedish.

GUTHRIE, WOODY (singer)

J429   Yurchenco, Henrietta. A mighty hard road; the Woody Guthrie story. New York, McGraw-Hill, 1970. 159 p. Discography: pp. 155-156.

GUY, JOE (JOSEPH LUKE; trumpet)

J430   Eyle, Willem Frederik van. Discography of Joe Guy. Zaandam, van Eyle, 1966. 3 p.

HALL, EDMOND (clarinet)

J431   Jepsen, Jørgen Grunnet. Edmond Hall. København, Jepsen, 1957.

HAMPTON, LIONEL (vibraharp, drums, piano, leader)

J432   Demeusy, Bertrand, and Otto Flückiger. Discography of Lionel Hampton Orchestra 1954-1958. Basel, Jazz Publications, 1963. 30 p.

J433   Flückiger, Otto. Discography of Lionel Hampton Orchestra 1951-1953. Reinach, Jazz Publications, 1961. 22 p.

J434   Jepsen, Jørgen Grunnet. Lionel Hampton 1947-1957. København, Jepsen, 1957. 16 p.

HARRIS, BARRY DOYLE (piano)

J435   Gardner, M. Barry Harris. *Jazz Monthly*, XIII (Nov. 1967), 31; (Dec. 1967), 31.

HARRIS, BILL (WILLARD PALMER; trombone)

J436   Edwards, Ernie, George Hall, and Bill Korst. Bill Harris discography. Whittier, Calif., Erngeobil, 1966. 30 p.

HARRISON, JIMMY (JAMES HENRY; trombone)

J437   Eyle, Willem Frederik van. Discography of Jimmy Harrison. Zaandam, van Eyle, 1966. 5 p.

HAWKINS, COLEMAN "BEAN" (tenor sax)

J438   Eyle, Willem Frederik van. Discography of Coleman Hawkins. Zaandam, van Eyle, 1966. 46 p.

Eyle, Willem Frederik van. Discography of Coleman Hawkins. Rev. ed. Zaandam, van Eyle, 1966. 46 p.

J439   Jepsen, Jørgen Grunnet. Coleman Hawkins 1947-1957. København, Jepsen, 1957. 12 p.

J440   McCarthy, Albert J. Coleman Hawkins. London, Cassell, 1963. 90 p. Includes record list.

HAWKINS, ERSKINE RAMSAY (trumpet, leader)
HENDERSON, HORACE (piano, leader)

J441   Edwards, Ernie, George Hall, and Bill Korst. Erskine Hawkins-Horace Henderson discography. Whittier, Calif., Erngeobil, 1965. 10 p.

HENDERSON, JAMES FLETCHER ("SMACK"; leader, composer, piano)

J442   Allen, W. C. Hendersonia. *Record Research*, #55 (Sep. 1963), 14; #56 (Nov. 1963), 12.

HENDERSON, JOE (tenor sax, leader)

J443   Gardner, M. Joe Henderson. *Jazz Monthly*, XIII (June 1967), 31.

HENRICHSEN, BØRGE ROGER (piano, trumpet, leader)

J444   Jørgensen, Birger. Børge Roger Henrichsen. København, C. Erichsen, 1962. 80 p. In Danish. Discography: pp. 68-75.

HENRY, ERNIE (ERNEST ALBERT; alto sax)

J445   Eyle, Willem Frederik van. Discography of Ernie Henry. Zaandam, van Eyle, 1966. 4 p.

HERMAN, WOODY (WOODROW CHARLES; clarinet, alto sax, leader, singer)

J446   Edwards, Ernie. Woody Herman discography, vol. 1: 1932-1946. Brande, Debut Records, 1959. 20 p.

J447   Edwards, Ernie. Woody Herman discography, vol. 2: 1946-1958. Brande, Debut Records, 1961. 32 p.

J448   Edwards, Ernie, George Hall, and Bill Korst. Woody Herman discography, vol. 1: 1932-1946. Whittier, Calif., Erngeobil, 1965. 26 p.

J449   Edwards, Ernie, George Hall, and Bill Korst. Woody Herman discography, vol. 2: 1946-1961. Whittier, Calif., Erngeobil, 1965. 32 p.

J450   Edwards, Ernie, George Hall, and Bill Korst. Woody Herman discography, vol. 3: 1959-1965. Whittier, Calif., Erngeobil, 1966. 17 p.

J451   Edwards, Ernie, George Hall, and Bill Korst. Woody Herman discography, vol. 1: 1932-1946. Whittier, Calif., Erngeobil, 1969.

J452   Edwards, Ernie, George Hall, Bill Korst, and other contributors. Woody Herman Alumni, vol. 1. [Eddie Bert, Conte Candoli, Serge Chaloff, Jerry Coker, Dick Collins, Don Fagerquist, Med Flory, Conrad Gozzo, Bob Graf, Urbie Green, Bill Harris, Herbie Haymer, Chubby Jackson, Richie Kamuca, Don Lanphere, Stan Levey, Lou Levey, Ray Linn, Sal Nistico, Cecil Payne, Flip Phillips, Nat Pierce, Red Rodney, Dick Ruedebusch, Herbie Steward, Cy Touff, plus Tony Aless, Joe Alexander, Billy Bauer, Bill Berry, Bill Bradley, Jimmy Cook, Mickey Folus, Art Mardigan, Dave Matthews, Jay

Migliori, Frank Rehak, Buddy Savitt, Dave Tough, Nick Travis.]
Whittier, Calif., Erngeobil, 1969. 61 p.

J453   Jepsen, Jørgen Grunnet. Woody Herman 1947-1957. København,
Jepsen, 1957.

HILL, ALEX (ALEXANDER; piano, composer)

J454   Eyle, Willem Frederik van. Discography of Alex Hill. Zaandam, van
Eyle, 1966. 2 p.

HODES, ART (ARTHUR W.; piano)

J455   Fairchild, R. Discography of Art Hodes. Ontario, Calif., Fairchild,
1962. 38 p.

HODGES, JOHNNY "RABBIT" (JOHN CORNELIUS; alto sax)

J456   Jepsen, Jørgen Grunnet. Johnny Hodges without Ellington. København, Jepsen, 1957. 14 p.

HÖLLERHAGEN, ERNST (clarinet, leader)

J457   Lehrer, Wolf. Ernst Höllerhagen. Eine Skizze. Bio-Diskographie.
Wanne-Eickel, Conrad, 1964. 21 p. In German.

J458   Muth, Wolfgang. Ernst Höllerhagen, ein deutscher Jazzmusiker.
Magdeburg, Jazz im Club, 1964. 28 p. In German.

HOLIDAY, BILLIE "LADY DAY" (real name, ELEANOR GOUGH McKAY; singer)

J459   Eyle, Willem Frederik van. Discography of Billie Holiday. Zaandam,
van Eyle, 1966. 17 p.

J460   Holiday, Billie, and William Dufty. Lady sings the blues. [Translation
of the English edition (New York, 1956) by Martin Schouten.]
Utrecht, Bruna, 1968. 192 p. In Dutch. Includes discography.

J461   Holiday, Billie, and William Dufty. Schwarze Lady, sings the Blues.
[Translation of *Lady sings the blues* (New York, 1956) by Werner
Burkhardt.] Hamburg, Rowohlt, 1964. 172 p. In German. Includes
discography.

J462   Jepsen, Jørgen Grunnet. Billie Holiday. New rev. ed. København,
Knudsen, 1969. 37 p.

HOPE, LYNN (saxophones)

J463   Rotante, A. Discography of Lynn Hope. *Record Research*, #79 (Oct. 1966), 9.

HOPKINS, SAM "LIGHTNIN'" (singer, guitar)

J464   Berg, Arne. Jazz rhythm & blues. Panorama special Lightnin' Hopkins discography. Stockholm, Berg, 196– ?

J465   Holt, John, Frank Scott, and Paul Oliver. Lightnin' Hopkins story and discography. London, Holt, 1965. 43 p. Includes discography.

HUBBARD, FREDDIE (trumpet, leader)

J466   Bower, R. Freddie Hubbard. *Jazz Monthly*, XI (Oct. 1965), 28-29; (Nov. 1965), 29-31; (Dec. 1965), 25-26.

HURT, MISSISSIPPI JOHN (singer)

J467   Kay, G. W. Mississippi John Hurt. *Jazz Journal*, XVII (Feb. 1964), 24-26.

HUTCHERSON, BOBBY (ROBERT; vibes, marimba)

J468   Wilbraham, R. J. Bobby Hutcherson. *Jazz Monthly*, XII (Feb. 1967), 26-28.

JACKSON, MAHALIA (singer)

J469   Hayes, C. J. Mahalia Jackson, a discography. *Matrix*, #62 (Dec. 1965), 3-5.

J470   Jackson, Mahalia, and Evan McLeod Wylie. Movin' on up. New York, Hawthorn Books, 1966. 219 p. Discography: pp. 215, 218-219.

J471   Uyldert, Herman. Vorstin van de gospel: Mahalia Jackson. Tielt, Den Haag, Lannoo, 1962. 96 p. In Dutch. Includes discography.

JACKSON, MILTON "BAGS" (vibraharp, piano, guitar)

J472   Jepsen, Jørgen Grunnet. Milt Jackson: a discography. København, Jepsen, 1957. 13 p.

J473   Wilbraham, R. J. Milt Jackson; a discography and biography. [Includes a discography of recordings made with the Modern Jazz Quartet.] London, Frognal Bookshop, 1968. 40 p.

JAFFE, NAT (piano)

J474   Eyle, Willem Frederik van. Discography of Nat Jaffe. Zaandam, van Eyle, 1966. 2 p.

JASPAR, BOBBY (ROBERT B.; tenor sax, clarinet, flute)

J475   Devoghelaere, Edmond. Bobby Jaspar; a biography, appreciation, record survey and complete discography. Antwerp, Labris, 1967. 124 p. Includes discography.

JAZZ COMPOSERS' ORCHESTRA

J476   Watson, R. The Jazz Composers' Orchestra: special review. *Pieces of Jazz*, #6 (1969), 5-8.

JOHANSSON, JAN (piano, guitar, composer)

J477   Rehnberg, B. Jan Johansson, a draft discography for 1956-1962. *Matrix*, #55 (Oct. 1964), 6-9.

JOHNSON, "BUNK" (WILLIAM GEARY; cornet, trumpet)

J478   Eyle, Willem Frederik van. Discography of Bunk Johnson. Zaandam, van Eyle, 1966. 6 p.

Eyle, Willem Frederik van. Discography of Bunk Johnson. Rev. ed. Zaandam, van Eyle, 1966. 6 p.

J479   Hopfe, Gerhard. Bunk Johnson. Ein Pionier des Jazz. Berlin [Eastern Sector], Hopfe, 1967. 25 p. In German. Includes discography.

JOHNSON, "J. J." (JAMES LOUIS; trombone, composer)

J480   Fini, Francesco. The Jay Jay Johnson complete discography. Imola, Italy, Galeati, 1962. 26 p.

J481   Jepsen, Jørgen Grunnet. Jay Jay Johnson: a discography. København, Jepsen, 1957. 17 p.

JOHNSON, PETE (piano)

J482   Fairchild, R. Pete Johnson discography. *Jazz Report*, III (Nov. 1962), 11-13; (Jan.-Feb. 1963), 11-12.

J483   Mauerer, Hans J. The Pete Johnson story. Frankfurt, Mauerer; New York, Wertheim, 1965. 78 p. Discography: pp. 57-73.

JOHNSON, ROBERT (singer, guitar)

J484   Charters, Samuel B. Robert Johnson. *Record Research*, #43 (May 1962), 12.

J485   Robert Johnson. Knutsford, Cheshire, England, Blues World, 1967. 24 p. Includes discography.

JOLSON, AL (ASA; singer, songwriter)

J486   Wigransky, Sidney David Pace. Jolsonography. Bournemouth, Eng., Barrie Anderton, 1971. 440 p. Includes discography.

JONES, QUINCY DELIGHT, JR. (composer, leader, trumpet, piano)

J487   Raben, E. Quincy Jones diskografi. *Orkester Journalen*, XXXIV (Nov. 1966), 32. In Swedish.

KEANE, "SHAKE" (ELLSWORTH McGRANAHAN; trumpet, fluegelhorn)

J488   Morgan, Alun. Shake Keane. *Jazz Monthly*, XI (Dec. 1965), 26-27.

KENTON, STAN (STANLEY NEWCOMB; leader, composer, piano)

J489   Edwards, Ernie. Discography of Stan Kenton and His Orchestra.
       [Two volumes covering respectively 1941-1952 and 1952-1962.]
       Brande, Debut Records, 1959, 1961. 2 v. (28 p., 25 p.)

J490   Jepsen, Jørgen Grunnet. Discography of Stan Kenton. New rev. ed.
       Brande, Debut Records, 1962. 2 v.

J491   Pirie, Christopher Anthony, and Siegfried Müller. Artistry in Kenton:
       a bio-discography of Stan Kenton and his music. Vol. 1. Vienna,
       Siegfried Müller, 1969. 359 p. Biography and discographical
       commentary.

       Pirie, Christopher Anthony, and Siegfried Müller. Artistry in Kenton:
       a bio-discography of Stan Kenton and his music. Rev. ed. Vienna,
       Siegfried Müller, 1969. 359 p. Biography and discographical
       commentary.

       Pirie, Christopher Anthony, and Siegfried Müller. Artistry in Kenton:
       a bio-discography of Stan Kenton and his music. 3d ed. Vienna,
       Siegfried Müller, 1971. 359 p. Biography and discographical
       commentary.

J492   Schulz-Köhn, Dietrich. Stan Kenton; ein Porträt. Wetzlar, Pegasus,
       1961. 48 p. In German. Discography: pp. 45-48.

J493   Sparke, Michael. The great Kenton arrangers. [Bill Holman, Johnny
       Richards, Gene Roland, Pete Rugolo, William Russo.] Whittier,
       Calif., Erngeobil, 1968. 70 p.

J494   Sparke, Michael, Pete Venudor, and Jack Hartley. Kenton on
       Capitol; a discography. Hounslow, Middlesex, Eng., Michael Sparke,
       1966. 134 p.

       Sparke, Michael, Pete Venudor, and Jack Hartley. Kenton on Capitol;
       a discography. 2d ed. Hounslow, Middlesex, Eng., Michael Sparke,
       1966. 108 p.

J495   Teubig, Klaus. Stan Kenton Discographie. [An addition to the
       "Stan Kenton Discographie" of Horst H. Lange, with AFRS trans-
       criptions, all radio transcriptions, and unknown Capitol recordings.]
       Hamburg, Teubig, 1963. 11 p. In German.

J496   Venudor, Pete, and Michael Sparke. The standard Kenton directory.
       Vol. 1: the forties, 1937-1949. Amsterdam, Venudor and Sparke,
       1968. 60 p.

KEPPARD, FREDDIE (trumpet)

J497   Eyle, Willem Frederik van. Discography of Freddie Keppard. Zaandam, van Eyle, 1966. 2 p.

KIRBY, JOHN (leader, bass)

J498   Hoefer, G. John Kirby. *Down Beat*, XXIX (Oct. 11, 1962), 27.

KIRKEBY, ED (leader, manager) AND THE CALIFORNIA RAMBLERS

J499   Backensto, W., and P. Armagnac. Ed Kirkeby's California Ramblers. *Record Research*, #66 (Feb. 1965), 6.

KOLLER, HANS (tenor sax, clarinet, baritone sax, alto sax)

J500   Kraner, Dietrich Heinz. Die Hans Koller Discographie 1947-1966. Graz, Kraner, 1967. 19 p. In German.

KONITZ, LEE (alto sax)

J501   Jepsen, Jørgen Grunnet. Discography of Lee Konitz/Gerry Mulligan. Brande, Debut Records, 1960. 21 p., 14 p.

KRUPA, GENE (drums, leader)

J502   Edwards, Ernie, George Hall, and Bill Korst. Gene Krupa and His Orchestra 1938-1951. Whittier, Calif., Erngeobil, 1968. 36 p.

KÜHN, JOACHIM (piano, leader)

J503   Tercinet, A. Joachim Kuehn. *Jazz Hot*, #273 (June 1971), 4-8. In French.

LACY, STEVE (real name, STEVEN LACKRITZ; soprano sax)

J504   Harrison, M. Steve Lacy [interview and discography] . *Jazz Monthly*, XII (Mar. 1966), 7-14.

LADNIER, TOMMY (THOMAS; trumpet)

J505　Eyle, Willem Frederik van. Discography of Tommy Ladnier. Zaandam, van Eyle, 1966. 10 p.

J506　Hillman, J. C. A discography [Tommy Ladnier]. *Jazz Journal*, XVIII (Aug. 1965), 9-10.

LAFITTE, GUY (tenor sax)

J507　Lafargue, P. A Guy Lafitte discography. *Jazz Monthly*, IX (Aug. 1963), 10-11; (Sep. 1963), 24-25; (Oct. 1963), 27.

LATEEF, YUSEF (real name, WILLIAM EVANS; tenor sax, flutes, oboe)

J508　Cooke, A. Yusef Lateef; a name discography. *Jazz Monthly*, IX (July 1963), 16-17.

LEADBELLY (real name, HUDDIE LEDBETTER; singer, guitar)

J509　Ledbetter, Huddie. The Leadbelly songbook. New York, Oak Publications, 1962. 96 p. Includes discography.

LEONARD, HARLAN (leader, alto sax, tenor sax)

J510　Simmen, J. Harlan Leonard and His Rockets. *Jazz Journal*, XVI (Aug. 1963), 4-6.

LEWIS, GEORGE (clarinet, leader)

J511　Jepsen, Jörgen Grunnet. George Lewis. København, Jepsen, 1957. 11 p.

J512　Kohno, Ryuji. The George Lewis discography including Bunk Johnson's [recordings]. Fujisawa, Kanagawa, The Dixieland Academy, 1966. 40 p.

J513　Stenbeck, L. George Lewis diskografi. *Orkester Journalen*, XXXIII (June 1965), 28; (July-Aug. 1965), 30. In Swedish.

LITTLE, BOOKER, JR. (trumpet)

J514   Walker, M. Booker Little. *Jazz Monthly*, XII (July 1966), 13-14.

LLOYD, CHARLES (tenor sax, flute, composer, leader)

J515   Wilbraham, R. J. Charles Lloyd. *Jazz Monthly*, XII (Dec. 1966), 24+

LOFTON, "CRIPPLE" CLARENCE (piano, singer)

J516   Eyle, Willem Frederik van. Discography of Cripple Clarence Lofton. Zaandam, van Eyle, 1966. 2 p.

Eyle, Willem Frederik van. Discography of Cripple Clarence Lofton. Rev. ed. Zaandam, van Eyle, 1966. 2 p.

LOUISIANA RHYTHM KINGS

J517   Waters, H. J. The Louisiana Rhythm Kings. *Record Research*, #44 (July 1962), 5-7.

LUNCEFORD, JIMMIE (JAMES MELVIN; leader)

J518   Edwards, Ernie, George Hall, and Bill Korst. The Jimmy Lunceford Band. Whittier, Calif., Erngeobil, 1965. 12 p.

Edwards, Ernie, George Hall, and Bill Korst. The Jimmy Lunceford Band. Rev. ed. Whittier, Calif., Erngeobil, 1965. 12 p.

J519   Fresia, E. Jimmie Lunceford. *Musica Jazz*, XVIII (July-Aug. 1962), 28-31. In Italian.

McGHEE, HOWARD (trumpet)

J520   Boenzli, Richard E. Discography of Howard McGhee. Basel, Jazz Publications, 1961. 32 p.

J521   Morgan, Alun. Discography [Howard McGhee]. *Jazz Journal*, XIX (Jan. 1966), 14; (Feb. 1966), 29.

McKINLEY, RAY (drums, singer, leader)

J522   Edwards, Ernie, Jr. Ray McKinley Orchestra. Whittier, Calif., Erngeobil, 1967. 19 p.

McKINNEY, WILLIAM (drums, leader) AND HIS COTTON PICKERS

J523   Chilton, John, and others. McKinney's. *Storyville*, #33 (Feb. 1971), 99-103.

McLEAN, JACKIE (JOHN LENWOOD; alto sax)

J524   Wilbraham, R. J. Jackie McLean; a biography and discography. London, Frognal Bookshop, 1968. 20 p.

McPHERSON, CHARLES (alto sax)

J525   Gardner, M. Charles McPherson discography. *Jazz Monthly*, #183 (May 1970), 25-27.

McSHANN, JAY "HOOTIE" (leader, piano)

J526   Niquet, B. Jay McShann ou la légende de K.C. *Jazz Hot*, #235 (Oct. 1967), 23-25. In French.

MANONE, JOSEPH "WINGY" (trumpet, singer, leader)

J527   Manone, Wingy, and Paul Vandervoort II. Trumpet on the wing. [Autobiography and discography; reprint of the New York, 1948 edition.] London, Jazz Book Club, 1964. 256 p. Includes discography.

MARES, PAUL (trumpet, leader)

J528   Eyle, Willem Frederik van. Discography of Paul Mares. Zaandam, van Eyle, 1966. 2 p.

MARMAROSA, "DODO" (MICHAEL; piano)

J529   Gibson, F. Dodo Marmarosa discography. *Jazz Journal*, XVIII (May 1965), 37; (June 1965), 25-26; (Dec. 1965), 43.

MARSH, WARNE MARION (tenor sax)

J530 Blomberg, L. Warne Marsh diskografi. *Orkester Journalen*, XXXVII (Feb. 1969), 30. In Swedish.

MATHIESEN, LEO (piano, cello, leader)

J531 Jørgensen, Birger. Leo Mathiesen. København, C. Erichsen, 1962. 76 p. In Danish. Includes discography.

MEMPHIS SLIM (real name, PETER CHATMAN; piano, singer, songwriter)

J532 Jazz Publications, ed. Discography of Memphis Slim. Basel, Jazz Publications, 1962. 12 p.

J533 Knight, B. Memphis Slim; discography. *Jazz Journal*, XV (Apr. 1962), 5-7.

J534 Rotante, A., and M. Chauvard. Memphis Slim—Peter Chatman revised discography. *Record Research*, #40 (Jan. 1962), 12.

METRONOME ALL STAR BANDS

J535 Kraner, Dietrich Heinz. The Metronome All Star Bands—a listing. *Matrix*, LXXVI (Apr. 1968), 3-6.

MILLER, GLENN (composer, leader, trombone)

J536 Edwards, Ernie, and Mike H. Morris. Glenn Miller Alumni, vol. 1. [Ray Anthony, Tex Beneke, Jerry Gray, Ray Eberle.] Whittier, Calif., Erngeobil, 1965. 60 p.

Edwards, Ernie, and Mike H. Morris. Glenn Miller Alumni, vol. 1. Rev. ed. Whittier, Calif., Erngeobil, 1969. 62 p.

J537 Edwards, Ernie, George Hall, Bill Korst, and Mike H. Morris. Glenn Miller Alumni, vol. 2. Whittier, Calif., Erngeobil, 1965. 53 p.

J538 Flower, John. Moonlight serenade: a bio-discography of the Glenn Miller civilian band. New Rochelle, N.Y., Arlington House, 1972. 554 p. Biography and discographical commentary.

MILLINDER, LUCKY (LUCIUS; leader)

J539   Demeusy, Bertrand, Otto Flückiger, Jørgen Grunnet Jepsen, and
        Kurt Mohr. Discography of Lucky Millinder 1941-1960. Basel, Jazz
        Publications, 1962. 26 p.

MINGUS, CHARLIE (CHARLES; bass, composer, leader, piano)

J540   Kraner, Dietrich Heinz. Mingus in Europe 1964—a listing of private
        recordings. *Discographical Forum*, X (Jan. 1969), 11.

J541   Wilbraham, Roy J. Charles Mingus; a biography and discography.
        London, Wilbraham, 1967. 33 p.

J542   Wilson, J. S. Mingus: the missing link. *New York Times*, CXIV (Oct.
        4, 1964, sec. 2), 25.

MITCHELL, GEORGE (trumpet)

J543   Eyle, Willem Frederik van. Discography of George Mitchell. Zaandam,
        van Eyle, 1966. 4 p.

MITCHELL, LES (leader) AND HIS JAZZ KINGS

J544   Conté, G. Les Mitchell's Jazz Kings. *Jazz Hot*, #244 (Nov. 1968),
        34-36. In French.

MITCHELL, LOUIS (drums, leader)

J545   Gillet, André V. Louis A. Mitchell. Bio-Disco-Bibliographie.
        Bruxelles, Gillet, 1966. 20 p. In French.

J546   Gillet, André V. The Mitchell's Jazz Kings—Discographie critique.
        [Same material but deluxe edition of the work J545 cited above.]
        Bruxelles, Gillet, 1966. 20 p. [plus 11 p. of photographs, etc.] In
        French.

MOBLEY, HANK (HENRY; tenor sax)

J547   Wilbraham, R. J. Hank Mobley discography. *Discographical Forum*,
        #13 (July 1969), 7-10; #16 (Jan. 1970), 7.

MONK, THELONIUS SPHERE (composer, piano)

J548   Jepsen, Jørgen Grunnet. A discography of Thelonius Monk and Bud
        Powell. New rev. ed. København, Knudsen, 1969. 44 p.

J549   Jepsen, Jørgen Grunnet. A discography of Thelonius Monk and
        Sonny Rollins. Brande, Debut Records, 1960. 27 p.

MONTGOMERY, "LITTLE BROTHER" (EURREAL; piano, singer)

J550   Zur Heide, Karl Gert. Deep South piano: the story of Little
        Brother Montgomery. London, Studio Vista, 1970. 112 p. Discog-
        raphy: pp. 105-107.

MOODY, JAMES (tenor sax, alto sax, flute, composer)

J551   Kuhn, Raymond. Discography of James Moody, with biographical
        notes. Basel, Jazz Publications, 1960. 16 p.

        Kuhn, Raymond. Supplement: corrections to the James Moody
        discography. Basel, Jazz Publications, 1961. 1 p.

MORTON, JELLY ROLL (real name, FERDINAND JOSEPH LA MENTHE; composer, piano, leader, singer)

J552   Ahlström, T. Jazz-diskoteket: Jelly Roll Morton. *Musikrevy*, XXVII
        (#5, 1972), 314-18. In Swedish.

J553   Carey, D., F. Dutton, and G. Hulme. Jelly Roll's Victor jazz. *Jazz
        Journal*, XV (June 1962), 8-10; (July 1962), 9-10.

J554   Davies, John R. T. B., and Laurie Wright. Morton's music: Jelly Roll
        Morton discography. New Orleans, Storyville, 1968. 38 p. [For
        addenda, see J559 below.]

J555   Eyle, Willem Frederik van. Discography of Jelly Roll Morton.
        Zaandam, van Eyle, 1966. 9 p.

        Eyle, Willem Frederik van. Discography of Jelly Roll Morton. Rev.
        ed. Zaandam, van Eyle, 1966. 9 p.

J556   Jepsen, Jørgen Grunnet. Discography of Jelly Roll Morton. [Two
        volumes covering respectively 1922-1929 and 1930-1940.] Brande,
        Debut Records, 1959. 2 v. (18 p., 21 p.)

J557   Lomax, Alan. Mister Jelly Roll. Les aventures de Jelly Roll Morton,
        Créole de la Nouvelle-Orléans, et inventeur du jazz. [Translation of
        Mister Jelly Roll (London, 1959) by Henri Parisot.] Paris,
        Flammarion, 1964. 362 p. In French. Includes discography.

J558   Lomax, Alan. Mister Jelly Roll; the fortunes of Jelly Roll Morton,
        New Orleans Creole and inventor of jazz. 2d ed. Berkeley, University
        of California Press, 1973. 318 p. Discography: pp. 297-318.

J559   Morton's music: addenda. *Storyville*, #17 (June-July 1968), 29-30.
        [Addenda to the publication by John Davies and Laurie Wright, J554
        above.]

J560   Williams, Martin T. Jelly Roll Morton. London, Cassell, 1962. 90 p.
        Includes record list.

MOSEHOLM, ERIK (bass, leader)

J561   Thomsen, Jens Schoustrup. Erik Moseholm. København, Erichsen,
        1962. 64 p. In Danish. Includes discography.

MOTEN, BENNY (CLARENCE LEMONT; bass)

J562   Eyle, Willem Frederik van. Discography of Bennie Moten. Zaandam,
        van Eyle, 1966. 3 p.

        Eyle, Willem Frederik van. Discography of Bennie Moten. Rev. ed.
        Zaandam, van Eyle, 1966. 3 p.

NAVARRO, "FATS" (THEODORE; trumpet)

J563   Eyle, Willem Frederik van. Discography of Fats Navarro. Zaandam,
        van Eyle, 1966. 7 p.

J564   Jepsen, Jørgen Grunnet. Fats Navarro: a discography. København,
        Jepsen, 1957. 11 p.

NEWTON, FRANKIE (WILLIAM FRANK; trumpet)

J565   Eyle, Willem Frederik van. Discography of Frankie Newton. Zaandam,
        van Eyle, 1966. 6 p.

NICHOLS, "RED" (ERNEST LORING; leader, cornet)

J566   Backensto, W. Red Nichols memorial issue. *Record Research*, #96-97 (Apr. 1969), whole issue. Includes discography.

NOONE, JIMMY (clarinet, leader)

J567   Eyle, Willem Frederik van. Discography of Jimmy Noone. Zaandam, van Eyle, 1966. 6 p.

OLIVER, "KING" (JOSEPH; cornet, leader)

J568   Eyle, Willem Frederik van. Discography of King Oliver. Zaandam, van Eyle, 1966. 11 p.

ORY, "KID" (EDWARD; trombone, leader, composer)

J569   Eyle, Willem Frederik van. Discography of Kid Ory. Zaandam, van Eyle, 1966. 14 p.

J570   Jepsen, Jørgen Grunnet. Kid Ory. København, Jepsen, 1957.

PAGE, "HOT LIPS" (ORAN; trumpet, singer, leader)

J571   Demeusy, Bertrand, Otto Flückiger, Jørgen Grunnet Jepsen, and Kurt Mohr. Hot Lips Page. Basel, Jazz Publications, 1961. 30 p.

Demeusy, Bertrand, Otto Flückiger, Jørgen Grunnet Jepsen, and Kurt Mohr. Hot Lips Page. Supplement. Basel, Jazz Publications, 1962. 1 p.

PAPA BUE (real name, ARNE BUE JENSEN; trombone, leader)

J572   Bendix, Ole. Papa Bue. København, Erichsen, 1962. 72 p. In Danish. Includes discography.

PARAMOUNT ORCHESTRAS

J573   Englund, Björn. Paramountorkesterns diskografi. *Orkester Journalen*, XXXVI (Dec. 1968), 44. In Swedish.

PARKER, CHARLIE "BIRD" (CHARLES CHRISTOPHER, JR.; alto sax, composer)

J574   Delormé, M. Discographie commentée des enregistrements publics de Charlie Parker. *Jazz Hot*, #207 (Mar. 1965), 30-35+ In French.

J575   Edwards, Ernie, George Hall, and Bill Korst. Charlie Parker. Whittier, Calif., Erngeobil, 1965.

J576   Gardner, M. Bargain Bird [discography of Charlie Parker on cut-price labels]. *Jazz Journal*, XX (June 1967), 8-11.

J577   Gardner, M., and F. Gibson. A discography of the 'live' recordings of Charlie Parker. *Jazz Journal*, XVII (June 1964), 29; (July 1964), 25.

J578   Gardner, M., and F. Gibson. A discography of the studio recordings of Charlie Parker. *Jazz Journal*, XVII (May 1964), 26-27.

J579   Jazz Publications, ed. Discography of Charlie Parker. Basel, Jazz Publications, 1962. 9 p.

J580   Jepsen, Jørgen Grunnet. Discography of Charlie Parker. Brande, Debut Records, 1959. 23 p.

       Jepsen, Jørgen Grunnet. Discography of Charlie Parker. 2d ed. Brande, Debut Records, 1960. 30 p.

J581   Jepsen, Jørgen Grunnet. A discography of Charlie Parker. København, Knudsen, 1969. 38 p.

J582   Reisner, Robert George. Bird: the legend of Charlie Parker. New York, Citadel, 1961. 450 p. New York, Citadel, 1962; New York, Bonanza Books, 1962; London, MacGibbon & Kee, 1963; London, Jazz Book Club, 1965. 256 p. Discography: pp. 241-256.

J583   Russell, Ross. Bird lives; the high life and hard times of Charlie (Yardbird) Parker. New York, Charterhouse, 1973. 404 p. Discography: pp. 384-388.

J584   Williams, Tony. Charlie Parker discography. *Discographical Forum*, #13 (July 1969), 13-17; #16 (Jan. 1970), 15-18.

PARKER, LEO (baritone sax)

J585   Eyle, Willem Frederik van. Discography of Leo Parker. Zaandam, van Eyle, 1966. 4 p.

J586   Jazz Publications, ed. Discography of Jimmy Smith and Leo Parker. Basel, Jazz Publications, 1962. 8 p.

PATTON, CHARLIE (CHARLES; singer, guitar)

J587   Evans, David. Charlie Patton. [Essay and discography.] Knutsford, Cheshire, Blues World, 1969. 20 p.

PAYNE, CECIL McKENZIE (baritone sax, alto sax)

J588   Gardner, M. Cecil Payne. *Jazz Monthly*, X (May 1964), 5-8; (June 1964), 5-7.

PEPPER, ART (ARTHUR EDWARD; alto sax, tenor sax)

J589   Edwards, Ernie, George Hall, and Bill Korst. Art Pepper. Whittier, Calif., Erngeobil, 1965. 24 p.

J590   Edwards, Ernie, and John Irwin. Art Pepper. Whittier, Calif., Erngeobil, 1969.

PERKINS, CARL (piano)

J591   Grigson, L., and A. Morgan. Carl Perkins. *Jazz Monthly*, VIII (July 1962), 11-15.

POWELL, BUD (EARL; piano, composer)

J592   Eyle, Willem Frederik van. Discography of Bud Powell. Zaandam, van Eyle, 1966. 10 p.

J593   Gardner, M. Bud Powell on record 1956-1966. *Jazz Monthly*, XIII (July 1967), 28-30.

J594   Jepsen, Jørgen Grunnet. Discography of Art Tatum/Bud Powell. Brande, Debut Records, 1961. 28 p.

QUEBEC, IKE ABRAMS (tenor sax)

J595   Eyle, Willem Frederik van. Discography of Ike Quebec. Zaandam, van Eyle, 1966. 5 p.

RAEBURN, BOYD (leader, composer, saxophones)

J596   Edwards, Ernie, George Hall, and Bill Korst. Boyd Raeburn and His Orchestra. [Also listings of Johnny Bothwell and George Handy.] Whittier, Calif., Erngeobil, 1966. 20 p.

J597   Hoefer, G. Volatile career and the controversial bands of Boyd Raeburn. *Down Beat*, XXIX (Apr. 16, 1962), 24-25.

J598   Jackson, A. Boyd Raeburn. *Jazz Monthly*, XII (Nov. 1966), 5-8.

RAINEY, MA (singer)

J599   Eyle, Willem Frederik van. Discography of Ma Rainey. Zaandam, van Eyle, 1966. 4 p.

J600   Stewart-Baxter, Derrick. Ma Rainey and the classic blues singers. London, Studio Vista; New York, Stein and Day, 1970. 112 p. Discography: pp. 106-110.

REINHARDT, DJANGO (JEAN BAPTISTE; guitar)

J601   Delaunay, Charles. Django Reinhardt. [Translated from the French edition (Paris, 1954) by Michael James.] London, Cassell, 1961. 247 p. Discography: pp. 163-241.

J602   Delaunay, Charles. Django Reinhardt. Souvenirs. 2d ed. Paris, le Terrain vague, 1968. 208 p. In French. Discography: pp. 165-199.

ROACH, MAX (MAXWELL; drums)

J603   Cooke, Ann. Max Roach; a name discography. *Jazz Monthly*, IX (June 1963), 15-18.

J604   Cooke, Jack. "We Insist!" The Max Roach group today and the "Freedom Now Suite." *Jazz Monthly*, VIII (July 1962), 3-4.

ROBINSON, ELZADIE

J605   Stewart-Baxter, Derrick. Blues on record [Elzadie Robinson]. *Jazz Journal*, XVII (Apr. 1964), 14.

ROBINSON, IKE (guitar, banjo, leader)

J606   Englund, Björn. Ikey Robinson; an introduction and discography.
        Jazz Monthly, VIII (Dec. 1962), 10-12.

RODNEY, RED (real name, ROBERT CHUDNICK; trumpet)

J607   Eyle, Willem Frederik van. Discography of Red Rodney. Zaandam,
        van Eyle, 1966. 8 p.

J608   Gibson, F. Red Rodney, a discography. *Jazz Journal*, XVI (Oct.
        1963), 10-12.

ROLLINS, SONNY (THEODORE WALTER; tenor sax)

J609   Jepsen, Jørgen Grunnet. Sonny Rollins: a discography. København,
        Jepsen, 1957. 11 p.

RUSSELL, GEORGE ALLAN (composer, drums)

J610   Discografia di George Russell. *Musica Jazz*, XXI (May 1965), 19.
        In Italian.

J611   Kraner, Dietrich Heinz. George Russell—a discography. *Matrix*, LXIX
        (Feb. 1967), 3-8.

RUSSELL, WILLIAM

J612   Lambert, E. William Russell's New Orleans recordings; some notes
        and reflections. *Jazz Monthly*, #183 (May 1970), 3-8.

SAVITT, JAN (leader) AND HIS TOP HATTERS

J613   Hall, George. Jan Savitt Top Hatters. Whittier, Calif., Erngeobil,
        1965. 16 p.

SAVOY BANDS

J614   Rust, Brian A. L. A discography of the Savoy bands of the twenties.
        Recorded Sound, #25 (Jan. 1967), 150-57, #26 (Apr. 1967), 193-95.

SCHIØPFFE, WILLIAM (drums, leader)

J615   Moseholm, Erik. William Schiøpffe. København, Erichsen, 1963.
        62 p. In Danish. Includes discography.

SHAW, ARTIE (real name, ARTHUR ARSHAWSKY; clarinet, composer, leader)

J616   Eyle, Willem Frederik van. Discography of Artie Shaw. Zaandam,
        van Eyle, 1966. 17 p.

SHAW, GENE (CLARENCE EUGENE; trumpet, leader)

J617   Gene Shaw—a discography. *Pieces of Jazz*, #7 (1969), 39-40.

SHEPP, ARCHIE (tenor sax)

J618   Walker, M. Archie Shepp. *Jazz Monthly*, XII (June 1966), 30-31.

SILVER, HORACE WARD MARTIN TAVARES (piano, composer)

J619   Gardner, Mark. Horace Silver discography with a brief biography.
        Droitwick, Worcestershire, Gardner, 1967. 22 p.

SLACK, FREDDIE (piano, composer, leader)

J620   Edwards, Ernie, George Hall, and Bill Korst. Freddie Slack. Whittier,
        Calif., Erngeobil, 1965. 17 p.

SMITH, BESSIE (singer, songwriter)

J621   Eyle, Willem Frederik van. Discography of Bessie Smith. Zaandam,
        van Eyle, 1966. 7 p.

        Eyle, Willem Frederik van. Discography of Bessie Smith. Rev. ed.
        Zaandam, van Eyle, 1966. 7 p.

SMITH, BIG MAYBELLE (MABEL; singer)

J622   Rotante, A. Big Maybelle; a discography of Big Maybelle Smith.
        Record Research, #60 (May-June 1964), 8-9.

SMITH, DEREK G. (piano)

J623   Morgan, Alun. Two 'name' discographies [Derek Smith and Tommy Whittle]. *Jazz Monthly*, IX (Dec. 1963), 26-27.

SMITH, "JABBO" (CLADYS; trumpet, singer, leader)

J624   Flückiger, Otto. Discography of Jabbo Smith. Basel, Jazz Publications, 1962. 8 p.

SMITH, MAMIE (singer)

J625   Mamie Smith; a provisional discography. *Record Research*, #57 (Jan. 1964), 8-12. [This item is a reprint, first appearing in *Discophile*, Nov. 1961.]

SMITH, WILLIE "THE LION" (real name, WILLIAM HENRY JOSEPH BERTHOL BONAPARTE BERTHOLOFF; piano, composer)

J626   Eyle, Willem Frederik van. Discography of Willie the Lion Smith. Zaandam, van Eyle, 1966. 11 p.

Eyle, Willem Frederik van. Discography of Willie the Lion Smith. Rev. ed. Zaandam, van Eyle, 1966. 11 p.

J627   Smith, Willie, and George Hoefer. Music on my mind; the memoirs of an American pianist. Garden City, N.Y., Doubleday, 1964; London, MacGibbon & Kee, 1965; London, Jazz Book Club, 1966. 318 p. Discography: pp. 302-311.

SNOWDEN, ELMER "POPS" (saxophones, guitar, banjo)

J628   Demeusy, Bertrand. Elmer Snowden discography. *Jazz Journal*, XVI (Apr. 1963), 15-16.

SULIEMAN, IDREES DAWUD (trumpet)

J629   Jepsen, Jørgen Grunnet. Idrees Sulieman diskografi. *Orkester Journalen*, XXXIII (Feb. 1965), 27-28. In Swedish.

TATUM, ART (ARTHUR; piano)

J630 Jepsen, Jørgen Grunnet. Art Tatum: a discography. København, Jepsen, 1957. 10 p.

J631 Spencer, R. Art Tatum; an appreciation. *Jazz Journal*, XIX (Aug. 1966), 6-10; (Sep. 1966), 11-16; (Oct. 1966), 13-16.

TAYLOR, CECIL PERCIVAL (piano, composer)

J632 Jepsen, Jørgen Grunnet. Cecil Taylor diskografi. *Orkester Journalen*, XXX (Dec. 1962), 48. In Swedish.

TEAGARDEN, JACK (WELDON JOHN; trombone, singer, leader)

J633 Wilson, J. S. Teagarden and his times—the early days documented. *High Fidelity*, XIII (June 1963), 86+

TERRY, CLARK (trumpet, fluegelhorn)

J634 Radzitzky, Carlos de. A 1960-1967 Clark Terry Discography; with biographical notes. Brasschaat, Jazzbox [Walter de Block], 1968. 48 p.

J635 Walker, M. Clark Terry discography. *Jazz Monthly*, VII (Jan. 1962), 18-19; (Feb. 1962), 28-29; (Mar. 1962), 30-31; (Apr. 1962), 29+

THARPE, SISTER ROSETTA (real name, ROSETTA NUBIN; singer, guitar)

J636 Hayes, C. J. Sister Rosetta Tharpe; a discography. *Matrix*, #77 (June 1968), 3-14.

THOMPSON, ELI "LUCKY" (tenor sax, soprano sax)

J637 Williams, Tony. Lucky Thompson discography and biography, part 1 (1944-1951). London, Williams, 1967. 31 p.

THORNHILL, CLAUDE (leader, composer, piano)

J638 Claude Thornhill and his orchestra. Rev. ed. Maryland, Jazz Discographies Unlimited, 1971.

J639   Crosbie, I. Prophet without honour [history of Claude Thornhill Orchestra]. *Jazz Journal*, XXIV (Apr. 1971), 28-31.

J640   Edwards, Ernie. A Claude Thornhill discography. *Jazz Monthly*, VIII (Jan. 1963), 13-14; (Mar. 1963), 16-17.

J641   Edwards, Ernie, George Hall, and Bill Korst. The sound of Claude Thornhill and his orchestra. Whittier, Calif., Erngeobil, 1965. 25 p.

Edwards, Ernie, George Hall, and Bill Korst. The sound of Claude Thornhill and his orchestra. 2d ed. Whittier, Calif., Erngeobil, 1967. 25 p.

TRISTANO, LENNIE (LEONARD JOSEPH; piano, composer)

J642   Eyle, Willem Frederik van. Discography of Lennie Tristano. Zaandam, van Eyle, 1966. 3 p.

TUCKER, GEORGE ANDREW (bass)

J643   Friedman, P. S. George Tucker discography. *Jazz Monthly*, #166 (Dec. 1968), 30-31; #167 (Jan. 1969), 30-31.

TWARDZIK, DICK (RICHARD; piano)

J644   Eyle, Willem Frederik van. Discography of Dick Twardzick [sic]. Zaandam, van Eyle, 1966. 2 p.

J645   Morgan, Alun. Dick Twardzik. *Jazz Monthly*, IX (Nov. 1963), 27.

TYNER, ALFRED McCOY (also known as SULAIMON SAUD; piano, composer)

J646   Bourne, Michael. McCoy Tyner. *Down Beat*, XL (#20, Dec. 6, 1973), 14-15.

VALENTINE, "KID" THOMAS (banjo)

J647   Bethell, T. Kid Thomas Valentine, a discography. *Jazz Report*, V (#4, 1966), 27-30; (#5, 1967), 33-36.

WALLER, "FATS" (THOMAS; piano, organ, singer, songwriter)

J648   Fox, Charles. Fats Waller. London, Cassell, 1960; New York, Barnes, 1961. 90 p. Includes record list.

J649   Kirkeby, W. T. Ed, Duncan P. Schiedt, and Sinclair Traill. Ain't misbehavin': the story of Fats Waller. London, Davies; New York, Dodd, Mead, 1966; London, Jazz Book Club, 1967. 248 p. Discography: pp. 233-248.

J650   Magnusson, Tor. An almost complete "Fats" Waller discography. Stockholm, Magnusson, 1964.

WALLINGTON, GEORGE (real name, GIORGIO FIGLIA; piano, songwriter)

J651   Gibson, F. George Wallington; a discography. *Jazz Journal*, XVII (Sep. 1964), 22-23.

J652   Morgan, Alun. George Wallington, a name discography. *Jazz Monthly*, IX (Nov. 1963), 25+

WATERS, ETHEL (singer)

J653   Niquet, B. Ethel Waters. *Le Point du Jazz*, #6 (Mar. 1972), 5-18. In French. Includes discography.

WATSON, LEO "SCAT" (singer)

J654   Magnusson, Tor. Leo "Scat" Watson diskografi. Göteborg, Magnusson, 1967. 6 p. In Swedish.

WEBSTER, FREDDIE (trumpet)

J655   Edwards, Ernie. Freddie Webster discography. *Discographical Forum*, #16 (Jan. 1970), 3-6+

WHITEMAN, PAUL (leader)

J656   Rust, Brian A. L. Paul Whiteman: a discography. *Recorded Sound* #28 (Oct. 1967), 255-58.

WILLIAMS, CLARENCE (composer, piano, leader)

J657　Lord, T., and others. Clarence Williams discography. *Storyville*, #17 (June-July 1968), 11-15; continues running in various issues of *Storyville* through 1968, 1969, and 1970.

WILLIAMS, JOHN (piano)

J658　Morgan, Alun. John Williams; the pianist from Vermont. [Biography and discography.] *Jazz Monthly*, VIII (Oct. 1962), 2-5; (Nov. 1962), 13-14.

WILLS, BOB (leader) AND HIS TEXAS PLAYBOYS

J659　Healy, B., and others. Bob Wills and His Texas Playboys; a bio-discography. *Record Research*, #80 (Nov. 1966), 3-5, #82 (Mar. 1967), 3-7.

WILSON, DICK (RICHARD; tenor sax)

J660　Eyle, Willem Frederik van. Discography of Dick Wilson. Zaandam, van Eyle, 1966. 4 p.

WITHERSPOON, JIMMY (JAMES; singer)

J661　Rotante, A. Jimmy Witherspoon discography. *Record Research*, #62 (Aug. 1964), 5-6; #63 (Sep. 1964), 7-8; #66 (Feb. 1965), 8-9; #67 (Apr. 1965), 10; #68 (May 1965), 7.

YANCEY, JIMMY (JAMES; piano)

J662　Eyle, Willem Frederik van. Discography of Jimmy Yancey. Zaandam, van Eyle, 1966. 2 p.

Eyle, Willem Frederik van. Discography of Jimmy Yancey. Rev. ed. Zaandam, van Eyle, 1966. 2 p.

YOUNG, LESTER WILLIS ("PREZ"; tenor sax, composer, clarinet)

J663　Jepsen, Jørgen Grunnet. Discography of Lester Young. Brande, Debut Records, 1959. 26 p.

Jepsen, Jørgen Grunnet. Discography of Lester Young. 2d ed. Brande, Debut Records, 1960. 26 p.

J664   Jepsen, Jørgen Grunnet. A discography of Lester Young. København, Knudsen, 1968. 45 p.

J665   Lester Young on record 1945-1949. *Jazz Monthly*, VIII (Apr. 1962), 23-24.

PART III

SUMMARY OF NATIONAL DISCOGRAPHIES, CATALOGS, AND MAJOR REVIEW SOURCES

SUMMARY OF NATIONAL DISCOGRAPHIES, CATALOGS, AND MAJOR REVIEW SOURCES

AUSTRIA

Reviews

S1 Österreichische Musikzeitschrift [Supplement: Phono]. Elisabeth Lafite, ed. 1946– . Monthly. 180 Schillings (Austrian)/year. Hegelgasse 13-22, 1010 Vienna, Austria. Contains reviews of classical records.

BELGIUM

National Discography

S2 Discothèque Nationale de Belgique. Catalogue général alphabétique. Brussels, Discothèque Nationale de Belgique, 1967-68. 2v. [Address: 320 Chaussée de Vleurgat, 1050 Brussels, Belgium]

Reviews

S3 La revue des disques et de la haute-fidélité. Marcel Doisy, ed. 1950– . 10 issues annually. 460 francs (Belgian)/year. Éditions Dereume, rue du Marché 69, B-1000 Brussels, Belgium. Contains reviews of classical and jazz records.

CANADA

Reviews

S4   Coda; Canada's jazz magazine. John Norris, ed. 1958– . Bimonthly. 3.50 dollars (Canadian)/year. Coda Publications, Box 87, Station J, Toronto M4J 4X8, Canada. Contains reviews of jazz records.

CZECHOSLOVAKIA

National Discography

S5   Bibliograficky Katalog CSSR. [Bibliography of Czech gramophone records.] Státni Knihovna CSSR, ed. 195– ? Quarterly. Státni Knihovna CSSR, Národni Knihovna Klementinum, Prague 1-190, Czechoslovakia. Catalog of all Czech records.

DENMARK

National Discography

S6   Nationaldiskoteket label discographies [78 rpm only]. København, Nationaldiskoteket. v. 1– . 1965– . [For volumes issued to date see *Danish His Master's Voice Records* and *Scandinavian His Master's Voice Records*.] [Address: Brede Hovedbygingen, 2800 Lyngby, Denmark]

Catalog

S7   Danske Grammofonplader. Nationaldiskoteket, ed. 195– ? Annual. Nationaldiskoteket, Brede Hovedbygingen, 2800 Lyngby, Denmark. Catalog of all Danish records.

Reviews

S8   Dansk Musiktidsskrift. Sven Erik Werner & Poul Nielsen, eds. 1925– . 8 issues annually. 54 kroner/yr. Möntergade 6A, DK 1116 Copenhagen K, Denmark. Contains reviews of classical records, mainly Danish and modern.

S9   High fidelity. 1968– . 11 issues annually. Linnésgade 6, 1161 Copenhagen K, Denmark. Contains reviews of classical, jazz, and popular records.

FINLAND

National Discography

S10   Suomalaisten Äänilevyjen Luettelo [Catalog of Finnish records]. Urpo Haapanen, ed. Helsinki, Finnish Institute of Recorded Sound, 1967-1970. 5 v. [Contents.–v. 1: 1902-1945.–v. 2: 1946-1966.– v. 3: 1967.–v. 4: 1968.–v. 5: 1969.]

Reviews

S11   Rondo. 1962– . Quarterly. c/o Raili Paloahde, Tyyppäläntie 6A, Jyväskylä, Finland. Contains survey of current Finnish records in Finnish.

FRANCE

National Discography

S12   La Discographie de France. Diapason, ed. 1964– . Bimonthly. Diapason, 103 rue d'Aguesseau, Boulogne, France. Functions like a bimonthly supplement to Diapason [S13 below].

Catalog

S13   Diapason; catalogue général de musique classique et de diction. 1964– . Annual. Diapason, 102 rue d'Aguesseau, Boulogne, France. Serves as annual cumulation of La Discographie de France [S12 above].

Reviews

S14   Bulletin du Hot Club de France. Hugues Panassié, ed. 1951–. 10 issues annually. Hugues Panassié, 65 Faubourg du Moustier, Montauban (Tarn-et-Garonne), France. Contains reviews of jazz records.

S15   Diapason. 1964– . Monthly. 61 rue La Fontaine, Paris 16ᵉ, France. Contains reviews of classical records.

S16   Harmonie. 1964– . Monthly. 27 Boulevard Malesherbes, Paris 8ᵉ, France. Contains reviews of classical records.

S17   Jazz hot. Charles Delaunay, ed. 1935– . 11 issues annually. 50 francs/year. 14 rue Chaptal, Paris 9ᵉ, France. Contains reviews of jazz records.

S18   Musique en jeu. Dominique Jameux, ed. 1970– . Quarterly. 55 francs/year. Éditions du Seuil, 27 rue Jacob, Paris 6ᵉ, France. Contains reviews of contemporary music records.

GERMANY (EAST)

National Discography

S19   Deutsche Nationalbibliographie. Das gesprochene Wort: Jahresverzeichnis der deutschen literarischen Schallplatten. 1965/66– . Annual. VEB Verlag für Buch- und Bibliotekswesen, Gerichtsweg 26, Postfach 130, 701 Leipzig, East Germany. An offprint from the Deutsche Nationalbibliographie which lists East German literary and documentary records.

GERMANY (WEST)

National Discographies

S20   Deutsche Bibliographie: Musikschallplatten. Berlin, Deutsche Bibliothek, Abteilung Deutsches Musikarchiv. v. 1– . In preparation. Replaces Deutsche Diskographie [S21 below]. [Address: Rüdesheimer Strasse 54-56, 1 Berlin 33, West Germany]

S21   Deutsche Diskographie. Berlin, Deutsche Bibliothek, Abteilung Deutsches Musikarchiv. v. 1-7. 1964-1970. Supersedes Deutsche Musik-Phonothek; superseded by Deutsche Bibliographie: Musikschallplatten [S20 above]. An inventory of deposit copies. [Address: Rüdesheimer Strasse 54-56, 1 Berlin 33, West Germany]

S22   Gemeinschafts-Katalog. Starnberg, Josef Keller Verlag. v. 1– . 1972– . Supersedes Der grosse Schallplatten Katalog [S23 below]. Annual with a supplement listing LPs, cassettes, and tapes. [Address: Josef Keller Verlag, Postfach 40, 8130 Starnberg, West Germany]

S23   Der grosse Schallplatten Katalog. Lüdenscheid, Linnepe. v. 1-8. 1964-1971. Title varies; superseded by Gemeinschafts-Katalog [S22 above]. Only LP records are listed.

Catalogs

S24 Bielefelder Katalog. 1953– . Semiannually. Bielefelder Verlagsanstalt KG, Ulmenstrasse 8, 48 Bielefeld, West Germany. Contains listings only of classical records.

S25 Bielefelder Katalog: Jazzplatten Katalog. 1953– . Annual. Bielefelder Verlagsanstalt KG, Ulmenstrasse 8, 48 Bielefeld, West Germany. Contains jazz LP records only.

S26 Bielefelder Katalog: Sprechplatten Katalog. 1953– . Annual. Bielefelder Verlagsanstalt KG, Ulmenstrasse 8, 48 Bielefeld, West Germany. Lists literary and documentary LPs.

Reviews

S27 Fono Forum; Zeitschrift für Schallplatte, Musikleben, Hifi-Wiedergabe. 1957– . Monthly. 44.40 Deutsche Marks/year. Bielefelder Verlagsanstalt KG, Ulmenstrasse 8, 48 Bielefeld, West Germany. Contains lists of new records and reviews.

S28 Hifi-Stereophonie; Zeitschrift für hochwertige Musikwiedergabe. Eberhard Knittel, ed. 1962– . Monthly. 40 Deutsche Marks/year. Verlag G. Braun GmbH, Karl-Friedrich-Strasse 14-18, 75 Karlsruhe, West Germany. Contains reviews of classical and popular records.

S29 Jazz Podium. Dieter Zimmerle, ed. 1952– . Monthly. 25 Deutsche Marks/year. Vogelsangstrasse 32, D-7000 Stuttgart 1, West Germany. Contains listings and reviews of new jazz records.

S30 Melos; Zeitschrift für neue Musik. Hans Oesch & Gerth-Wolfgang Baruch, eds. 1920– . Bimonthly. 26.40 Deutsche Marks/year. Verlag B. Schott's Söhne, Weihergarten, Postfach 3640, D-65 Mainz, West Germany. Contains reviews of contemporary music records.

S31 Musica; Zweimonatsschrift für alle Gebiete des Musiklebens. Wolfram Schwinger, ed. 1947– . Bimonthly. 24 Deutsche Marks/year. Bärenreiter Verlag Karl Vötterle KG, Heinrich-Schütz-Allee 29-31, 35 Kassel-Wilhelmshöhe, West Germany. Contains reviews of new classical records.

S32 Der Musikmarkt. Jürgen Sauermann, ed. 1959– . Semimonthly. 40.80 Deutsche Marks/year. Josef Keller Verlag, Seebrite 9, 8136 Kempfenhausen, West Germany. Contains reviews of new records.

S33 Opern Welt; die deutsche Opernzeitschrift. 1963– . Monthly. 68 Deutsche Marks/year. Erhard Friedrich Verlag, 3001 Velb Er Bei Hannover, West Germany. Contains reviews of new opera records.

GREAT BRITAIN

Catalogs

S34 The gramophone; classical record catalogue. 1953– . Quarterly. General Gramophone Publications, Ltd., 177-179 Kenton Road, Kenton, Middlesex HA3 OHA, England. Lists only classical LP records.

S35 The gramophone; popular record catalogue, artist section. 1953– . Quarterly. General Gramophone Publications, Ltd., 177-179 Kenton Road, Kenton, Middlesex HA 3 OHA, England.

S36 The gramophone; popular record catalogue, title section. 1953– . Quarterly. General Gramophone Publications, Ltd., 177-179 Kenton Road, Kenton, Middlesex HA3 OHA, England.

S37 The gramophone; spoken word and miscellaneous catalogue. 1953– . Annual. General Gramophone Publications, Ltd., 177-179 Kenton Road, Kenton, Middlesex HA3 OHA, England.

S38 The new records. 19??– . Monthly. Francis Anthony Ltd., 20 East Hill Street, Austell, Cornwall, England.

S39 Pop singles. 1967– . Quarterly. Christopher Foss Catalogues, 34a Paddington Street, London W1, England.

Reviews

S40 Blues unlimited. Simon Napier & Mike Leadbitter, eds. 1963– . 10 issues annually. 2.00 pounds/year 38a Sackville Rd., Bexhill-on-Sea, Sussex, England. Contains reviews of jazz and blues records.

S41 Discographical forum. Malcolm Walker, ed. 1960– . Bimonthly. 13 shillings/year. Malcolm Walker, 98 a Oakley Street, Chelsea, London SW 3, England. Contains record reviews and discographies.

S42 The gramophone. Malcolm Walker, ed. 1923– . Monthly. 3.60 pounds/year. General Gramophone Publications, Ltd., 177-179 Kenton Road, Kenton, Middlesex HA3 OHA, England. Contains record reviews.

S43   Hi-fi news & record review. John Crabbe, ed. 1956– . Monthly. 3.24 pounds/year. Link House Publications, Ltd., Link House, Dingwall Avenue, Croydon CR9 2TA, England. Contains record reviews.

S44   Jazz and blues [formerly Jazz monthly]. Albert J. McCarthy, ed. 1955– . Monthly. 50 shillings/year. Hanover Books, Ltd., 61 Berner's Street, London W1P 3AE, England. Contains reviews of jazz and blues records.

S45   Jazz journal. Sinclair Traill, ed. 1948– . Monthly. 2.85 pounds/year. Novello & Co., Ltd., The Cottage, 27 Willow Vale, London W12 OPA, England. Contains reviews of jazz records.

S46   The monthly letter. 1931– . Monthly. Hand-made Gramophones, Ltd., 26 Soho Square, London W1V 6BR, England. Contains listings and reviews of classical records.

S47   Music week [formerly Record retailer and Record & tape retailer]. 195– ? Weekly. 10 pounds/year. Billboard Publications, Ltd., 7 Carnaby Street, London W1V 1PG, England. Contains listings, charts, advertising, and record reviews.

S48   The musical times. Stanley Sadie, ed. 1844– . Monthly. 3.00 pounds/year. Novello & Co., Ltd., 27 Soho Square, London W1V 6BR, England. Contains reviews of new classical records.

S49   Opera. Harold Rosenthal, ed. 1950– . Monthly. 100 shillings/year. Seymour Press, Ltd., 334 Brixton Road, London S.W.9, England. Contains reviews of new opera records.

S50   The record collector; a magazine for collectors of recorded vocal art. James F. E. Dennis, ed. 1948– . Monthly. 2.50 pounds/year. James F. E. Dennis, 17 St. Nicholas Street, Ipswich, 1P1 1TW Suffolk, England. Discographies and commentary on 78 rpm records.

S51   Records and recording. Trevor Richardson, ed. 1957– . Monthly. 4.20 pounds/year. Hansom Books, Ltd., 75 Victoria Street, London SW1H OHZ, England. Contains listings and reviews of new records.

HUNGARY

National Discographies

S52   Magyar könyvészet [Hungarian bibliography]. Budapest, Országos Széchényi Könytár. v. 1-9. 1961-1969. Forms annual cumulations of Magyar nemzeti bibliográfia [S53 below] ; superseded by Magyar zeneművek bibliográfiája [S54 below] . Contains listings of books, scores, and maps as well as records published in Hungary. [Address: Országos Széchényi Könytár, PF 486, Budapest 5, Hungary]

S53 Magyar nemzeti bibliográfia [Hungarian national bibliography]. Budapest, Országos Széchényi Könytár. Biweekly. 1946-1969. Cumulated annually from 1961 by the Magyar könyvészet [S52 above] ; superseded by Magyar zeneművek bibliográfiája [S54 below]. Includes music records published in Hungary 1961-1969. [Address: Országos Széchényi Könytár, PF 486, Budapest 5, Hungary]

S54 Magyar zeneművek bibliográfiája [Hungarian music bibliography]. Budapest, Országos Széchényi Könytár. Quarterly. 1970– . Supersedes Magyar könyvészet [S52 above] and Magyar nemzeti bibliográfia [S53 above] . Lists scores and music records published since 1970. [Address: Országos Széchényi Könytár, PF 486, Budapest 5, Hungary]

Reviews

S55 Hanglemez [Record]. 1969– . Monthly? Magyar Hanglemezgyártó Vallalat, Budapest, Hungary. Contains reviews of new records.

S56 Kóta [Score]. 1971– . Bimonthly. Council of Hungarian Choruses, Budapest, Hungary. Contains reviews of new records.

S57 Studia musicologica. B. Szabolcsi, ed. 1961– . 9 issues annually. 1500 forints/year. Academia Scientiarum Hungaricae, Országhaz u. 9, Budapest 1, Hungary. Contains reviews of new classical records.

S58 Vigilia. György Ronay, ed. 1935– . Monthly. 100 forints/year. Actio Catholica, V. Kossuth Lajos u. 1, H-1053 Budapest, Hungary. Contains reviews of new recordings since 1967.

ITALY

Catalog

S59 Angelicum santandrea; catalogo generale dischi microsolco [formerly Santandrea]. 1953– . Bimonthly. 4000 lira/year. Angelicum santandrea, Piazza San Angelo 2, I-20121 Milan, Italy. Includes 45 rpm records as well as LPs.

Reviews

S60   Discoteca alta fedeltá; revista di dischi e musica e alta fedeltá
      [formerly Discoteca] . Ornella Zanuso Mauri, ed. 1959– . Monthly.
      5000 lira/year. Esperto S.p.A., Via Martignoni, I-20124 Milan,
      Italy. Contains reviews of classical records.

S61   Musica e dischi. Mario De Luigi, Jr., ed. 1945– . Monthly. 5000
      lira/year. Corriere Internazionale della Musica, Via Carducci 8,
      I-20123 Milan, Italy. Contains listings and reviews of classical,
      jazz, and popular records.

S62   Nuova rivista musicale italiana. Leonardo Pinzauti, ed. 1967– .
      Bimonthly. 7500 lira/year. ERI Edizioni RAI Radiotelevisione
      Italiana, Via del Babuino 51, 10097 Rome, Italy. Contains reviews
      of classical records.

JAPAN

Catalog

S63   Music in Japan. 1967– ? Annual. Japan Phonograph Record Asso-
      ciation, 8-9, 2 Chome, Tsukiji, Chuo-ku, Tokyo, Japan. Contains
      45 and LP records of Japanese music by major recording companies
      in annual listing.

NETHERLANDS

Catalogs

S64   Donemus. Audio visual series 1961-1965, vol. 1: 10-inch records.
      Amsterdam, Donemus, 1966. Lists records of music by Dutch con-
      temporary composers which are available with scores. [Address:
      Donemus, Jacob Obrechtstraat 51, Amsterdam, The Netherlands]

S65   Donemus. Audio visual series 1966-1970, vol. 2: 12-inch mono and
      stereo records. Amsterdam, Donemus, 1971. Lists records of music
      by Dutch contemporary composers which are available with scores.
      [Address: Donemus, Jacob Obrechtstraat 51, Amsterdam, The
      Netherlands]

S66   Telstar LP catalogus. 196– ? Annual. Telgram, Postbox 70, Weert,
      The Netherlands. Contains listings of records of Dutch popular
      music.

Reviews

S67 Disk; kritisch maandblad vor discofielen. J. de Kruijff & F. Versteeg, eds. 1967– . Monthly. 44 florins/year. Misset/Fonorama, Postbus 26, Amersfoort, The Netherlands. Contains reviews of classical records.

S68 Luister [Listen]. 1952– . Monthly. 25 florins/year. Drukkerij Onnes B.V., Postbus 43, Amersfoort, The Netherlands. Contains reviews of classical records.

S69 Mens en melodie [Man and melody]. 1945– . Monthly. 26 florins/ year. Uitgeverij Het Spectrum N.V., Postbus 2073, Utrecht, The Netherlands. Contains reviews of classical, contemporary, ethnic, and folk records.

S70 Orgel [Organ]. 1903– . Monthly. Nederlandse Organisten Vereniging, Rodenrijslaan 15A, Rotterdam 11, The Netherlands. Contains reviews of classical and contemporary organ music and organ records.

POLAND

Catalog

S71 Polish record catalogue. 1964?– . Annual? Ars Polona, 7 Krakowskia Przedmiescie, Warsaw, Poland. Lists records published in Poland.

Reviews

S72 Jazz. Jozef Balcerak, ed. 1956– . Monthly. 4.50 dollars (U.S.)/year. Krajowe Wydawnictwo Czasopism, Noakowskiego 14, 00-666 Warsaw, Poland. Contains reviews of jazz records.

S73 Ruch muzyczny [Musical life]. Ludwik Erhardt, ed. 1957– . Biweekly. 135 zlotys/year. RSW Prasa-ksiazka-Ruch, ul Senatorska 13-15, Warsaw, Poland. Contains reviews of Polish classical records.

SWEDEN

National Discography

S74 STIM [Swedish Music Information Center]. Svensk ton på skiva och band [Swedish music on record and tape]. Stockholm, STIM.

Biennial. 196– ? A selected discography of Swedish classical, jazz, and folk music on record. [Address: STIM, Tegnérlunden 3, 11161 Stockholm, Sweden]

SWITZERLAND

National Discography

S75   Schweizerisches Musik-Archiv. Schweizer Musik auf Schallplatten. Zürich, Schweizerisches Musik-Archiv. Biennial. 196– ? Lists classical music records only.

UNITED STATES

Catalogs

S76   Schwann-1 record & tape guide [formerly Schwann long playing record catalog and Long playing record catalog]. 1949– . Monthly. 95 cents/issue. W. Schwann, Inc., 137 Newbury Street, Boston, Mass. 02116, U.S.A. Lists stereo classical music, current jazz and popular music, etc.

S77   Schwann-2 record & tape guide [formerly Schwann supplementary catalog]. 1965– . Semiannually. 85 cents/issue. W. Schwann, Inc., 137 Newbury Street, Boston, Mass. 02116, U.S.A. Lists mono classical records, jazz and pop over 2 years old, international pop and folk, spoken, educational, religious records, etc.

S78   Schwann artist issue. Occasional: recent issues have been 1958, 1960, 1963, 1966, and 1970. 1.75 dollars/issue. W. Schwann, Inc., 137 Newbury Street, Boston, Mass. 02116, U.S.A. Classical records only.

S79   Schwann children's record & tape guide. Occasional: recent issues have been 1972/73 and 1973/74. 40 cents/issue. W. Schwann, Inc., 137 Newbury Street, Boston, Mass. 02116, U.S.A.

S80   Schwann country and western tape & record catalog. Occasional: most recent issue is 1970/71. 75 cents/issue. W. Schwann, Inc., 137 Newbury Street, Boston, Mass. 02116, U.S.A.

Reviews

S81   American record guide. James Lyons, ed. 1934— . Monthly. 6.00 dollars/year. Box 319, Radio City Station, New York, N.Y. 10019, U.S.A. Contains reviews of classical records.

S82   Blues research. 1959— . Irregular. Record Research, 65 Grand Avenue, Brooklyn, N.Y. 11205, U.S.A. Issues contain label discographies of blues records.

S83   Down beat. Jack Maher, ed. 1934— . Biweekly. 9.00 dollars/year. Maher Publications, Inc., 222 W. Adams Street, Chicago, Ill. 60606, U.S.A. Contains reviews of jazz records.

S84   Ethnomusicology [formerly Ethnomusicology newsletter]. Norma McLeod, ed. 1953— . 3 issues annually. 15 dollars/year. Society for Ethnomusicology, Israel J. Katz, Treasurer, Center for Studies in Ethnomusicology, Department of Music, Columbia University, New York, N.Y. 10027, U.S.A. Includes some reviews of jazz and blues records as well as reviews of ethnic and folk records.

S85   High fidelity [incorporating Musical America since 1965]. Leonard Marcus, ed. 1951— . Monthly. 7.95 dollars/year. Billboard Publications, Inc., 165 W. 46th Street, New York, N.Y. 10036, U.S.A. Contains record reviews.

S86   The musical quarterly. Paul Henry Lang, ed. 1915— . Quarterly. 9 dollars/year. G. Schirmer, Inc., 866 Third Ave., New York, N.Y. 10022, U.S.A. Contains reviews of classical records.

S87   Music Library Association. Notes. Frank C. Campbell, ed. 1934— . Quarterly. 10 dollars, individual/year; 15 dollars, institution/year. Music Library Association, 343 S. Main Street, Room 205, Ann Arbor, Mich. 48108, U.S.A. Contains record review index for classical and popular records.

S88   Stereo review [formerly Hifi/stereo review]. William Anderson, ed. 1958— . Monthly. 7 dollars/year. Ziff-Davis Publishing Co., 1 Park Ave., New York, N.Y. 10016, U.S.A. Contains reviews of classical and pop records.

INDEX

This index is inclusive of authors, distinctive monographic titles, series, and subjects—all within a single alphabetical sequence. Subjects are in capitals. Series entries are identified by [series] if the word series is not part of the title. Indexing was not done for titles where a personal name was the most distinctive element of the title (e.g., *Pablo Casals; a biography*, or *A discography of Charlie Parker*) as well as all titles appearing within periodicals. Authors and subjects with multiple surnames have been indexed under incorrect or less often used name forms, as well as those used by this author, as an aid in easily locating them.

The sequence proceeds alphabetically and word-by-word with these exceptions (observed in many library catalogs), as follows:

1) The umlaut over a vowel (e.g., ä) in German adds an "e" directly after it (i.e., ae; e.g., Händel spells as Haendel).

2) All Mc's are found under Mac.

3) Abbreviations will be found as though the word were fully spelled out (e.g., St. becomes Saint).

4) Articles at the beginning of a title are disregarded in all languages.

5) Multiple surnames will be found as if run together (e.g., De Lerma will be found as if spelled Delerma).

6) Initials (e.g., BBC, BIRS, RCA) come at the beginning of their initial letter.

7) Identical authors precede identical subjects; identical subjects precede identical titles.